W9-AMX-050

The American Sign Language Handshape Dictionary

Richard A. Tennant
Marianne Gluszak Brown

Illustrated by
Valerie Nelson-Metlay

Clerc Books
Gallaudet University Press
Washington, D.C.

Clerc Books
An imprint of Gallaudet University Press
Washington, DC 20002

Library of Congress Cataloging-in-Publication Data

Tennant, Richard A.
    The American Sign Language Handshape Dictionary / Richard A.
Tennant, Marianne Gluszak Brown ; illustrated by Valerie Nelson-Metlay
       p.   cm.
    Includes index.
    ISBN 1-56368-043-2
    1. American Sign Language—Dictionaries.   I. Brown, Marianne Gluszak.
II. Title.
HV2475.T46   1998
419—dc21   97-48389
                                               CIP

Design and Production
Victory Productions, Inc.

Design: Victoria Porras
Cover Design: Victoria Porras & Karin Daigle
Production: Karin Daigle

This work is dedicated to those who struggle to learn to communicate with others, and to those teachers who devote themselves to bringing these desires to fruition.

R. T.

To the Deaf community that has nurtured me since birth, and to all who seek to understand the beauty of American Sign Language.

M. G. B.

Contents

Preface

The American Sign Language Handshape Dictionary departs from most sign language dictionaries in that it is organized by the various shapes of the hands used to form signs rather than in English alphabetical word order. This unique format allows users to search for a sign that they recognize but whose meaning they have forgotten or for the meaning of a new sign they have seen for the very first time.

The American Sign Language Handshape Dictionary will be especially helpful to new sign language students, and it will be a handy reference for people who know some signs but want to increase their vocabulary. The dictionary will also be valuable to Deaf people who want to know the various English words that are used to signify the same concept conveyed in a particular sign. Finally, the Index of English Glosses provides an English to American Sign Language (ASL) listing of all the signs in the book so that new signers can look up a word in English to learn the conceptually correct sign to use to express a specific idea. This dual-language feature enables users to go from ASL to English or English to ASL easily and quickly.

Introduction

American Sign Language (ASL) is a visual/gestural language. It is a *natural* language, meaning that it has developed naturally over time by its users, Deaf people. ASL has all of the features of any language; that is, it is a rule-governed system using symbols to represent meaning. In ASL, the symbols are specific hand movements and configurations that are modified by facial expressions to convey meaning. These gestures or symbols are called *signs*.

Contrary to common belief, ASL is not derived from any spoken language, nor is it a visual code representing English. It is a unique and distinct language, one that does not depend on speech or sound. ASL has its own grammar, sentence construction, idiomatic usage, slang, style, and regional variations—the characteristics that define any language.

American Sign Language is the shared language that unites Deaf people in what is known as the Deaf community. *Deaf* with a capital *D* is used in publications to recognize the cultural and linguistic affiliation of Deaf people who are members of the Deaf community, whereas *deaf* with a lowercase *d* is used to refer to deaf people who do not embrace ASL or involve themselves with the values, organizations, and events that are heralded by signing Deaf people. The Deaf community is not bound by geographic borders, but rather comprises those people who elect to become members by using ASL as their preferred mode of communication and by accepting the cultural identity of Deaf people. It is difficult to give an accurate number of how many people are in the Deaf community because census takers typically lump together all people who have a hearing loss. Many researchers believe that approximately 10 percent of the general population has some degree of hearing loss and that 1 percent of that number represents Deaf people, for a total of about half a million people in the Deaf community.

The people most likely to be native users of ASL are those who have Deaf parents. People who lose their hearing as infants, before they begin to speak, may become native signers if they are exposed to ASL at an early age. These people, who are unable to hear English and learn it naturally, must be taught English through formal means. Hearing children of Deaf parents also acquire ASL as a first language. However, their enculturation tends to cross the cultures of the Deaf and hearing worlds. These children, like their Deaf counterparts, are often referred to as bicultural and bilingual.

History of Sign Language in America

Not much is known about deaf people who came to America before the beginning of the nineteenth century, although evidence suggests that they brought the sign languages of their native countries with them. Because there were no schools specifically for them and traveling was difficult, deaf people probably had very little contact with one another.

This situation began to change in the early 1800s when Thomas Hopkins Gallaudet, a Connecticut clergyman, embarked on a voyage abroad at the request of a Hartford physician who had a deaf daughter. Gallaudet had heard that successful methods of educating deaf children were being used in Europe, and he was eager to learn these teaching methods and bring them back to America so that he could open a school for children who were deaf. After a lukewarm welcome by the administrators of the school for the deaf in England, Gallaudet moved on to the Royal Institution for the Deaf in Paris, where he was well received. He studied French signs and methods of teaching deaf children using sign language. When Gallaudet was ready to return to Hartford, he contracted with Laurent Clerc, a graduate of the Royal Institution and one of the best teachers at the school in Paris, to return with him to America. Clerc played an important role in the emergence of early versions of ASL by bringing French Sign Language to the United States to intermingle with existing sign languages.

Gallaudet and Clerc established the first permanent school for deaf children in the United States. The school opened in Hartford, Connecticut, in 1817. This event is viewed as a milestone for the Deaf community in that it brought large numbers of Deaf people together for the first time. The school became a forum for sharing ideas, experiences, beliefs, and values unique to Deaf life. The founding of this school helped to create, develop, and nurture an enduring sense of community—the Deaf community.

American Sign Language, formed of a fusion between sign languages already in existence (including the newly imported French Sign Language), did what most languages do: it evolved. It was flexible enough to be able to respond to the ever-changing American society, and today it has evolved into one of the richest sign languages in the world. We are indebted to Gallaudet, to early Deaf pioneers, to the French for the head start they gave us, and for the conditions here in the United States that have nurtured ASL.

Signs—The Vocabulary of American Sign Language

A sign is a gesture or movement that conveys a concept. Each sign is made with a specific hand configuration or handshape, placed at various locations on or near the signer's body. If the handshape, movement, or location changes, the meaning of the sign also changes. Signs are the basic semantic units of sign languages, much as words are the basic semantic units of spoken languages.

The signs of ASL are formed with one hand or two hands. When a sign is formed using only one hand, the hand used is determined by the signer's natural dominance. The same is true for two-hand signs in which only one hand moves. The hand that moves is called the *dominant* hand, while the other hand is called the *passive* hand. The illustrations in this dictionary show models with a right-hand dominance.

Two-hand signs can be produced in one of three ways: (1) both hands form identical handshapes and both hands move; (2) both hands form identical handshapes but only the dominant hand moves; or (3) the hands form

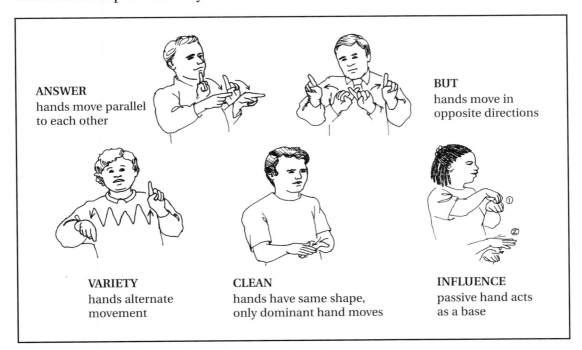

ANSWER
hands move parallel to each other

BUT
hands move in opposite directions

VARIETY
hands alternate movement

CLEAN
hands have same shape, only dominant hand moves

INFLUENCE
passive hand acts as a base

Figure 1. Examples of how two-hand signs can be formed.

different handshapes and only the dominant hand moves, while the passive hand is restricted to a limited set of handshapes (see figure 1).

When both hands move, a *symmetry* condition exists, which means that the handshapes and movements must be identical. These movements may be made either in unison or alternatingly. In addition, when the hands move in unison the movement can be parallel or in opposite directions. For two-hand signs in which the handshapes are not identical, a *dominance* condition exists in that the passive hand remains static while the dominant hand executes the sign. The handshape of the dominant hand is more significant than the shape of the passive hand. The dominant hand carries the essential information whereas the other hand acts primarily as a base and, as such, is usually stationary and limited in the handshapes that it can have. The dominant hand can display any of approximately 150 different handshapes, but the passive hand can assume only about seven handshapes. Because the passive hand plays a lesser role, that hand is often less carefully articulated.

Native signers are naturally consistent in their adherence to the rules regarding symmetry and dominance. Someone who does not observe these rules is awkward to watch, particularly if the person alternatingly uses the left and the right hand for one-hand signs.

Parameters of a Sign

Every sign is a composite of basic components or *parameters*. The parameters of a sign are handshape, palm orientation, location, movement, and nonmanual features or signals. If one of these five parameters changes, a completely different sign may be formed. You will notice that the sign descriptions written for each sign illustration in this dictionary include each of these parameters (see figure 2).

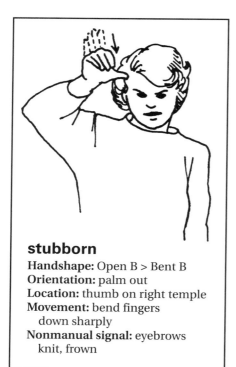

stubborn
Handshape: Open B > Bent B
Orientation: palm out
Location: thumb on right temple
Movement: bend fingers
   down sharply
Nonmanual signal: eyebrows
   knit, frown

Figure 2. All sign descriptions include the five parameters of a sign.

Handshape

The handshape is probably the most apparent parameter of a sign. It is the configuration the hand assumes when beginning to make a sign. The most frequently used handshapes are the letters of the American Manual Alphabet and the manual numbers (see pages 20 and 26); however, linguists have identified a large number of discrete handshapes. In order to make this book as accessible as possible, the signs have been organized using forty of the possible handshapes. Handshapes that are quite similar to each other (for example, K and P) have been arbitrarily grouped under one of these handshapes.

Palm Orientation

The next parameter of a sign is its orientation, or the direction in which the hand is turned. The direction that the palm of the hand faces (up, down, left, or right) is a useful way of describing the orientation because once the palm is described, the direction of the fingers and back of the hand is obvious.

Location

Signs are formed on or near only certain areas of the body. Approximately 75 percent of all signs are formed in the head and neck area because there they can be seen more easily. For the same reason, over time, signs that used to be formed near the waist or elbows have moved up and in toward the chest. The location of a sign frequently contributes to its meaning. For example, many signs that denote feelings are formed near the heart, whereas signs related to cognitive concepts are formed near the head.

Movement

Much of the meaning of signs may be expressed through movement. The direction in which a sign moves may indicate the doer or recipient of the action. For example, if the sign HELP[1] moves from the signer toward another person, help is offered to that person. If the sign moves in toward the signer, another person might be helping the signer. The repetition of the movement may indicate several things—the frequency of an action, the plurality of a noun, or the distinction between a noun and a verb. The size of the movement may indicate volume or size. And the speed or vigor of the movement combined with the appropriate nonmanual signals may convey many adverbial aspects of what is being expressed. Generally, the signs in this book show basic movements to which a skilled signer may add the semantic variations.

---

[1] ASL signs are indicated by using small capital letters for the English glosses of root signs.

Nonmanual Signals

If you have executed each of the first four parameters, you can succeed in correctly making a sign. However, being a good signer involves more than just executing signs correctly. In spoken languages, additional semantic information is carried through one's tone of voice. In sign language, additional semantic information is carried through one's body and facial expressions. This nonmanual parameter occurs at the same time that the sign is being executed to contribute to its meaning. The signed message is quite different if you shake your head no or nod your head yes while signing HAPPY. When one signs using all of the parameters including the nonmanual parameter, there is a complete thought—a sentence. Without the nonmanual parameter, there is merely a string of signs.

Some attempt has been made in this book to illustrate or to describe the nonmanual parameter of each sign, although often the nonmanual signals are dictated by the context in which the sign is used. Keep in mind that while the dictionary offers an extensive inventory of "root" signs, the nonmanual signals as well as the signs themselves can be inflected and combined in myriad ways, producing more variations than can be shown in a printed dictionary. Because sign language is three-dimensional, and because grammatical inflections and nonmanual signals are expressed simultaneously with the signs, it is difficult to present ASL in the two-dimensional medium of a book. It is important that you take a sign class to become aware of the nuances of this beautiful language. And to supplement that instruction, you should interact with the Deaf community to acquire a deeper appreciation of the language in the context of its people and their culture.

Figure 3. The signing space

Signing Space

When Deaf people sign, they use a defined space that approximates a rectangle. This rectangle starts at waist height, extends to slightly above one's head, reaches out no more than a foot in front of the body, and rarely extends more than a foot left or right beyond the torso (see figure 3). This area provides for optimum viewing of signs as they are formed. The signing space becomes proportionately larger and the signs may be exaggerated when signing to large audiences. Likewise, the signing space may become more confined for purposes of more rapid signing or in order to be secretive.

Grammatical Features

American Sign Language, like all languages, has definite rules of grammar. These rules specify how signs can be used and combined in order to allow for communication. Some of the basic features are discussed here as an introduction to the sophistication and versatility of ASL as a language.

Verb Types

Most verbs are explicitly signed along with the subject and object of the sentence. These *regular* verbs cannot take advantage of variable movement and space to create modifications on the root sign. However, some verbs can use space to incorporate both the subject and object of the sentence in the verb sign itself. These *directional* verbs use movement to or from the signer to express who or what gives or receives the action. Examples of directional verbs are GIVE, INFORM, DEFEND, and BORROW. Directional verbs are very efficient since an entire sentence is expressed with the use of one sign (see figure 4). With some directional verbs, the palm orientation may reverse. For example, for the sign PITY, the palm faces in toward the body when signing YOU-PITY-ME and faces out toward the referent when signing I-PITY-YOU.

Locational verbs are signed on or near the area of the body to which the action refers. Signing HURT near the mouth indicates a toothache; near the head, a headache; and so on. Similarly, signing SURGERY near the appendix versus signing it near the heart gives clear information about what kind of surgery was performed.

Noun/Verb Pairs

Signs for related ASL nouns and verbs (i.e., are based on the same concept) are formed in very similar ways. In a two-dimensional illustration, the signs may actually

ASL: I-GIVE-YOU
English: I give it to you.

ASL: YOU-GIVE-ME
English: You give it to me.

Figure 4. Directional verbs allow the signer to incorporate the subject and object of the sentence into the verb.

FLY

AIRPLANE

Figure 5. The only difference between some noun and verb signs is indicated in the movement.

look identical because the difference in movements cannot be shown easily. Typically the verb forms have a single large movement, whereas their noun counterparts are often signed smaller and with a double movement (see figure 5). Some examples of ASL noun/verb pairs are AIRPLANE and FLY, CHAIR and SIT, and FOOD and EAT.

In this dictionary, you may notice that only the noun or only the verb form of a sign is illustrated. The difference between the two forms is indicated by the notation *SM* (single movement) or *DM* (double movement) after the English entry for the sign. It is up to you, the user, to remember that the single movement, typically used for verbs, is larger than the double movement, which is usually several small quick movements. Because there are many noun/verb pairs in ASL, it would have been repetitive to illustrate each noun and verb since in the illustration they would look identical except for the arrow.

Agent Markers

The *agent marker* is a sign added to a root sign to indicate that one is referring to a person (see figure 6). The agent marker is referred to as the *-er* sign, and it often marks the distinction between a noun and a verb (for example, TEACH + agent marker =TEACHER). It also conveys the same idea as the inflections *-an*, *-ist*, *-ent*, and *-or* in

TEACH + AGENT MARKER = TEACHER

Figure 6. The agent marker is added to a noun sign to indicate a person. This allows the signer to specify an occupation or nationality.

English (for example, STUDY + agent marker = STUDENT; POLITICS + agent marker = POLITICIAN).

Plurals

There are several ways to show the plurality of people and objects. One of the most common techniques is to repeat the noun sign a number of times. Signs that are made in space off the body are likely candidates for this way of making the sign plural. Sometimes the sign will be moved slightly to the right while it is being repeated.

ASL singular:	BOOK I HAVE.
English:	I have a book.
ASL plural:	BOOK, BOOK I HAVE.
English:	I have some books.

Some signs cannot be pluralized by repeating the sign. In such cases, there are several other ways to express plurals, including adding a plural pronoun, a number, or a quantifying sign (for example, MANY) to the noun sign.

ASL singular:	MAN I SEE.
English:	I see a man.

Pronoun

ASL plural:	MAN *THEY* I SEE.
English:	I see some men.

Number

ASL plural:	MAN *THREE* I SEE.
English:	I see three men.

Quantifier

ASL plural:	MAN *SEVERAL* I SEE.
English:	I see several men.

Comparatives

ASL has two methods of comparing two persons, places, things, or ideas. One method makes use of space. When discussing the first item being compared, the signer shifts the shoulders toward the right, looks in

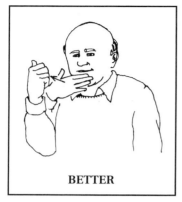

BETTER

BEST

Figure 7. The difference between the comparative and superlative form can be shown in the degree of movement.

that direction, and signs everything related to that item on that side of the body. Then when discussing the second item, the signer shifts left, looks left, and signs toward the left for the other item. This shifting continues throughout the conversation as the signer refers to either item. An example of this method would be as follows:

ASL:	CANDY (shift body right), ICE CREAM (shift body left), ME LIKE BOTH (body center).
English:	I like both candy and ice cream!

The second way of comparing items is to add an inflection to the root adjective describing the two items. The inflection sign for the comparative form (*-er*) is made by jerking the thumb of the Open A hand upward a short distance; the superlative form (*-est*) is made by a larger movement upward (see figure 7). These movements are accompanied by appropriate facial expressions, and they can be exaggerated to show just how much difference is indicated in the comparison.

Variation in Sign Language

Language is the creation of the community of people who use it and shape it. Yet, subgroups exist within any community. Factors such as gender, geography, race, socioeconomic background, level of education, and age, play a role in creating language variations. These kinds of variations do not prevent speakers or signers of different backgrounds from being able to converse with one another, rather they identify certain characteristics about the individuals. For instance, a particular sign may reveal which school for the deaf the person attended. The manner of signing or the pace of signing may indicate the region someone comes from—the Midwest, Southeast, and so on.

Changes in Signs

Over time and through use, signs change. Some of the changes are a result of the personal and practical needs of the current users. After all, a language must possess the flexibility and creativity necessary to express new ideas, inventions, and events. For example, ASL has signs for *microwave* as well as adaptations of the old signs TELEPHONE and WASH-CLOTHES to reflect modern appliances. Other changes have occurred to make signs easier to produce or recognize. One such change is that signs now are produced in a smaller space closer to the center of the body than years ago. SUPPORT and HELP are examples of signs that have moved from being formed on the arm to being formed on the hand held in front of the chest.

Still other changes are due to the trend to use one-hand signs when there is an identical two-hand version. This is particularly true of *iconic* signs (signs that visually resemble the concept they represent) that used to require both hands, but now require only one hand; for example, COW, DEVIL, or CAT (see figure 8). Following the pattern of all languages, ASL is evolving to allow quick, easy, and concise communication.

Many times people prefer to use one-hand signs for conversational purposes because it frees the signer to use the passive hand for another activity like holding a drink or a baby. In two-hand signs where there is a dominance condition, the passive hand is not typically dropped, though it can be if the signer's left hand is occupied.

In this dictionary, not all one-hand and two-hand variations are illustrated. The book would have become too unwieldy if all possible permutations had been included.

CAT

CAT

Figure 8. One of the changes ASL has undergone is a preference for one-hand over two-hand signs.

Fingerspelling

The American Manual Alphabet has a handshape to represent each letter of the English alphabet (see figure 9). *Fingerspelling* uses the manual alphabet to provide a visual representation of English words. Because fingerspelling is derived from English, its role in ASL is generally limited to proper names of people and places, brand names, and titles. Technical terms are fingerspelled only if no sign currently exists and the English term is important to know. However, a combination of signs may be enough to carry the concept until a more efficient sign is created by the Deaf community.

The following list describes how to fingerspell properly. When following the techniques on the list, keep in mind that fingerspelling should feel comfortable. Take your time, perhaps practice in front of a mirror to view both the expressive and receptive perspectives simultaneously, and above all—relax.

1. Raise the dominant hand so that the elbow is about waist high.

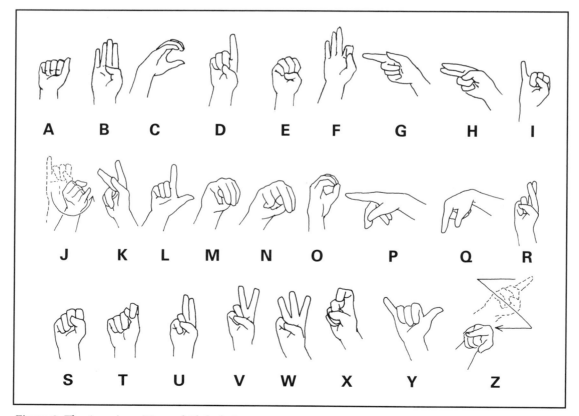

Figure 9. The American Manual Alphabet

2. The palm should face forward and slightly toward the left (except for letters G and H, where the palm faces the body).

3. The hand should be approximately eight to ten inches in front of the chest.

4. The hand moves slightly toward the right while spelling.

5. Spelling should be rhythmic. The focus should not be on the individual letters.

6. Do not bounce the elbow or twist the wrist.

7. Hold the last letter of a word for an extra beat before spelling the next.

Reading fingerspelling seems to be more difficult for learners to master than doing the fingerspelling. Historically, the emphasis in instruction has been on expressing rather than receiving. This leaves many students without concrete advice on developing and maintaining good receptive skills.

Think about good readers. Readers do not read text letter by letter! Readers see whole words and the configuration of words or phrases. In addition, they use context. The principles of learning how to read text apply to reading fingerspelling as well. Don't look for individual letters when someone is fingerspelling, rather look for clues to help you make an educated guess.

Here is a list of techniques that may help you improve your receptive skills.

1. Maintain eye contact. Resist the temptation to look at the signer's hand.

2. Use clues such as the length of a word, its position in the sentence, the configuration of the word, easily recognized letters, and context.

3. Sometimes a phonetic approach is useful.

Below are some exercises that may help either to break bad reading habits or prevent any from developing.

1. Starting with three-letter words, say the word and spell it simultaneously. Then try progressively harder words, again making sure to begin and end vocalization and spelling at the same time.

2. With a partner, tell each other stories with a lot of contextual clues. For instance, talk about your experience at a pet shop trying to choose a dog, and be sure your partner understands the topic before moving on with the story. Narrow the field to help your partner hone in on the kinds of words that are likely to appear in your story. For example, give plenty of clues about the appearance and behavior of the dog's breed before spelling it. Fingerspell the type (for example, collie), at a moderate to fast clip. If your partner misses the word you might want to give more clues before spelling it again.

Do not fingerspell the words slowly under any circumstances. Encourage your partner to see the whole word by asking her to guess. Remember, it is very important that you not let your partner look at your hand while you spell. Doing this kind of exercise routinely will help you build confidence in your ability to successfully read fingerspelled words. Remember, often there are a lot of clues to aid in making intelligent guesses. This is what Deaf people have learned to do. You can do it too!

Fingerspelled Loan Signs

Borrowing from both ASL and English, fingerspelled *loan* signs are a combination of English letters and ASL movements. For example, although there are several signs in ASL for *dog,* the loan sign #DOG[2] is a D handshape twisting into the G handshape, omitting the letter *o.* The sign itself does not appear as ordinary fingerspelling; it has taken on a unique character of its own, heavily defined by its movement and use of space. Loan signs begin as fingerspelled English words, and through repeated usage over time they change so that they look more like ASL signs. Fingerspelled loan signs tend to keep the first and last letter of the word and delete the medial letters. Some examples of loan signs are #JOB, #WHAT, and #BACK. Many fingerspelled loan signs only have two letters that are either an abbreviation of the English word or the whole word. Some examples of two-letter loan signs are #HA, #NG (for "no good"), #OK, and #NO.

---

[2] The # symbol is used to show the difference between a fingerspelled loan sign and a regular sign. The fingerspelled word is written with hyphens between the letters (ex., D-O-G).

Conclusion

All living human languages, as we have said, are constantly changing, and ASL is no exception. In this dictionary, we offer a description of ASL as it now exists. Loan words to describe new processes and technologies, borrowed terms from sign languages elsewhere in the world, and the inventiveness of its native speakers will doubtless alter and enrich ASL in the coming years, and we look forward to keeping up with that growth.

How to Use This Dictionary

When studying a foreign language, it is usually necessary to acquire a two-way dictionary. To study German, for example, you would want to have an English–German, German–English dictionary close at hand. The primary purpose of *The ASL Handshape Dictionary* is to provide sign language students with the ASL equivalent of a two-way dictionary. The signs are arranged by the shape the hand assumes when beginning to make a sign. This allows students to locate a sign they know, or have just seen, to find out its meaning. At the same time the book offers students, through its comprehensive index of English glosses, the means for locating a sign that is needed to express an English concept.

If a sign is a symbol that represents a concept, then what is the best way to convey a translation of that concept? The concept could be illustrated, but many concepts are abstract and difficult to convey in a picture. Thus, in most sign language dictionaries, English words, or *glosses,* appear with each sign illustration as an attempt to translate the meaning of the sign. Most of the sign illustrations in this dictionary include more than one English gloss. These English words may not represent all possible instances in which the sign may be used. Sometimes remarks or parts of speech are given in parentheses with an English gloss to specify the meaning or appropriate use of the sign. Sometimes such limits for using a sign can be derived by looking at the other glosses in the list. For example, by examining the glosses for the sign DRUM, you would see that you cannot appropriately use that sign to mean "drumming up business" because the other gloss with the illustration is "play drums." This makes it clear that the sign is intended to convey the concept of a musical instrument. Remarks accompanying the sign description may also be of help in choosing an appropriate gloss for the context you are trying to convey.

In many sign language dictionaries the sign illustrations are arranged in the alphabetical order of their English glosses or meanings. In such an alphabetical arrangement there is no method of locating a sign that one remembers or observes in order to discover its meaning. This dictionary presents signs in a logical order, by handshape, so that a known or observed sign can be quickly located without reference to an English word or gloss.

A second advantage of this dictionary's arrangement is that teachers of sign language can find groups of signs that use the same initial handshape displayed in one place. The convenience of these handshape categories enables a sign language teacher to present signs in a unique and logical organization. It also offers students a helpful memory device.

A third advantage of this dictionary is its generous array of glosses available to assist Deaf people who seek to increase their English vocabulary. When looking up signs whose concepts are already familiar to them, Deaf people may find among the glosses other English words that can be used to represent the signed concept.

General Arrangement of the Dictionary

This dictionary is divided into three major sections, each with a specific purpose. The first section contains illustrations of one-hand signs and their English glosses. The signs are arranged in order of the initial handshape that is used in producing the sign. The second section contains the two-hand signs and their English glosses, and once again, the signs are arranged in order of the initial handshape. Each illustration in both of these sections is accompanied by its equivalent English glosses (meanings) and a sign description. Each description includes the handshape, palm orientation, location, movement, and when appropriate, nonmanual signals. Notes are included with some descriptions to give suggestions as to the sign's use, alternate variations, or preferred signs.

Most of the illustrations include arrows that indicate how the hands move. A double-headed arrow or a double arrow is used when the movement is repeated. Many signs move from an initial position to a final position. In this dictionary, the first position is sometimes represented by dotted hands and the final position by solid hands. When signs have two distinct parts, as in compound signs, the two positions are numbered to show the sequence of production.

As we mentioned in an earlier section, an *agent marker* is an inflection added to a root sign to indicate that a sign refers to a person. In this dictionary, the signs that can be formed with an agent marker do not have separate entries. Instead, they are listed in italics within parentheses after the glosses for the root sign to indicate that the agent marker must be added to form that inflected sign. They are also listed in the index of English glosses.

The final section of this book looks like an index; it is an alphabetical listing of the English glosses encountered in the previous sections. Each entry in the listing directs the user to the page where the illustration for that word appears. By using this index, the user can quickly find the illustration needed to translate the English word or concept into sign.

Organization of the Handshape Sections

American Sign Language, unlike many spoken languages, does not have a written form. A sign conveys a concept, not an English word, and the production of a sign involves five parameters that need to be described: the handshape, the palm orientation, the location, the movement, and the nonmanual signals. The signs in a dictionary have to be ordered by one of these components so they can be easily located.

As we have said, the primary order of the signs in this dictionary is the initial handshape that the hands assume when beginning to execute the sign. The signs are categorized under forty handshapes. Most of the handshapes are taken from the American Manual Alphabet (see figure 9 on p. 20); some are modifications of these handshapes (for example, Bent B, Flattened O). A few handshapes are taken from the number signs (see figure 10). In addition to the handshapes from the American Manual Alphabet and numbers, we selected L-I and 1-I as symbols to represent the handshapes combining L and I as in the sign I-LOVE-YOU, and 1 and I as in the handshape used for the sign MOCK.

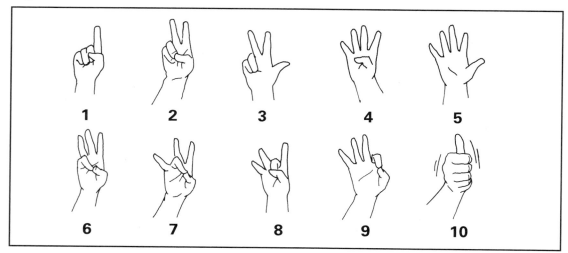

Figure 10. The Manual Numbers

Some letters of the American Manual Alphabet and some number handshapes are not included among the handshapes. The reason for this is that some handshapes are identical except for palm orientation (for example, H and U, K and P, 2 and V). In the context of forming a sign, palm orientation is determined by the sign, not by the handshape. The decision as to which of two identical handshapes was selected and which was eliminated was arbitrary.

The chart shown in figure 11 contains the handshapes used in this dictionary in the order in which they are arranged. For the sake of convenience, this ordering will be referred to as *morphologic order* because it is neither truly alphabetic nor numeric but a selective combination of both. The handshapes and their order are fundamental to the use of this dictionary.

Ordering of Signs within Handshape Sections

The number of hands used to make a sign is one of the easiest things to observe about sign production. This dictionary is divided into two handshape sections: the one-hand signs and the two-hand signs. This organization helps narrow the search for a sign to one of two large locations in the book. The handshape at the top of the even-numbered pages indicates the handshape of the first sign on the page. The handshape at the top of odd-numbered pages indicates the handshape of the last sign on the page.

One-Hand Signs

The illustrations for signs made with only one hand are presented in the first section of the dictionary. The signs follow the morphologic order of handshapes presented in figure 11, beginning with the signs that are made with an A handshape followed by those beginning with an Open A handshape, and so on. The signs within each handshape category are ordered in a specific sequence to assist the user in finding a sign. The signs presented first are those that have no change in handshape during sign production. For example, in the sign ANY, the handshape Open A stays the same, and therefore the sign ANY appears toward the beginning of the Open A handshape category. However, in the sign LADY, the handshape changes from Open A to 5 during the execution of the sign, so appears sequentially after all of the signs in which the handshape does not change. These changes in handshape are indicated by an arrowhead (>) between the handshapes; therefore, LADY appears under Open A > 5.

The one-hand signs have one more level of ordering—signs that are formed in space and do not touch the body appear before those signs that do

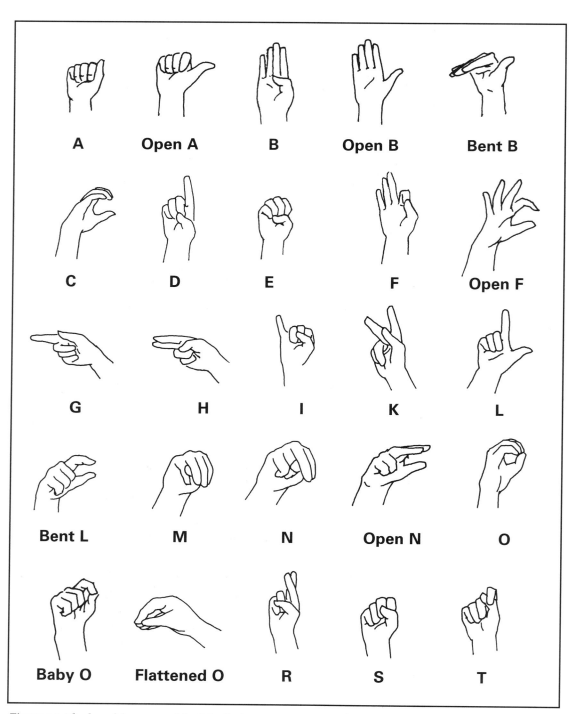

A Open A B Open B Bent B

C D E F Open F

G H I K L

Bent L M N Open N O

Baby O Flattened O R S T

Figure 11. The handshapes used in this dictionary are presented in morphological order.

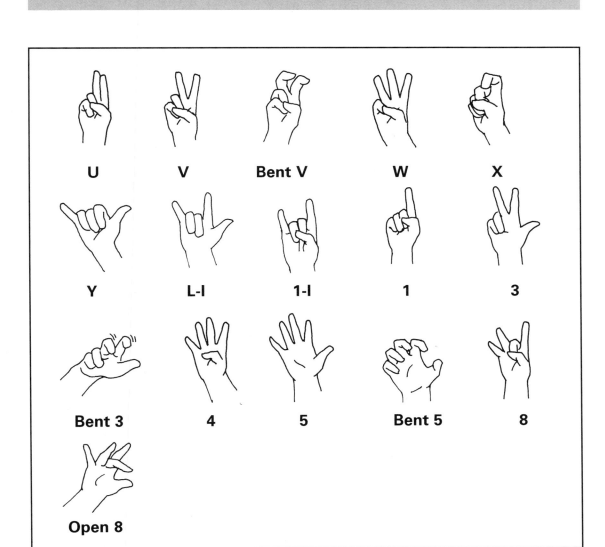

Figure 11 — continued

touch the body. Within the group of signs that touch the body, the ones that are formed on the head or neck precede those that touch the torso. Although this arrangement may not be important for small handshape categories, it will be very useful for quickly locating a particular sign in the handshape categories that contain many illustrations.

Two-Hand Signs

The section containing illustrations of signs in which two hands are used follows the one-hand signs section. The signs in the two-hand section follow the same morphologic order of handshapes as the one-hand signs. Remember that for two-hand signs, the order is determined by the initial handshape of the dominant hand. The dominant hand is assumed to be the right hand in this book.

As with one-hand signs, two-hand signs are presented within each handshape category in a specific sequence. Signs in which both hands have identical handshapes and both hands move appear first. These signs are identified by listing the handshape for each hand separated by a colon (A : A, the first A being the handshape for the dominant hand and the second A being the handshape for the passive hand). These signs are further ordered to assist the user, so that signs in which the movement occurs simultaneously are presented before signs in which the movement is alternating (first one hand moves and then the other hand makes an identical movement).

These signs are followed by two-hand signs that have identical handshapes, but only the *dominant* hand moves. Again, the handshapes for these signs are listed by the dominant handshape first, followed by a colon and the handshape of the passive hand (for example, Open B : Open B for the sign PIE; see figure 12).

For most two-hand signs the dominant hand is a different handshape from the passive hand. These signs appear after the signs with identical handshapes. Ordered first by the handshape of the dominant hand, the signs are further arranged in the morphologic order of the passive hand, so that A : Open B comes before A : L, which comes before A : 1.

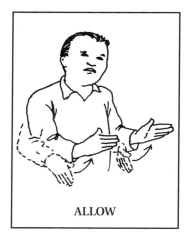
ALLOW

ANCESTORS

CLEAN

Figure 12. *The two-hand signs are ordered so that signs with identical hand movement are followed by signs with alternating hand movement, which are then followed by signs in which only the dominant hand moves.*

As with the signs in the one-hand sign section, two-hand signs some-times change handshapes while the sign is being produced. The change may take place only in the dominant hand or in both hands; however, the hand-shape of the passive hand never changes alone. These signs in which the handshape changes follow the signs with no handshape changes.

In summary, the two-hand signs are presented in the following sequence:

1. Hands have the same handshapes and move simultaneously;

2. Hands have the same handshapes and move alternatingly;

3. Hands have the same handshapes, but only the dominant hand moves;

4. Hands have different handshapes, and the hands are ordered first by the handshape and movement of the dominant hand and second by the handshape of the passive hand.

This order is important for locating signs in very large handshape categories.

Additional Role of the Passive Hand

There are some signs in which the passive hand or arm serves only as a base for the dominant hand's movement. For example, the signs used for periods of time in a day use the passive arm to represent the horizon, whereas the dominant hand represents the sun's movement in relation to the horizon. The handshape of the passive hand is immaterial and does not contribute to the meaning of the sign. In forming these signs, the passive hand may assume one of a number of handshapes, usually an Open B, B, S, or a loose unformed handshape. In this dictionary, the signs formed in this manner are ordered under the passive handshape shown in the artist's illustration.

Compounds

One additional group of signs may be presented at the end of a hand-shape category. These are signs classified as *compounds*. Compound signs are created by combining two basic signs into one new sign with a distinct meaning of its own. For example, the sign WIFE is made up of the signs FEMALE (a one-hand sign with an A handshape) and MARRY—two separate

Figure 13. WIFE *is a compound sign made from* FEMALE + MARRY.

signs that have merged to become WIFE (see figure 13). In compound signs, the changes in handshapes are usually more complicated than regular signs, so they are presented at the end of the handshape category designated by the initial handshape of the first of the two signs being combined. In the case of WIFE, the sign is located at the end of all of the A signs in the one-hand section of the dictionary, even though two hands are used in the second part of the sign.

Techniques for Using the Handshape Sections

The following examples provide step-by-step guidelines for using the one-hand and two-hand sections of the dictionary. To get the greatest benefit from these examples, follow the instructions below and locate each sign as directed.

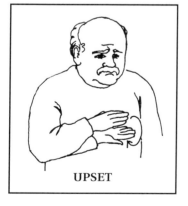

Example 1

Suppose you saw this sign and wanted to locate it in the dictionary. Your thinking should be as follows:

a. The sign is a one-hand sign. *(Go to the one-hand signs in the first section of the dictionary.)*

b. The sign has an Open B handshape. *(Go to the Open B category, which is located after B.)*

c. You observed that the hand touched the torso, so you would skip through the Open B category past the signs produced in space, past the signs that touch the head, until you reach those signs that touch the torso. *(Go through Open B until you come to those signs that touch the body.)* With quick perusal of the signs that touch the torso, you will easily find the illustration and learn that the English gloss for that sign is "upset."

Example 2

Suppose you had seen the following sign:

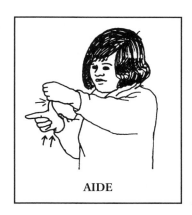

AIDE

a. The sign uses two hands. *(Go to the two-hand sign section of the dictionary.)*

b. The dominant hand has an L handshape and the passive hand has an S handshape. *(Go to the handshape category of the dominant hand—L).* Observe that the two-hand signs in each category begin with those signs in which both hands have the same shape (in this category, it is L : L).

c. After the signs having identical handshapes, the signs are arranged in the morphological order of the shape of the passive hand (for example, S). *(Go through the L category until you come to L : S.)* In this case, AIDE is the only sign with L : S handshapes.

Example 3

Try to find a sign in which the handshape changes.

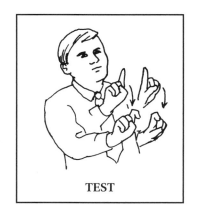

TEST

a. You observe that both hands begin with a 1 handshape and then both change to an X handshape. *(Go to the 1 handshape category in the two-hand section.)*

b. The 1 handshape category begins with all of the signs having identical handshapes on both hands (1 : 1). These are followed by the signs that begin 1 : 1 and then change handshapes. The signs are listed in the morphological order of the handshape formed after the change, in this case X. *(Skip through the 1 : 1 signs; then page through the signs that have a change in handshape until you come to 1 > X : 1 > X. If you come to the signs whose passive handshape is no longer 1, you have gone too far.)* You should easily locate the illustration of the sign for which you were looking and discover that its English gloss is "test."

Example 4

Suppose you see a sign that begins as a one-hand sign and then changes to a two-hand sign. You guess that it is a compound sign.

HUSBAND

a. To find compound signs in this dictionary, you must pay attention only to the hand-shapes used at the beginning of the sign. You can see that this sign begins as a one-hand sign. *(Go to the one-hand sign section.)*

b. The first handshape in the sign is a Flattened O. *(Go to the Flattened O handshape category.)*

c. The compound signs are at the end of a handshape category. *(Go to the end of the Flattened O handshape category.)* You find that the first sign in the compound is MALE and that the second sign is MARRIAGE. Together, these signs form the sign HUSBAND.

Example 5

You see a two-hand sign in which the passive hand or arm merely serves as a base for the dominant hand. How do you find the sign?

SHEEP

a. The dominant hand has a V handshape, and you think that the passive hand has an Open B handshape. The passive hand could also be a B or S or relaxed hand without changing the meaning of the sign. *(Go to the two-hand section of the book. Then find the V : Open B signs.)*

b. The passive signs are at the end of the V : Open B signs, but before the compound signs, if there are any. The word *passive* is given after the handshape to indicate that it doesn't matter what shape the passive hand uses. *(Go to the end of the V : Open B handshape category until you come to signs designated as passive.)*

c. You should easily find the illustration for the sign SHEEP. If you cannot find the correct illustration, then you should proceed to look under B or S. (There are no relaxed hand handshape categories in this dictionary.)

Additional Clues

Sometimes you may look for a sign and not find it under the handshape category where you think it should be. The following list contains possible reasons why this might happen.

1. This dictionary contains about one-fourth of all the possible handshapes. Each sign has been categorized by the handshape it most closely resembles in its initial position.

2. This book is arranged by the initial handshape(s); sometimes it may be the final position of the sign that you remember.

3. The book contains only a few of the multitude of regional variations for signs.

4. Deaf people and other skilled signers often truncate their signs for more efficient and rapid communication.

5. You may have looked under the two-hand section for a sign that can be signed with one hand, or vice versa (for example, COW).

6. With compound signs, each part of the sign is typically signed rapidly and with less complete articulation (BROTHER is a compound of BOY and SAME, yet when signed together, SAME looks different than when it is signed alone).

7. Some handshapes are quite similar to others, especially when you observe someone signing rapidly. Figure 14 shows handshape "look-alikes." This information may help you find a sign under a different handshape than you expected.

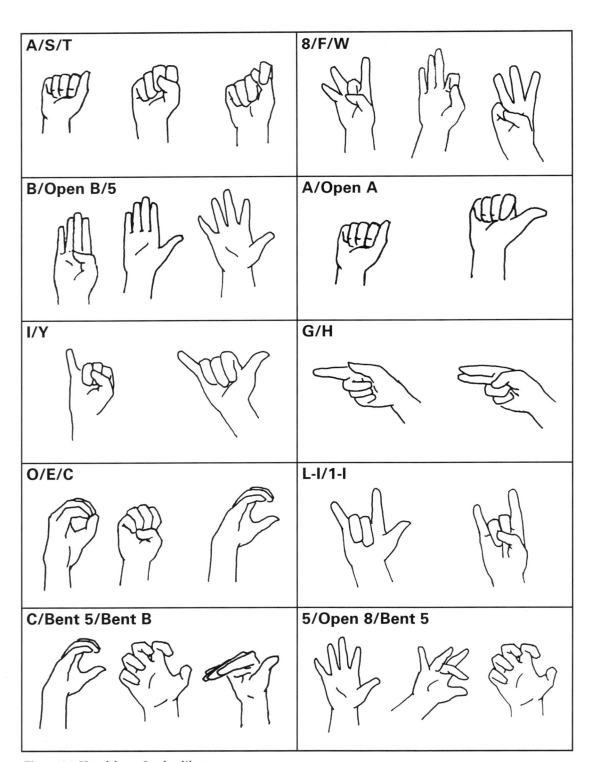

Figure 14. Handshape Look-alikes

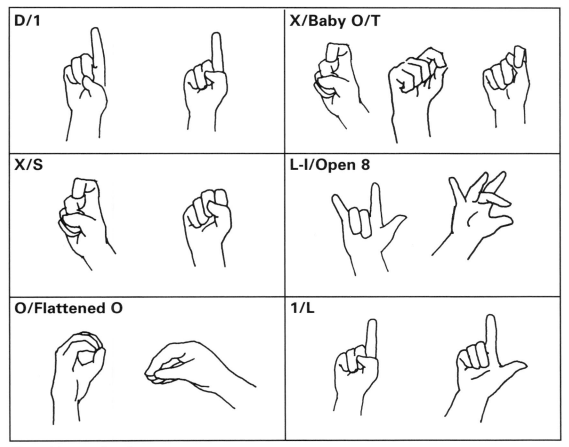

Figure 14 — continued

Organization of the Index of English Glosses

The Index of English Glosses section of this dictionary is an alphabetical listing of English words and phrases that appear as glosses with the sign illustrations in the handshape sections. Some words list more than one entry. These entries lead to several signs that can be used to express either the same or various meanings of those words. These entries usually have additional information (part of speech, synonym, meaning) to assist in identifying which entry may be the appropriate choice for the usage needed.

Information about the handshape for each sign is also given for each gloss entry. The handshape(s) of the sign may help the user further identify which of the identical entries is the one being sought.

One-Hand
Signs

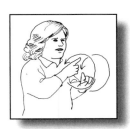

purse

Handshape: A
Orientation: palm in
Location: neutral space
Movement: double bounce hand down
Note: This sign is similar to SUITCASE, which is made with an S handshape.

Africa, African

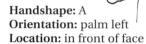

Handshape: A
Orientation: palm left
Location: in front of face
Movement: circle thumb around face
Note: This sign is disparaging to African Americans. See page 139 for the preferred sign.

dumb, stupid

Handshape: A
Orientation: palm in
Location: near forehead
Movement: move hand in and hit forehead

audiology *(audiologist)*

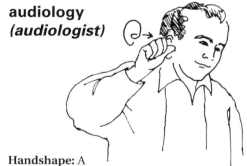

Handshape: A
Orientation: palm out
Location: near right ear
Movement: move thumb forward and make small circles around the ear

menstruate, period

Handshape: A
Orientation: palm left
Location: right cheek
Movement: double bounce fingers against cheek
Nonmanual signal: puff air into right cheek

aunt

Handshape: A
Orientation: palm out
Location: right cheek
Movement: move thumb down cheek in two short movements
Note: Movement may be circular.

patient, bear, long-suffering, patience, stand, tolerance, withstand

Handshape: A
Orientation: palm left
Location: lips
Movement: move thumb down to chin

private, confidential, privacy, secret, top-secret

Handshape: A
Orientation: palm left
Location: near chin
Movement: gently tap chin twice

am

Handshape: A
Orientation: palm left
Location: mouth
Movement: move thumb straight out from mouth
Note: Use this sign only when signing manual English.

Canada, Canadian

Handshape: A
Orientation: palm in
Location: below right shoulder
Movement: double bounce hand off chest
Note: The hand grasps clothing.

assembly (legislative body)

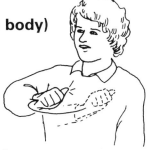

Handshape: A
Orientation: palm left, back of thumb against chest
Location: left side of chest
Movement: arc hand from left side of chest to right side of chest

attitude

Handshape: A
Orientation: palm left
Location: below left shoulder
Movement: make small circular movement, ending with thumb on chest

**zip (SM),
zipper (DM)**

Handshape: A
Orientation: palm in
Location: waist
Movement: move hand up the chest

**sorry,
apologize,
regret,
remorse,
repent**

Handshape: A
Orientation: palm in
Location: center of chest
Movement: circle hand on chest
Nonmanual signal: head and eyes
  lowered; "sad" expression

**several,
a few**

Handshape: A > 6
Orientation: palm up
Location: neutral space
Movement: sweep thumb across fingertips
  from index finger to little finger

**commute,
back and forth,
day student,
round-trip**

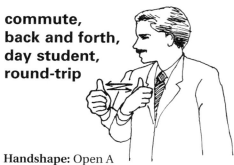

Handshape: Open A
Orientation: palm left
Location: neutral space
Movement: move hand forward and
  back twice

**another, else,
elsewhere,
other**

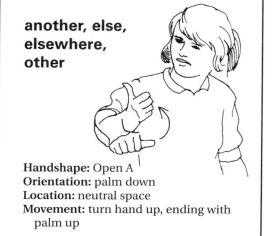

Handshape: Open A
Orientation: palm down
Location: neutral space
Movement: turn hand up, ending with
  palm up

any

Handshape: Open A
Orientation: palm left
Location: neutral space
Movement: turn hand down, ending
  with palm down

turn down, deny, reject

Handshape: Open A
Orientation: palm left
Location: neutral space
Movement: twist wrist, ending with thumb pointing down

herself, himself, itself

Handshape: Open A
Orientation: palm left
Location: neutral space
Movement: double bounce toward referent
Nonmanual signal: eyes on the person to whom you are speaking

yourself

Handshape: Open A
Orientation: palm left
Location: neutral space
Movement: double bounce toward referent
Nonmanual signal: eyes on referent

yourselves

Handshape: Open A
Orientation: palm left
Location: neutral space
Movement: arc thumb from left to right in front of chest
Nonmanual signal: eyes on people to whom you are speaking

themselves

Handshape: Open A
Orientation: palm left
Location: neutral space
Movement: arc thumb right to left toward referents
Nonmanual signal: eyes on person to whom you are speaking

bye, good luck, take care

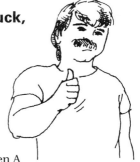

Handshape: Open A
Orientation: palm left
Location: neutral space
Movement: double bounce hand forward toward referent

chief, superior, -er, -est

Handshape: Open A
Orientation: palm in
Location: above right shoulder
Movement: jerk thumb upward above shoulder
Note: The hand makes a larger movement upward to indicate a higher status.

refuse, won't

Handshape: Open A
Orientation: palm left
Location: in front of right shoulder
Movement: jerk thumb sharply toward right shoulder
Nonmanual signal: head shakes "no"

daily, common, everyday, ordinary, usual

Handshape: Open A
Orientation: palm left
Location: right cheek
Movement: brush knuckles down cheek twice

yesterday

Handshape: Open A
Orientation: palm out
Location: near mouth
Movement: arc thumb back to touch cheek
Nonmanual signal: right shoulder lifts up; head tilts right; "cz" mouth movement

tomorrow

Handshape: Open A
Orientation: palm left
Location: right cheek
Movement: twist wrist forward
Nonmanual signal: right shoulder lifts up; head tilts right; "cz" mouth movement

nut, peanut

Handshape: Open A
Orientation: palm left
Location: thumb under front teeth
Movement: flick thumb forward with short double movement

drink (alcoholic beverage)

Handshape: Open A
Orientation: palm left
Location: near mouth
Movement: move thumb in toward mouth twice

India

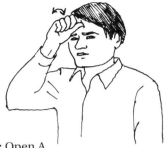

Handshape: Open A
Orientation: palm left
Location: forehead
Movement: twist thumb back and forth on forehead in small, quick movements

girl

Handshape: Open A
Orientation: palm left
Location: thumb on cheek
Movement: brush thumb forward on cheek twice

not, don't

Handshape: Open A
Orientation: palm left
Location: under chin
Movement: thrust hand forward
Nonmanual signal: head shakes "no"

myself, self

Handshape: Open A
Orientation: palm right
Location: chest
Movement: double bounce hand on chest

ourselves

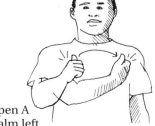

Handshape: Open A
Orientation: palm left
Location: thumb below right shoulder
Movement: arc hand across chest, ending with knuckles on left chest area, palm right
Nonmanual signal: eyes on persons to whom you are speaking

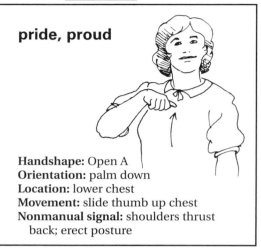

pride, proud

Handshape: Open A
Orientation: palm down
Location: lower chest
Movement: slide thumb up chest
Nonmanual signal: shoulders thrust back; erect posture

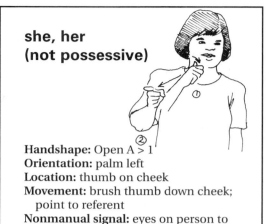

she, her (not possessive)

Handshape: Open A > 1
Orientation: palm left
Location: thumb on cheek
Movement: brush thumb down cheek; point to referent
Nonmanual signal: eyes on person to whom you are speaking

a few days ago

Handshape: Open A > 3
Orientation: palm down
Location: thumb on cheek
Movement: flip hand back while changing to 3 handshape

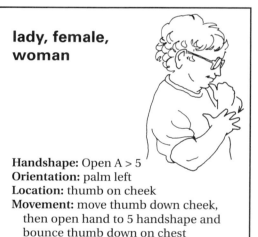

lady, female, woman

Handshape: Open A > 5
Orientation: palm left
Location: thumb on cheek
Movement: move thumb down cheek, then open hand to 5 handshape and bounce thumb down on chest

anything (compound: any + thing)

Handshape: Open A > Open B
Orientation: palm up
Location: neutral space
Movement: twist wrist down, then change to Open B handshape and flip hand up

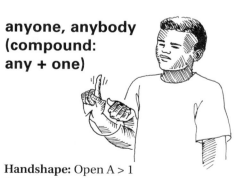

anyone, anybody (compound: any + one)

Handshape: Open A > 1
Orientation: palm up
Location: neutral space
Movement: twist wrist down and change hand to 1 handshape, palm forward

daughter (compound: girl + baby)

Handshape: Open A > Open B : passive
Orientation: palm left
Location: thumb on cheek
Movement: brush thumb down cheek, then change hand to Open B handshape and move arm down, ending with back of right arm on top of left arm

wife (compound: girl + marry)

Handshape: Open A > C : C
Orientation: palm left
Location: thumb on cheek
Movement: brush thumb down cheek, then change to C handshape and clasp left hand

sister (compound: girl + same)

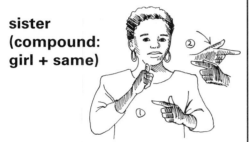

Handshape: Open A > L : L
Orientation: right palm left, left palm right
Location: right thumb on cheek
Movement: move thumb down cheek, then change hand to L handshape and bring hand down on top of left hand

blue

Handshape: B
Orientation: palm left
Location: neutral space
Movement: twist wrist back and forth twice

never

Handshape: B
Orientation: palm left
Location: in front of face
Movement: move hand down with large wavy motion
Nonmanual signal: head shakes "no"

humble

Handshape: B
Orientation: palm left
Location: in front of face
Movement: arc hand down
Nonmanual signal: head lowered

hospital

Handshape: B
Orientation: palm left
Location: forehead
Movement: arc hand from right to left side of forehead

firefighter, fireman

Handshape: B
Orientation: palm out
Location: middle of forehead
Movement: tap forehead twice

fever

Handshape: B
Orientation: palm out
Location: near forehead
Movement: lay back of hand lightly on forehead
Nonmanual signal: "sick" expression

Australia, Australian

Handshape: B
Orientation: palm left
Location: index finger on forehead
Movement: flip hand back, ending with palm out
Note: See page 363 for the preferred sign.

bastard

Handshape: B
Orientation: palm left
Location: near forehead
Movement: hit forehead sharply with edge of hand

hello, hi, greet

Handshape: B
Orientation: palm left
Location: forehead
Movement: move hand forward and tilt fingers forward
Nonmanual signal: head tilts back; smile

be

Handshape: B
Orientation: palm left
Location: mouth
Movement: move hand straight out, away from mouth
Note: Use this sign only when signing manual English.

bachelor

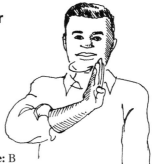

Handshape: B
Orientation: palm left
Location: right side of chin
Movement: arc hand from right to left side of chin

beer

Handshape: B
Orientation: palm out
Location: cheek
Movement: brush index finger down cheek twice

brown

Handshape: B
Orientation: palm out
Location: cheek
Movement: slide index finger down cheek

bullshit, brownnose

Handshape: B
Orientation: palm left
Location: nose
Movement: slide index finger up and down nose twice

lie *(liar)*, slander

Handshape: B
Orientation: palm down
Location: chin
Movement: move hand right to left across chin

full, fed up, up to here

Handshape: B
Orientation: palm down
Location: under chin
Movement: bring back of hand up sharply and hit chin
Nonmanual signal: head tilts back

bite

Handshape: B
Orientation: palm down
Location: mouth
Movement: put edge of hand between teeth

bitch

Handshape: B
Orientation: palm left
Location: near mouth
Movement: hit mouth sharply with index finger

board (group of persons)

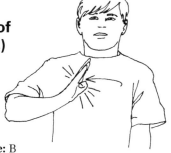

Handshape: B
Orientation: palm left
Location: chest
Movement: arc hand from left to right side of chest

your, yours (singular)

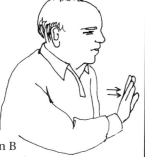

Handshape: Open B
Orientation: palm out
Location: neutral space
Movement: double bounce hand forward toward referent
Nonmanual signal: eyes on referent

his, her, its

Handshape: Open B
Orientation: palm out
Location: neutral space
Movement: move hand toward referent
Nonmanual signal: eyes on person to whom you are speaking

yours (plural)

Handshape: Open B
Orientation: palm out
Location: neutral space
Movement: move hand in arc from left to right
Nonmanual signal: eyes on people to whom you are speaking

theirs, their

Handshape: Open B
Orientation: palm out
Location: neutral space
Movement: point hand toward referents and make a small arc from left to right
Nonmanual signal: eyes on person to whom you are speaking

call (for attention)

Handshape: Open B
Orientation: palm angled out
Location: neutral space
Movement: double bounce hand down
Nonmanual signal: "earnest" expression

thing, object

Handshape: Open B
Orientation: palm up
Location: neutral space
Movement: bounce hand to the right
Note: This sign can also be made with a double bounce to the right.

welcome, employ, hire

Handshape: Open B
Orientation: palm left
Location: neutral space
Movement: swing hand down and in toward chest, ending palm up

get away, away

Handshape: Open B
Orientation: palm in
Location: neutral space
Movement: flip hand out sharply
Nonmanual signal: "angry" expression

come here

Handshape: Open B
Orientation: palm in, fingers angled up
Location: neutral space
Movement: bend wrist in toward chest

**grow up,
all my life,
childhood,
raised,
reared,
upbringing**

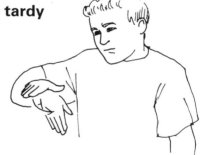

Handshape: Open B
Orientation: palm down
Location: neutral space
Movement: move hand up to eye level
Nonmanual signal: head tilts back;
    eyes watch hand movement

**not yet,
haven't**

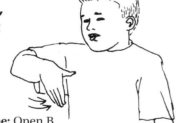

Handshape: Open B
Orientation: palm in, fingers down
Location: neutral space
Movement: swing fingers back toward
    body twice
Nonmanual signal: mouth open;
    tongue protruding

late, tardy

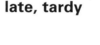

Handshape: Open B
Orientation: palm down
Location: neutral space
Movement: swing fingers back

**hello, hi (SM);
good-bye,
so long (DM)**

Handshape: Open B
Orientation: palm out
Location: near right shoulder
Movement: wave hand from side to side

**will, shall,
would**

Handshape: Open B
Orientation: palm left
Location: near head
Movement: move hand forward while
    tipping fingers forward

future, later on, someday

Handshape: Open B
Orientation: palm left
Location: near head
Movement: move hand forward in double arc

formerly, ages ago, ancestors, ancient, former, previously

Handshape: Open B
Orientation: palm left
Location: near head
Movement: circle hand back twice
Nonmanual signal: right shoulder up

God

Handshape: Open B
Orientation: palm left
Location: above head
Movement: arc hand down in front of face
Nonmanual signal: head tilts back; eyes gaze up and follow hand movement

lecture, oration, presentation, speech, testimony

Handshape: Open B
Orientation: palm left
Location: near head
Movement: shake hand forward and back from wrist several times

elephant

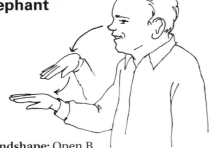

Handshape: Open B
Orientation: palm down
Location: near nose
Movement: move hand down and forward, tracing the shape of a trunk

mirror

Handshape: Open B
Orientation: palm left
Location: near face
Movement: rotate palm forward and back twice
Nonmanual signal: eyes watch hand movement

apparent, appear, seem

Handshape: Open B
Orientation: palm out
Location: near face
Movement: twist palm slightly in

smell, fragrant, odor

Handshape: Open B
Orientation: palm in
Location: in front of face
Movement: circle hand up toward nose
Nonmanual signal: wrinkle nose; purse lips

in front of, front

Handshape: Open B
Orientation: palm in
Location: in front of face
Movement: double bounce hand
   toward face

overlook, incognito, invisible

Handshape: Open B
Orientation: palm in
Location: in front of right eye
Movement: move hand down across face

don't know

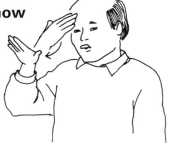

Handshape: Open B
Orientation: palm in, fingers up
Location: forehead
Movement: flip hand out and down
Nonmanual signal: head shakes "no"

hat

Handshape: Open B
Orientation: palm down
Location: top of head
Movement: tap top of head twice

cabbage, lettuce

Handshape: Open B
Orientation: palm left
Location: temple
Movement: hit temple with heel of hand twice

bed, sleep

Handshape: Open B
Orientation: palm left
Location: cheek
Movement: rest cheek on palm
Nonmanual signal: head tilts right

hear, listen

Handshape: Open B
Orientation: palm left
Location: near ear
Movement: bring hand back behind ear
Nonmanual signal: head tilts left

call (to get attention)

Handshape: Open B
Orientation: palm left
Location: near mouth
Movement: move hand back to right side of mouth
Nonmanual signal: head tilts back, mouth opens

whisper (hearing people)

Handshape: Open B
Orientation: palm left
Location: in front of mouth
Movement: move hand back to left side of mouth
Nonmanual signal: head and body tilt to the right

frustrated

Handshape: Open B
Orientation: palm out
Location: near mouth
Movement: smack back of hand against mouth
Nonmanual signal: "frustrated" expression

thank you, thanks

Handshape: Open B
Orientation: palm in
Location: mouth
Movement: move hand forward
Nonmanual signal: head bows; smile

napkin

Handshape: Open B
Orientation: palm in
Location: mouth
Movement: brush hand across mouth twice

ice cream

Handshape: Open B
Orientation: palm in
Location: mouth
Movement: brush hand down lips twice

sweet, adorable

Handshape: Open B
Orientation: palm in
Location: chin
Movement: brush fingertips down chin twice

bad, evil, wicked

Handshape: Open B
Orientation: palm in, fingers angled up
Location: mouth
Movement: move hand out, then turn hand over and sharply bend wrist down

my (SM); mine (DM)

Handshape: Open B
Orientation: palm in
Location: chest
Movement: pat chest with palm

our, ours

Handshape: Open B
Orientation: palm left
Location: thumb near right shoulder
Movement: arc hand across chest, ending with palm right
Nonmanual signal: eyes pan the eyes of all the referents

willing, acquiesce, admit, confess, consent, give in, yield

Handshape: Open B
Orientation: palm in
Location: palm on chest
Movement: move hand out a short distance
Nonmanual signal: body leans forward

happy, delight, glad, joy, merry

Handshape: Open B
Orientation: palm in
Location: chest
Movement: brush hand up in a circular motion twice
Nonmanual signal: smile

upset

Handshape: Open B
Orientation: palm down
Location: index finger on chest
Movement: flip hand over, ending with palm up
Nonmanual signal: "angry" or "sad" expression

please, appreciate, enjoy

Handshape: Open B
Orientation: palm in
Location: palm on chest
Movement: make small circles on chest
Nonmanual signal: smile

because

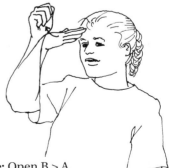

Handshape: Open B > A
Orientation: palm in
Location: fingertips on forehead
Movement: arc hand up, closing to A handshape

forget

Handshape: Open B > A
Orientation: palm in
Location: fingertips on forehead
Movement: slide fingers across and off forehead, closing to A handshape
Nonmanual signal: head tilts back

better

Handshape: Open B > A
Orientation: palm in
Location: mouth
Movement: move hand out to the right, closing to A handshape
Note: Exaggerate movement upward to form the superlative form, "best."

prefer, rather

Handshape: Open B > A
Orientation: palm in
Location: chest
Movement: arc hand up to the right, closing to A handshape

dog

Handshape: Open B > A
Orientation: palm left
Location: right thigh
Movement: smack thigh, then move hand up and snap fingers twice
Nonmanual signal: lips pursed

stubborn, obstinate, persistent

Handshape: Open B > Bent B
Orientation: palm out
Location: thumb on right temple
Movement: bend fingers down sharply
Nonmanual signal: eyebrows knit, frown

sleepy

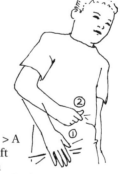

Handshape: Open B > Bent B
Orientation: palm in, fingers up
Location: in front of face
Movement: bend fingers down twice
Nonmanual signal: droopy eyes

pig

Handshape: Open B > Bent B
Orientation: palm down
Location: under chin
Movement: bend fingers down and up twice

dweeb, jerk, nerd

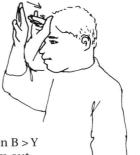

Handshape: Open B > Y
Orientation: palm out
Location: near forehead
Movement: bring hand back against forehead while changing to Y handshape
Nonmanual signal: tongue protrudes

why

Handshape: Open B > Y
Orientation: palm in
Location: fingertips on forehead
Movement: move hand forward and down while changing to Y handshape
Nonmanual signal: "questioning" expression
Note: See page 115 for a variation of this sign.

**pollution
(compound: smell + mix)**

Handshape: Open B > 5 : 5
Orientation: right palm in; left palm up
Location: right hand in front of mouth; left hand in neutral space
Movement: brush hand up toward nose, then change to 5 handshape, palm down above left palm, and move hands in circular motion

BENT B ✿ 1-Hand SIGNS

short, small (height)

Handshape: Bent B
Orientation: palm down
Location: neutral space
Movement: move hand down
Nonmanual signal: eyes follow hand

child

Handshape: Bent B
Orientation: palm down
Location: neutral space
Movement: move hand down a short distance

adult, tall, big

Handshape: Bent B
Orientation: palm down
Location: neutral space
Movement: move hand up
Nonmanual signal: eyes follow hand

back, behind, rear

Handshape: Bent B
Orientation: palm in
Location: above right shoulder
Movement: double bounce hand back over right shoulder

past, ago, ex-, last, previous, was

Handshape: Bent B
Orientation: palm in
Location: in front of right shoulder
Movement: move hand back over right shoulder

know (SM); aware, conscious, familiar, knowledge, mental, recognize (DM)

Handshape: Bent B
Orientation: palm in
Location: near temple
Movement: tap temple with fingertips

head

Handshape: Bent B
Orientation: palm down
Location: temple
Movement: move fingertips from right temple to right cheek

broke, penniless

Handshape: Bent B
Orientation: palm down
Location: near neck
Movement: strike side of neck with side of hand
Nonmanual signal: head tilts left

ashamed, bashful, shame, shy

Handshape: Bent B
Orientation: palm down
Location: knuckles on cheek
Movement: twist hand up
Nonmanual signal: head tilts right; eyes lowered

blouse

Handshape: Bent B
Orientation: palm in
Location: fingertips on chest
Movement: arc hand down to waist, ending with palm up

me (dramatic)

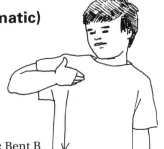

Handshape: Bent B
Orientation: palm up
Location: fingertips on chest
Movement: slide hand down chest to waist
Nonmanual signal: shoulders thrust back; erect posture

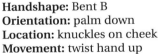

member

Handshape: Bent B
Orientation: palm in
Location: fingertips on left side of chest
Movement: arc hand across to right side of chest

breasts

Handshape: Bent B
Orientation: palm in
Location: fingertips on left breast
Movement: arc hand across to right breast

pig (insult)

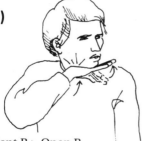

Handshape: Bent B > Open B
Orientation: palm down
Location: under chin
Movement: smack hand up sharply to hit chin while straightening fingers
Nonmanual signal: "disgusted" expression

force, coerce, compel, impel

Handshape: C
Orientation: palm out
Location: neutral space
Movement: move hand forward and bend wrist down

conservative

Handshape: C
Orientation: palm out
Location: neutral space
Movement: shake hand gently side to side

Chicago

Handshape: C
Orientation: palm left
Location: neutral space
Movement: move hand to the right and down

Christmas

Handshape: C
Orientation: palm out
Location: neutral space
Movement: swing hand in a semicircle, ending with palm in
Note: See page 64 for a variation of this sign

strange, curious, odd, queer, weird

Handshape: C
Orientation: palm left
Location: near right eye
Movement: bend wrist down, ending with palm down in front of chin
Nonmanual signal: head tilts right; frown with "puzzled" expression

examine, investigate, look for, probe, search, seek

Handshape: C
Orientation: palm left
Location: near face
Movement: circle hand to the left in front of face at least twice
Nonmanual signal: head and body move slightly left with each circular movement; eyes scan room
Note: When referring to a more thorough examination, use both hands in an alternating movement.

cousin (male)

Handshape: C
Orientation: palm left
Location: near temple
Movement: twist wrist back and forth
Note: The sign for a female cousin is made near the chin.

computer

Handshape: C
Orientation: palm left
Location: right temple
Movement: double bounce thumb against temple

sun

Handshape: C
Orientation: palm left
Location: near right temple
Movement: double bounce fingertips
   against temple
Nonmanual signal: head tilts left

genius

Handshape: C
Orientation: palm left
Location: near forehead
Movement: move hand back, ending
   with thumb on forehead
Nonmanual signal: puffed cheeks

**concept,
cognitive**

Handshape: C
Orientation: palm in
Location: thumb on forehead
Movement: move hand out

choke, gag

Handshape: C
Orientation: palm in
Location: fingertips on neck
Movement: shake hand slightly from side
   to side
Nonmanual signal: "choking" expression

**Christmas,
Santa Claus**

Handshape: C
Orientation: palm left
Location: chin
Movement: arc hand down to chest,
   ending with palm up
Note: See page 63 for a variation of this
   sign.

**drink,
beverage**

Handshape: C
Orientation: palm left
Location: thumb on mouth
Movement: tilt hand up

cafeteria

Handshape: C
Orientation: palm left
Location: index finger on left side of chin
Movement: slide index finger down left
side of chin, then down right side of chin

beard

Handshape: C
Orientation: palm in
Location: fingertips on right side of chin
Movement: slide fingers across to left side
of chin

appetite, hunger, hungry, wish (SM); passion, lust (DM)

Handshape: C
Orientation: palm in
Location: fingertips on chest
Movement: slide fingertips slowly
down chest; for "passion" and "lust,"
make shorter, faster movements

cop, guard, patrol, police, security

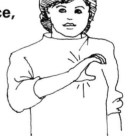

Handshape: C
Orientation: palm left
Location: chest
Movement: double bounce side of hand
on chest

character

Handshape: C
Orientation: palm left
Location: near chest
Movement: move hand in a small circle,
then drop hand on chest

Congress, committee, council

Handshape: C
Orientation: palm left
Location: left side of chest
Movement: arc hand across to right side
of chest

complain, object (SM); complain, grievance, objection (DM)

Handshape: C
Orientation: palm in
Location: chest
Movement: double bounce fingertips against chest

Christ (Christian)

Handshape: C
Orientation: palm left
Location: below left shoulder
Movement: move hand across body down to right side of waist

cough

Handshape: C
Orientation: palm in
Location: fingertips on chest
Movement: rock hand up and down
Nonmanual signal: shoulders rounded; "sick" expression

pension, allowance, dividend, royalty, subscription, welfare

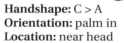

Handshape: C > A
Orientation: palm in
Location: near head
Movement: bring hand down in short, quick double motion while changing to A handshape
Nonmanual signal: lips pursed

boy

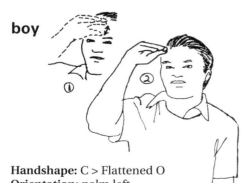

Handshape: C > Flattened O
Orientation: palm left
Location: near forehead
Movement: close fingertips and thumb together twice

man, male

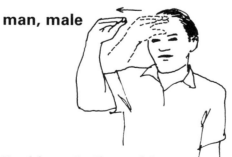

Handshape: C > Flattened O
Orientation: palm left
Location: near forehead
Movement: move hand forward, closing fingertips and thumb

milk, dairy

Handshape: C > S
Orientation: palm left
Location: neutral space
Movement: open and close fist twice

guess, assume, estimate, miss

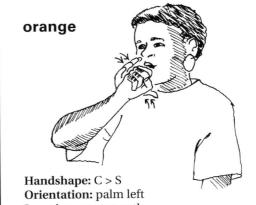

Handshape: C > S
Orientation: palm left
Location: right side of face
Movement: arc hand across face, closing to S handshape

old, age, antique

Handshape: C > S
Orientation: palm left
Location: index finger on chin
Movement: move hand down while changing to S handshape

orange

Handshape: C > S
Orientation: palm left
Location: near mouth
Movement: open and close fist twice

democrat

Handshape: D
Orientation: palm out
Location: neutral space
Movement: shake hand back and forth, gently

dinner

Handshape: D
Orientation: palm in
Location: near chin
Movement: tap chin twice with fingertips

detective

Handshape: D
Orientation: palm down
Location: chest
Movement: brush fingertips down
    chest twice

east

Handshape: E
Orientation: palm out
Location: neutral space
Movement: move hand right

elevator

Handshape: E
Orientation: palm left
Location: neutral space
Movement: move hand up and down

Easter

Handshape: E
Orientation: palm out
Location: near head
Movement: twist wrist back and forth
    with small movement

Europe

Handshape: E
Orientation: palm in
Location: near forehead
Movement: move hand in small circle

french fries

Handshape: F
Orientation: palm down
Location: neutral space
Movement: bounce hand from left to right

Friday

Handshape: F
Orientation: palm in
Location: neutral space
Movement: move hand in gentle circular motion

every Friday, Fridays

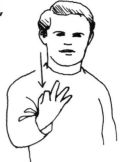

Handshape: F
Orientation: palm in
Location: in front of face
Movement: move hand down

pepper

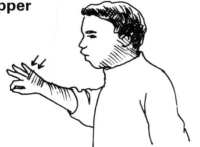

Handshape: F
Orientation: palm down
Location: neutral space
Movement: double bounce hand down

fine (texture)

Handshape: F
Orientation: palm out
Location: neutral space
Movement: rub index finger and thumb together several times

furniture

Handshape: F
Orientation: palm out
Location: neutral space
Movement: shake hand slightly side to side

preach (minister, pastor, preacher), sermon

Handshape: F
Orientation: palm out
Location: near right shoulder
Movement: double bounce hand forward
Nonmanual signal: lips pursed

find, discover

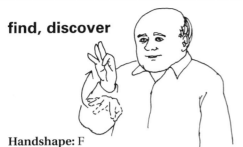

Handshape: F
Orientation: palm down
Location: neutral space
Movement: bend wrist up, ending with palm out
Nonmanual signal: head tilts back; mouth open

France, French

Handshape: F
Orientation: palm out
Location: near head
Movement: swing hand in a semicircle, ending with palm in

in the nick of time

Handshape: F
Orientation: palm in
Location: thumb and index fingertips on right eyebrow
Movement: move hand out in a short, quick motion
Nonmanual signal: right shoulder lifts up; head tilts right; "cz" mouth movement

hair

Handshape: F
Orientation: palm left
Location: head
Movement: grasp hair and pull up twice, using short, quick motions

Native American, American Indian, Indian

Handshape: F
Orientation: palm left
Location: near chin
Movement: bounce thumb and index fingertips back along cheek toward ear

earring

Handshape: F
Orientation: palm left
Location: right earlobe
Movement: wiggle earlobe several times

very close, nearby

Handshape: F
Orientation: palm in
Location: thumb and index fingertips on nose
Movement: twist hand sharply out and bend wrist down
Nonmanual signal: right shoulder lifts up; head tilts right; "cz" mouth movement

fox

Handshape: F
Orientation: palm left
Location: thumb and index fingertips on nose
Movement: twist wrist back and forth

fruit

Handshape: F
Orientation: palm left
Location: thumb and index fingertips on cheek
Movement: twist hand forward twice

cat

Handshape: F
Orientation: palm left
Location: cheek
Movement: brush index finger and thumb back toward ear twice
Note: See page 223 for a two-hand variation of this sign.

soon

Handshape: F
Orientation: palm in
Location: chin
Movement: tap chin twice
Nonmanual signal: right shoulder lifts up; head tilts right; "cz" mouth movement

knack, expert

Handshape: F
Orientation: palm in
Location: near chin
Movement: bring hand in to hit chin
Nonmanual signal: lips taut

curious

Handshape: F
Orientation: palm in
Location: neck
Movement: grasp skin of neck and pull side to side
Nonmanual signal: body leans forward; head tilts right; eyebrows knit

volunteer, apply, candidate

Handshape: F
Orientation: palm in
Location: chest
Movement: grasp shirt fabric and tug twice
Nonmanual signal: right shoulder raised

benefit, advantage

Handshape: F
Orientation: palm down
Location: on chest
Movement: brush thumb and index fingertips down chest

profit, commission, gain

Handshape: F
Orientation: palm down
Location: ribs
Movement: brush thumb and index fingertips down body
Nonmanual signal: right shoulder raised

pill, capsule, take a pill

Handshape: F > Open F
Orientation: palm in
Location: near mouth
Movement: move hand toward mouth and flick open index finger and thumb twice
Nonmanual signal: mouth open

appoint, choose, select

Handshape: Open F > F
Orientation: palm down
Location: neutral space
Movement: bend wrist back, closing to F handshape

skunk

Handshape: Open F > G
Orientation: palm in
Location: nose
Movement: press nostrils together, then change to G handshape and move hand up head, ending with hand on top of head, palm out

green

Handshape: G
Orientation: palm up
Location: neutral space
Movement: twist hand up and down several times

quiz

Handshape: G
Orientation: palm out
Location: neutral space
Movement: trace the shape of a question mark with fingers, ending with palm down

small, little bit, slight, tiny

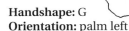

Handshape: G
Orientation: palm left
Location: near face
Movement: bring hand back slightly toward face
Nonmanual signal: "cz" mouth movement; right shoulder and head tilt to right side

turkey

Handshape: G
Orientation: palm down
Location: chin
Movement: swing fingers back and forth twice

priest, clergy (SM); collar (DM)

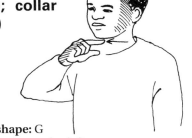

Handshape: G
Orientation: palm left
Location: neck
Movement: move hand left to right across neck

Thanksgiving

Handshape: G
Orientation: palm down
Location: index finger on mouth
Movement: move hand down to center of chest

queen

Handshape: G
Orientation: palm down
Location: index finger and thumb on chest
Movement: move hand diagonally across body, ending at right side of waist

guilt, conscience, guilty

Handshape: G
Orientation: palm left
Location: below left shoulder
Movement: tap index finger and thumb against chest

what-to-do, what

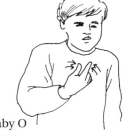

Handshape: G > Baby O
Orientation: palm up
Location: neutral space
Movement: bring index finger and thumb together twice
Nonmanual signal: body leans forward, head tilts right, "puzzled" expression

lots to do, busy

Handshape: G > Baby O
Orientation: palm up
Location: neutral space
Movement: move hand in small circles while opening and closing index finger and thumb
Nonmanual signal: trill lips

Gallaudet

Handshape: G > Baby O
Orientation: palm right
Location: thumb and index fingertips near right eye
Movement: move hand back and close index finger and thumb

glasses, eyeglasses

Handshape: G > Baby O
Orientation: palm left
Location: thumb and index fingertips near right eye
Movement: move hand right, closing index finger and thumb twice

bird, chicken

Handshape: G > Baby O
Orientation: palm out
Location: index finger against cheek
Movement: close and open index finger and thumb twice

pin (jewelry)

Handshape: G > Baby O
Orientation: palm in
Location: thumb on chest
Movement: close index finger against thumb

Thursday

Handshape: H
Orientation: palm in
Location: neutral space
Movement: move hand in gentle circular motion

every Thursday, Thursdays

Handshape: H
Orientation: palm in
Location: in front of face
Movement: move hand down

zap, got ya! (slang)

Handshape: H
Orientation: palm out
Location: neutral space
Movement: bend hand forward and back quickly

hard of hearing

Handshape: H
Orientation: palm left
Location: neutral space
Movement: bounce hand down from left to right

history

Handshape: H
Orientation: palm left
Location: neutral space
Movement: shake hand up and down twice

use, utilize, wear

Handshape: H
Orientation: palm out
Location: neutral space
Movement: move hand in a circle
Note: See page 237 for a two-hand variation of this sign.

hell

Handshape: H
Orientation: palm in
Location: below left shoulder
Movement: make sharp movement down across body, ending in front of right side of waist

high, inebriated, stoned

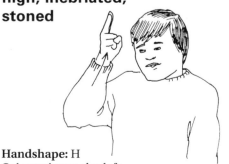

Handshape: H
Orientation: palm left
Location: near forehead
Movement: move hand up

Catholic

Handshape: H
Orientation: palm in
Location: near forehead
Movement: trace shape of cross near forehead

uncle

Handshape: H
Orientation: palm out
Location: near temple
Movement: brush hands down temple twice
Note: Movement may be circular.

handsome, Hawaii, Hawaiian

Handshape: H
Orientation: palm in
Location: near face
Movement: circle fingers counterclockwise around face

horse

Handshape: H
Orientation: palm out
Location: thumb on right temple
Movement: bend index and middle fingers twice
Note: This may be signed with both hands, using the same handshape and movement.

Latin

Handshape: H
Orientation: palm in
Location: fingertips on forehead
Movement: move hand down to tip of nose
Note: See page 84 for a variation of this sign.

honor

Handshape: H
Orientation: palm left
Location: index finger on forehead
Movement: arc hand forward
Nonmanual signal: head slowly moves up in reverence

necktie, tie

Handshape: H
Orientation: palm in
Location: neck
Movement: arc hand down to center of chest

us

Handshape: H
Orientation: palm left
Location: thumb on right side of chest
Movement: arc hand across to left side of chest, ending palm in
Note: Use this sign only when signing manual English.

hospital

Handshape: H
Orientation: palm in
Location: left upper arm
Movement: use fingertips to trace shape of cross on arm

candy, cute, sugar

Handshape: H > N
Orientation: palm in
Location: chin
Movement: brush fingers down chin twice, ending in N handshape

funny, amusing, comical, humorous

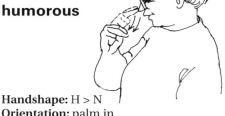

Handshape: H > N
Orientation: palm in
Location: nose
Movement: brush fingers down nose twice while bending them
Nonmanual signal: smile

high school

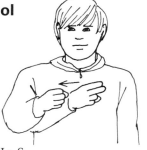

Handshape: H > S
Orientation: palm in
Location: neutral space
Movement: move hand right, closing to S handshape

United States

Handshape: H > S
Orientation: palm out
Location: neutral space
Movement: move hand forward, closing to S handshape

insurance

Handshape: I
Orientation: palm out
Location: neutral space
Movement: shake hand slightly side to side

Italy, Italian, Pepsi

Handshape: I
Orientation: palm in
Location: near forehead
Movement: trace a cross near center of forehead
Note: See page 86 for the preferred sign for Italy.

imagine, conceive, theory

Handshape: I
Orientation: palm in
Location: fingertip on forehead
Movement: spiral hand forward and up

idea

Handshape: I
Orientation: palm in
Location: fingertip on forehead
Movement: move hand up and out

paranoid

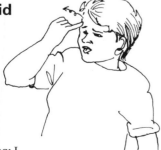

Handshape: I
Orientation: palm in
Location: fingertip on forehead
Movement: move hand out in small spirals
Nonmanual signal: tongue protruding

if, suppose, what if

Handshape: I
Orientation: palm in
Location: below eye
Movement: tap little finger against face twice
Nonmanual signal: head tilts right, "frowning" expression

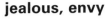
jealous, envy

Handshape: I
Orientation: palm out
Location: fingertip near right corner of mouth
Movement: twist hand back, ending with palm in
Nonmanual signal: head tilts right, "angry" expression

Japan, Japanese

Handshape: I
Orientation: palm left
Location: eye
Movement: twist hand back, ending with palm in
Note: See page 249 for the preferred sign.

Israel, Israeli

Handshape: I
Orientation: palm in
Location: chin
Movement: slide index finger down left side of chin, then down right side of chin

I

Handshape: I
Orientation: palm left
Location: chest
Movement: hit thumb side of hand against chest

kitchen

Handshape: K
Orientation: palm left
Location: neutral space
Movement: shake hand slightly side to side

Philadelphia

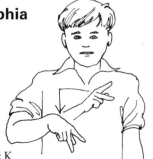

Handshape: K
Orientation: palm left
Location: neutral space
Movement: move hand to the right and down

purple

Handshape: K
Orientation: palm down
Location: neutral space
Movement: twist hand side to side twice

philosophy

Handshape: K
Orientation: palm down
Location: near forehead
Movement: bend wrist down slightly twice

two of us, we (two)

Handshape: K
Orientation: palm in
Location: neutral space
Movement: bend wrist forward and back between self and referent

politics

Handshape: K
Orientation: palm left
Location: near temple
Movement: circle hand near the head; then touch right temple with middle finger

paranoid

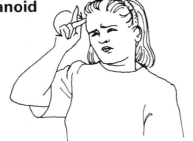

Handshape: K
Orientation: palm left
Location: middle finger on temple
Movement: twist wrist forward and back twice

poison

Handshape: K
Orientation: palm in
Location: middle finger on chin
Movement: twist hand slightly twice

pink

Handshape: K
Orientation: palm in
Location: chin
Movement: brush middle finger down chin twice

parents

Handshape: K
Orientation: palm left
Location: middle finger on right temple
Movement: move middle finger down to right side of mouth

peach

Handshape: K
Orientation: palm down
Location: index finger on cheek
Movement: circle hand forward on cheek

cake

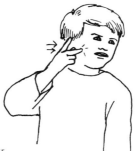

Handshape: K
Orientation: palm in
Location: cheek
Movement: brush cheek twice with middle finger

penis, pee, urine

Handshape: K
Orientation: palm in
Location: nose
Movement: tap nose twice with middle finger

king

Handshape: K
Orientation: palm down
Location: index finger on chest
Movement: move hand down across body, ending on right side of waist
Nonmanual signal: shoulders thrust back, erect posture

patient (ill person)

Handshape: K
Orientation: palm in
Location: left upper arm
Movement: trace shape of a cross with middle finger

personality

Handshape: K
Orientation: palm down
Location: chest
Movement: move hand in small circle, then drop thumb on chest

drill (tool)

Handshape: L
Orientation: palm in, index finger pointing down
Location: neutral space
Movement: bounce hand up and down several times while moving hand left

landlord

Handshape: L
Orientation: palm down, index finger pointing forward
Location: neutral space
Movement: arc hand from left to right

left (direction)

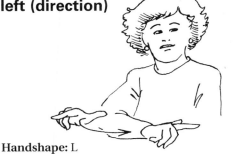

Handshape: L
Orientation: palm down, index finger pointing forward
Location: neutral space
Movement: move hand left

library

Handshape: L
Orientation: palm out
Location: neutral space
Movement: move hand in a circle

hair dryer

Handshape: L
Orientation: palm down, index finger pointing at head
Location: near head
Movement: move hand in a circle
Nonmanual signal: head tilts left

second, endorse

Handshape: L
Orientation: palm left, index finger pointing up
Location: above right shoulder
Movement: twist wrist forward, ending with index finger pointing forward

Latin

Handshape: L
Orientation: palm left
Location: thumb on forehead
Movement: move thumb down to nose
Note: See page 77 for a variation of this sign.

Lincoln

Handshape: L
Orientation: palm out
Location: right side of forehead
Movement: tap forehead twice with thumb

lemon

Handshape: L
Orientation: palm left
Location: chin
Movement: twist wrist and brush thumb down chin twice

lunch

Handshape: L
Orientation: palm left
Location: chin
Movement: tap chin twice with thumb

Lord, landlord

Handshape: L
Orientation: palm down,
  index finger pointing left
Location: thumb below left shoulder
Movement: move hand down across
  body, ending with thumb on right
  side of waist

lazy

Handshape: L
Orientation: palm in
Location: below left shoulder
Movement: tap chest twice
Nonmanual signal: mouth open,
  tongue protruding

legislature

Handshape: L
Orientation: palm down, index finger
  pointing left
Location: thumb on chest
Movement: arc hand across to right
  side of chest

shoot

Handshape: L > Bent L
Orientation: palm left, index finger
  points at referent
Location: neutral space
Movement: bend thumb down twice

laugh

Handshape: L > Bent L
Orientation: palm in
Location: cheek
Movement: bend index finger down,
  brushing cheek twice

who, whom

Handshape: L > Bent L
Orientation: palm left
Location: thumb on chin
Movement: bend index finger down twice

because

Handshape: L > Bent L
Orientation: palm in
Location: index finger on forehead
Movement: wipe index finger across
   forehead to the right, then bend finger

Coke, Coca-Cola

Handshape: L > Bent L
Orientation: palm in
Location: index finger on left arm
Movement: bend thumb down twice

drink (liquor), shot (liquor)

Handshape: Bent L
Orientation: palm left
Location: neutral space
Movement: tip hand back toward mouth
Nonmanual signal: head tips back

moon

Handshape: Bent L
Orientation: palm left
Location: thumb on forehead
Movement: arc hand up and to right

Italy

Handshape: Bent L > Baby O
Orientation: palm out
Location: neutral space
Movement: move hand down in wavy motion,
   closing thumb and index finger
Note: This is the preferred sign for Italy, used
   by Italians.

interest

Handshape: Bent L > A
Orientation: palm in
Location: near nose
Movement: move hand out, closing to
   A handshape
Nonmanual signal: body leans forward

Monday

Handshape: M
Orientation: palm in
Location: neutral space
Movement: move hand in gentle
   circular motion
Note: The palm may face forward.

every Monday, Mondays

Handshape: M
Orientation: palm in
Location: in front of face
Movement: move hand down

Boy Scout

Handshape: M
Orientation: palm out, fingertips
   angled up
Location: near forehead
Movement: tap forehead twice with
   index finger

Mormon

Handshape: M
Orientation: palm left
Location: cheek
Movement: brush fingertips down
   cheek twice

member

Handshape: M
Orientation: palm in
Location: fingertips below left
   shoulder chest
Movement: arc hand across to right
   side of chest

north

Handshape: N
Orientation: palm in
Location: neutral space
Movement: move hand up

nephew

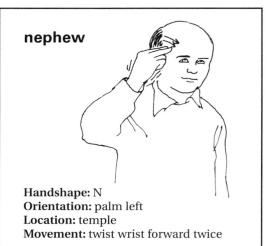

Handshape: N
Orientation: palm left
Location: temple
Movement: twist wrist forward twice

niece

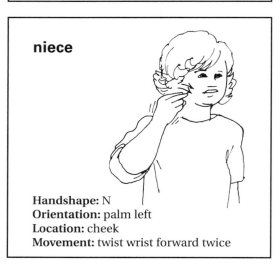

Handshape: N
Orientation: palm left
Location: cheek
Movement: twist wrist forward twice

duck

Handshape: Open N > N
Orientation: palm out
Location: cheek
Movement: close fingers to thumb twice

Thanksgiving

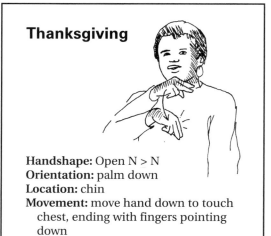

Handshape: Open N > N
Orientation: palm down
Location: chin
Movement: move hand down to touch
    chest, ending with fingers pointing
    down

no

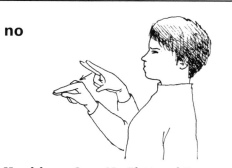

Handshape: Open N > Flattened O
Orientation: palm out
Location: neutral space
Movement: close fingers sharply to thumb
Nonmanual signal: head shakes "no"

gray

Handshape: O
Orientation: palm left
Location: neutral space
Movement: twist hand around, ending with palm in

seasoning, spice

Handshape: O
Orientation: palm right
Location: neutral space
Movement: bounce hand down twice

none, zip

Handshape: O
Orientation: palm left
Location: neutral space
Movement: move hand forward

zero

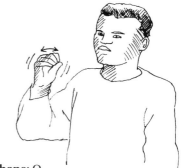

Handshape: O
Orientation: palm left
Location: neutral space
Movement: shake hand side to side

percent

Handshape: O
Orientation: palm left
Location: neutral space
Movement: move hand right and then down

opinion

Handshape: O
Orientation: palm left
Location: forehead
Movement: circle hand out from forehead twice

orphan

Handshape: O
Orientation: palm left
Location: thumb and index finger on forehead
Movement: move hand down to chin

frog

Handshape: O > V
Orientation: palm down
Location: under chin
Movement: flick fingers out into V handshape

warm

Handshape: O > 5
Orientation: palm in
Location: fingertips on chin
Movement: move hand out, opening to 5 handshape, palm up

point, period

Handshape: Baby O
Orientation: palm out
Location: neutral space
Movement: sharply bend wrist forward

thus, therefore

Handshape: Baby O
Orientation: palm out
Location: neutral space
Movement: draw top part of a triangle

cap (clothing)

Handshape: Baby O
Orientation: palm left
Location: forehead
Movement: move hand down slightly

cold (virus)

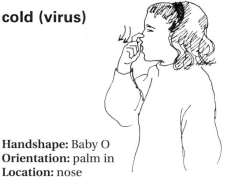

Handshape: Baby O
Orientation: palm in
Location: nose
Movement: brush fingers down each
   side of nose twice
Nonmanual signal: droopy eyes

a little, slightly

Handshape: Baby O > A
Orientation: palm up
Location: neutral space
Movement: flick thumb off index finger
   twice
Nonmanual signal: right shoulder raised

tattle

Handshape: Baby O > 1
Orientation: palm down
Location: mouth
Movement: move hand out, flicking
   index finger out

ponder, cogitate, deliberate, mull over

Handshape: Flattened O
Orientation: palm in
Location: near forehead
Movement: circle hand while randomly
   tapping fingertips on thumb
Nonmanual signal: "pensive" expression

flower

Handshape: Flattened O
Orientation: palm left
Location: right side of nose
Movement: arc hand around to left
   side of nose

home

Handshape: Flattened O
Orientation: palm in
Location: chin
Movement: bounce hand up right cheek

kiss

Handshape: Flattened O
Orientation: palm in
Location: mouth
Movement: twist the wrist out and
    move hand toward referent

**eat (SM);
food (DM)**

Handshape: Flattened O
Orientation: palm in
Location: mouth
Movement: double bounce hand
    against mouth

give, supply

Handshape: Flattened O
Orientation: palm in
Location: chest
Movement: bend wrist out, ending with
    palm up
Note: See page 258 for a two-hand
    variation of this sign.

own

Handshape: Flattened O
Orientation: palm left
Location: chest
Movement: hit hand against chest

**send, dispatch,
mail to**

Handshape: Flattened O > 5
Orientation: palm out
Location: neutral space
Movement: move hand out while
    opening to 5 handshape

lamp, light

Handshape: Flattened O > 5
Orientation: palm left
Location: near head
Movement: drop hand down toward
    face while opening to 5 handshape

shower

Handshape: Flattened O > 5
Orientation: palm left
Location: near head
Movement: bend hand down toward
    face while flicking fingers open twice
Nonmanual signal: head tilts left

inform, information, news, notify

Handshape: Flattened O > 5
Orientation: palm in
Location: forehead
Movement: drop hand down and out
    while opening to 5 handshape

gentleman, man

Handshape: Flattened O > 5
Orientation: palm left
Location: forehead
Movement: move hand down to chest
    while opening to 5 handshape

ignore, disregard, don't care, indifferent

Handshape: Flattened O > 5
Orientation: palm in
Location: nose
Movement: twist hand sharply out
    while opening to 5 handshape

white person, Caucasian, pale

Handshape: Flattened O > 5
Orientation: palm in
Location: chest
Movement: snap hand up and open to 5
    handshape, ending with palm in front
    of face

breakfast
(compound: eat + morning)

Handshape: Flattened O > Open B : passive
Orientation: palms in
Location: right hand near mouth; left hand in
    neutral space
Movement: bring right hand to mouth, then
    place left hand inside crook of right arm and
    bring right forearm up

lunch
(compound: eat + noon)

Handshape: Flattened O > Open B : passive
Orientation: right palm in; left palm down
Location: right hand near mouth; left hand in
    neutral space
Movement: bring right hand to mouth, then
    place right elbow on back of left hand

dinner
(compound: eat + night)

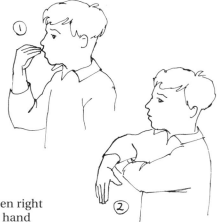

Handshape: Flattened O > Open B : passive
Orientation: right palm in; left palm down
Location: right hand near mouth; left hand in
    neutral space
Movement: bring right hand to mouth, then open right
    hand while bringing right arm down over left hand

husband
(compound: man + marry)

Handshape: Flattened O > C : C
Orientation: right palm left; left palm up
Location: right hand on forehead; left hand in
   neutral space
Movement: move right hand down, opening to C
   handshape, and clasp hands together

son
(compound: boy + baby)

Handshape: Flattened O > Open B : Open B
Orientation: right palm left; left palm up
Location: right hand on forehead; left hand in neutral
   space
Movement: move right hand down, opening to Open B
   handshape, and lay right arm inside left arm

brother
(compound: boy + same)

Handshape: Flattened O > L : L
Orientation: right palm left; left palm right
Location: right hand on forehead; left
   hand in neutral space
Movement: move right hand down,
   opening to L handshape, and place
   hand on top of left hand

right
(direction)

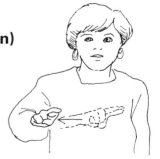

Handshape: R
Orientation: palm down
Location: neutral space
Movement: move hand right

rest room, railroad

Handshape: R
Orientation: palm down
Location: neutral space
Movement: arc hand from left to right

reason, rational, rationale, realize

Handshape: R
Orientation: palm in
Location: forehead
Movement: move hand in small circles

rat

Handshape: R
Orientation: palm left
Location: nose
Movement: brush fingers across nose twice

respect

Handshape: R
Orientation: palm in
Location: fingertips on forehead
Movement: arc hand out and up
Nonmanual signal: head slowly lifts up

are

Handshape: R
Orientation: palm left
Location: mouth
Movement: move hand straight out
Note: Use this sign only when signing manual English.

restaurant

Handshape: R
Orientation: palm in
Location: chin
Movement: brush fingers down right side of chin, then down left side of chin

religious, religion

Handshape: R
Orientation: palm in
Location: fingertips on chest
Movement: twist hand out, ending with fingers pointing forward

yes

Handshape: S
Orientation: palm out
Location: neutral space
Movement: bend wrist down twice
Nonmanual signal: slight nod of head up and down

south

Handshape: S
Orientation: palm in
Location: neutral space
Movement: move hand down

punch, hit

Handshape: S
Orientation: palm left
Location: neutral space
Movement: push hand out sharply

Saturday

Handshape: S
Orientation: palm in
Location: neutral space
Movement: move hand in gentle circular motion

every Saturday, Saturdays

Handshape: S
Orientation: palm in
Location: in front of face
Movement: move hand down

disobey, rebel, strike

Handshape: S
Orientation: palm in
Location: in front of head
Movement: twist hand around sharply
Nonmanual signal: pursed lips

carrot

Handshape: S
Orientation: palm down
Location: near mouth
Movement: bring hand in toward mouth in slow bounces
Nonmanual signal: teeth chatter

ice cream

Handshape: S
Orientation: palm left
Location: near mouth
Movement: brush hand down chin twice
Nonmanual signal: mouth open, tongue protruding

hang (by a rope)

Handshape: S
Orientation: palm out
Location: near neck
Movement: pull hand up sharply to the right
Nonmanual signal: head tilts left
Note: See page 114 for a variation of this sign.

baggage, luggage, suitcase

Handshape: S
Orientation: palm in
Location: neutral space
Movement: double bounce hand down
Note: This sign is similar to PURSE, which is made with an A handshape.

metal

Handshape: S
Orientation: palm left
Location: under chin
Movement: brush index-finger knuckle under chin twice

baloney, bull (slang), bullshit

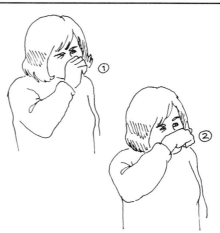

Handshape: S
Orientation: palm left
Location: nose
Movement: twist hand down twice
Nonmanual signal: "disbelieving"
  expression, head tilts right

cough

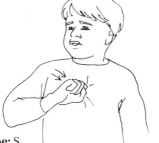

Handshape: S
Orientation: palm left
Location: chest
Movement: bounce hand off chest twice
Nonmanual signal: shoulders rounded;
  "sick" expression

Senate

Handshape: S
Orientation: palm left
Location: below left shoulder
Movement: arc hand across to right
  side of chest

tough, gang

Handshape: S
Orientation: palm right
Location: below right shoulder
Movement: brush hand down against
  chest twice
Nonmanual signal: right shoulder raises and
  leans forward; "tough-guy" expression

throw (away), discard

Handshape: S > H
Orientation: palm in
Location: neutral space
Movement: flick fingers open to H hand-
  shape while moving hand forward

understand, comprehend

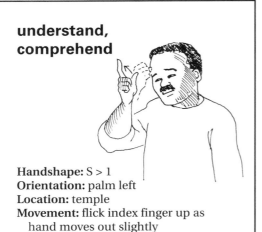

Handshape: S > 1
Orientation: palm left
Location: temple
Movement: flick index finger up as
  hand moves out slightly

drop, forget it

Handshape: S > 5
Orientation: palm down
Location: neutral space
Movement: bend wrist down and flick
  fingers out

gamble

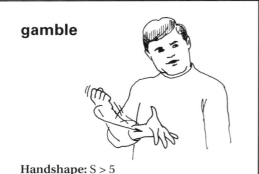

Handshape: S > 5
Orientation: palm up
Location: neutral space
Movement: shake hand slightly side to side,
  then throw it down, flicking fingers out

nothing, deny (not true)

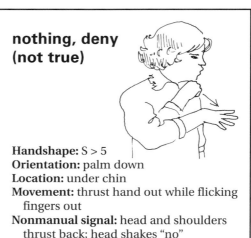

Handshape: S > 5
Orientation: palm down
Location: under chin
Movement: thrust hand out while flicking
  fingers out
Nonmanual signal: head and shoulders
  thrust back; head shakes "no"

poetry (ASL)

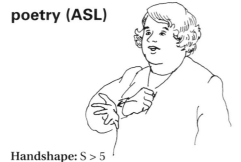

Handshape: S > 5
Orientation: palm in
Location: chest
Movement: arc hand out, opening to
  5 handshape

toilet, bathroom, rest room

Handshape: T
Orientation: palm out
Location: neutral space
Movement: shake hand slightly side to side

Tuesday

Handshape: T
Orientation: palm in
Location: neutral space
Movement: move hand in gentle
circular motion

every Tuesday, Tuesdays

Handshape: T
Orientation: palm in
Location: in front of face
Movement: move hand down

tan

Handshape: T
Orientation: palm out
Location: cheek
Movement: move hand down cheek

twins

Handshape: T
Orientation: palm left
Location: left side of chin
Movement: bounce hand around to
right side of chin

Thursday

Handshape: T > H
Orientation: palm left
Location: neutral space
Movement: twist hand around,
changing to H handshape

every Thursday, Thursdays

Handshape: T > H
Orientation: palm left
Location: in front of face
Movement: move hand down while
changing into H handshape

fast, immediate, rapid, right away, suddenly, swift

Handshape: T > Bent L
Orientation: palm left
Location: neutral space
Movement: bend hand forward while flicking thumb off index finger

delete, remove, eliminate

Handshape: T > Bent L
Orientation: palm left
Location: neutral space
Movement: flick thumb off index finger

look, gaze, observe, watch, witness, view

Handshape: V
Orientation: palm out
Location: neutral space
Movement: double bounce hand toward referent
Nonmanual signal: eyes follow referent

contempt, disdain, disrespect, look down on, scorn

Handshape: V
Orientation: palm out
Location: neutral space
Movement: bend wrist down, ending with fingers angled down
Nonmanual signal: head and eyes lowered; "patronizing" expression

vanilla, vitamin

Handshape: V
Orientation: palm out
Location: neutral space
Movement: shake hand slightly side to side

switch, trade places, vice-versa

Handshape: V
Orientation: palm down
Location: neutral space
Movement: flip hand over, ending with palm up

misunderstand, misconception

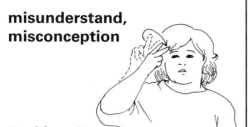

Handshape: V
Orientation: palm out
Location: index finger on forehead
Movement: flip hand over, ending with middle finger on forehead
Nonmanual signal: head back; mouth open; tongue protruding

ignorant, dumb, stupid

Handshape: V
Orientation: palm out
Location: forehead
Movement: smack hand sharply against forehead
Nonmanual signal: mouth open; tongue protruding

hindsight

Handshape: V
Orientation: palm down
Location: near eye
Movement: arc hand back toward ear

see, perceive

Handshape: V
Orientation: palm in
Location: near eye
Movement: move hand out to the left
Nonmanual signal: eyes follow fingers toward referent

speechread, lipread

Handshape: V
Orientation: palm in
Location: near mouth
Movement: shake hand side to side

careless, reckless

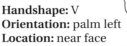

Handshape: V
Orientation: palm left
Location: near face
Movement: move hand across face twice
Nonmanual signal: head tilts back; mouth open; tongue protruding
Note: Sign may be formed with both hands moving past each other in front of the face.

smoke (v.)

Handshape: V
Orientation: palm in
Location: mouth
Movement: move hand out and back twice
Nonmanual signal: mouth in sucking position

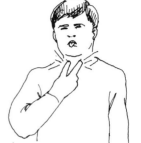

stuck, trapped

Handshape: V
Orientation: palm in
Location: neck
Movement: poke neck with index and middle fingers
Nonmanual signal: head back; mouth open; tongue protruding

voice

Handshape: V
Orientation: palm in
Location: fingertips on neck
Movement: brush fingers up and off neck

scissors

Handshape: V > H
Orientation: palm in
Location: neutral space
Movement: close and open fingers several times

haircut *(barber, beautician)*

Handshape: V > H
Orientation: palm left
Location: near head
Movement: close and open fingers while moving hand back along hairline

pizza

Handshape: Bent V
Orientation: palm out
Location: neutral space
Movement: zigzag hand down

tour, journey, travel, trip

Handshape: Bent V
Orientation: palm out
Location: neutral space
Movement: move hand in a circle

stairs

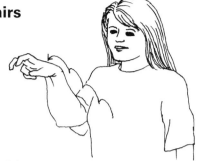

Handshape: Bent V
Orientation: palm down
Location: neutral space
Movement: spiral hand up in small arcs

snake

Handshape: Bent V
Orientation: palm in
Location: near mouth
Movement: twist hand around and
  move hand down in a wavy motion

blind

Handshape: Bent V
Orientation: palm in
Location: near eyes
Movement: bring hand in to eyes

speech, oral

Handshape: Bent V
Orientation: palm in
Location: near mouth
Movement: circle mouth with index
  and middle fingers

doubt, cynical, don't believe, skeptical

Handshape: Bent V
Orientation: palm in
Location: near eyes
Movement: bend fingers down twice
Nonmanual signal: head tilts right;
  "disbelieving" expression

nervy, nerve, rude

Handshape: Bent V
Orientation: palm out
Location: knuckles on cheek
Movement: swing wrist out and to the left
Nonmanual signal: "annoyed" expression

goat

Handshape: Bent V
Orientation: palm in
Location: fingertips on chin
Movement: arc hand up, ending with bent fingertips on forehead

strict, stern

Handshape: Bent V
Orientation: palm left
Location: near nose
Movement: sharply tap index finger against nose
Nonmanual signal: shoulders thrust back; erect posture; "stern" expression

gum, chewing gum

Handshape: Bent V > V
Orientation: palm left
Location: fingertips on cheek
Movement: straighten and bend fingers twice

west

Handshape: W
Orientation: palm out
Location: neutral space
Movement: move hand left

Wednesday

Handshape: W
Orientation: palm in
Location: neutral space
Movement: move hand in gentle circular motion

every Wednesday, Wednesdays

Handshape: W
Orientation: palm in
Location: in front of face
Movement: move hand down

baptism, christening

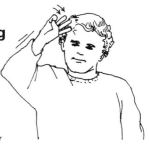

Handshape: W
Orientation: palm out
Location: forehead
Movement: tap forehead twice with index finger
Nonmanual signal: head tilts left

weird

Handshape: W
Orientation: palm left
Location: right side of face
Movement: bend fingers down and up while moving hand left
Nonmanual signal: "scornful" expression

wine

Handshape: W
Orientation: palm left
Location: cheek
Movement: move hand in small circle

water

Handshape: W
Orientation: palm left
Location: chin
Movement: double bounce index finger against chin

Washington (state), George Washington

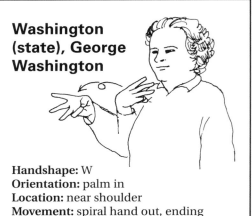

Handshape: W
Orientation: palm in
Location: near shoulder
Movement: spiral hand out, ending with palm left

we

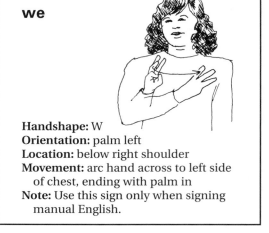

Handshape: W
Orientation: palm left
Location: below right shoulder
Movement: arc hand across to left side of chest, ending with palm in
Note: Use this sign only when signing manual English.

ocean, river (compound: water + waves)

Handshape: W > Open B : Open B
Orientation: right palm left; left palm down
Location: right index finger on chin; left hand in neutral space
Movement: tap right index finger against chin, then bring hand down, opening to Open B handshape and move both hands forward in wavy motion

flood (compound: water + rise)

Handshape: W > Open B : Open B
Orientation: right palm left; left palm down
Location: right index finger on chin; left hand in neutral space
Movement: tap right index finger against chin, then bring hand down, opening to Open B handshape, palm down, and raise hands

pond
(compound: water + circular body)

Handshape: W > Bent L : Bent L
Orientation: right palm left; left palm right
Location: right index finger on chin; left hand in neutral space
Movement: tap right index finger against chin, then bring hand down, opening to Bent L handshape, palms facing, and move hands apart to show size of pond

celebrate, cheer, hurray, triumph, victory

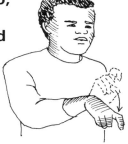

Handshape: X
Orientation: palm in
Location: near shoulder
Movement: move hand in a circle
Nonmanual signal: "happy" expression
Note: See page 255 for a two-hand variation of this sign.

give, acquiesce, donate

Handshape: X
Orientation: palm left
Location: neutral space
Movement: bend arm down

must, have to, obligated to, ought, should (SM); need, necessary, vital (DM)

Handshape: X
Orientation: palm out
Location: neutral space
Movement: bend wrist down

fool, sucker

Handshape: X
Orientation: palm in
Location: near mouth
Movement: double bounce hand in
Nonmanual signal: mouth open; tongue protruding

wise

Handshape: X
Orientation: palm down
Location: forehead
Movement: double bounce hand down

eagle

Handshape: X
Orientation: palm out
Location: nose
Movement: tap nose twice with index
finger

Egypt

Handshape: X
Orientation: palm out
Location: forehead
Movement: double bounce hand on
forehead

doll

Handshape: X
Orientation: palm left
Location: nose
Movement: brush index finger down
nose twice

**addiction,
hooked**

Handshape: X
Orientation: palm in
Location: index finger on side of mouth
Movement: pull index finger sharply to right
Nonmanual signal: head tilts right; mouth
open; tongue protruding

**recently, a
little while
ago, lately**

Handshape: X
Orientation: palm in
Location: index finger on cheek
Movement: bend index finger slightly
against cheek
Nonmanual signal: right shoulder lifts up;
head tilts right; "cz" mouth movement

chewing gum, gum

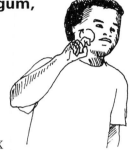

Handshape: X
Orientation: palm out
Location: index finger on cheek
Movement: move index finger in a
small circle

envious

Handshape: X
Orientation: palm in
Location: index finger between teeth
Movement: twist hand slightly side to side
Nonmanual signal: head tilts right; right
shoulder leans forward; eyes lower

china, glass

Handshape: X
Orientation: palm in
Location: mouth
Movement: tap index finger against
front teeth twice

hearing aid

Handshape: X
Orientation: palm out
Location: ear
Movement: double bounce hand
against ear

dry, boring, dull

Handshape: X
Orientation: palm left
Location: chin
Movement: wipe index finger across
chin to the right
Nonmanual signal: "pained" expression

sex

Handshape: X
Orientation: palm out
Location: index finger on temple
Movement: bounce hand down to
lower cheek

apple

Handshape: X
Orientation: palm down
Location: index finger against cheek
Movement: twist hand slightly forward twice

onion

Handshape: X
Orientation: palm out
Location: index finger on corner of right eye
Movement: twist hand slightly forward twice

rubber, condom

Handshape: X
Orientation: palm out
Location: cheek
Movement: brush side of index finger down cheek twice

metal

Handshape: X
Orientation: palm left
Location: under chin
Movement: brush index finger off chin twice

detective

Handshape: X
Orientation: palm down
Location: below left shoulder
Movement: brush index finger down chest twice

query, ask, inquire, question (v.), quiz

Handshape: X > 1
Orientation: palm out
Location: neutral space
Movement: use index finger to draw a question mark, changing to 1 handshape

oh, I see

Handshape: Y
Orientation: palm out
Location: neutral space
Movement: double bounce hand down
Nonmanual signal: head tilts back;
  mouth open; eyes widen

yellow

Handshape: Y
Orientation: palm left
Location: neutral space
Movement: twist wrist back and forth
  several times

stay, remain, still

Handshape: Y
Orientation: palm down
Location: neutral space
Movement: move hand down sharply

me too, in common, same

Handshape: Y
Orientation: palm down
Location: neutral space
Movement: move arm out and back
  toward referent twice

cow

Handshape: Y
Orientation: palm out
Location: thumb on right temple
Movement: bend wrist down and up twice
Note: See page 302 for a two-hand
  variation of this sign.

drunk

Handshape: Y
Orientation: palm left
Location: right side of face
Movement: move hand across face,
  ending with palm down

blond

Handshape: Y
Orientation: palm left
Location: right side of head
Movement: turn hand out and to the right

**telephone (n.),
phone (n.) (SM);
telephone (v.),
phone (v.) (DM)**

Handshape: Y
Orientation: palm left
Location: thumb at ear and little finger at mouth
Movement: double bounce hand on cheek

**Holland,
Dutch,
The
Netherlands**

Handshape: Y
Orientation: palm left
Location: thumb at forehead
Movement: arc thumb down and off nose

**silly, absurd,
folly, foolish,
ridiculous**

Handshape: Y
Orientation: palm left
Location: near nose
Movement: brush thumb across nose twice
Nonmanual signal: head tilts right; mouth open; tongue protruding

**hang
(by a rope)**

Handshape: Y
Orientation: palm out
Location: neck
Movement: pull hand up sharply to right
Nonmanual signal: head tilts left; mouth open; tongue protruding
Note: See page 98 for a variation of this sign.

shave

Handshape: Y
Orientation: palm left
Location: thumb on left cheek
Movement: slide thumb across chin and up right cheek

error, wrong (SM); mistake, incorrect (DM)

Handshape: Y
Orientation: palm in
Location: chin
Movement: hit knuckles against chin
Nonmanual signal: mouth open; tongue protruding

yesterday

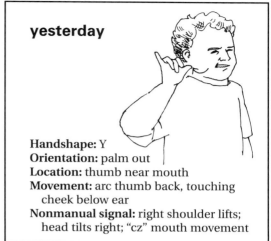

Handshape: Y
Orientation: palm out
Location: thumb near mouth
Movement: arc thumb back, touching cheek below ear
Nonmanual signal: right shoulder lifts; head tilts right; "cz" mouth movement

that one

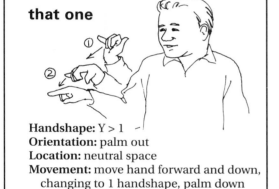

Handshape: Y > 1
Orientation: palm out
Location: neutral space
Movement: move hand forward and down, changing to 1 handshape, palm down
Nonmanual signal: change from "th" mouth to open mouth as head tilts back

I love you

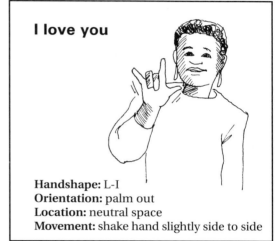

Handshape: L-I
Orientation: palm out
Location: neutral space
Movement: shake hand slightly side to side

fly (SM); airplane, airport, plane (pilot, flier, aviator) (DM)

Handshape: L-I
Orientation: palm down
Location: neutral space
Movement: double bounce hand to the right

why

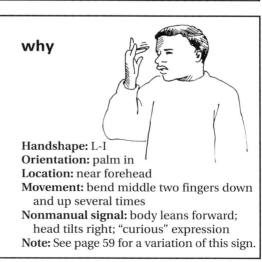

Handshape: L-I
Orientation: palm in
Location: near forehead
Movement: bend middle two fingers down and up several times
Nonmanual signal: body leans forward; head tilts right; "curious" expression
Note: See page 59 for a variation of this sign.

gold, California

Handshape: L-I
Orientation: palm left
Location: index finger at ear
Movement: swing hand around, changing to Y handshape, palm down

Halloween

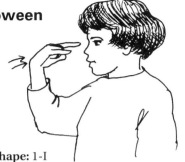

Handshape: 1-I
Orientation: palm in
Location: near eyes
Movement: double bounce hand in toward eyes

kid

Handshape: 1-I
Orientation: palm down
Location: under nose
Movement: twist wrist down twice

stuck-up, conceited, high society, snob

Handshape: 1-I
Orientation: palm left
Location: index fingertip under nose
Movement: brush index finger up tip of nose twice
Nonmanual signal: head tilts back

sophisticated, prim

Handshape: 1-I
Orientation: palm left
Location: chin
Movement: brush index finger up chin twice
Nonmanual signal: shoulders thrust back; erect posture

one

Handshape: 1
Orientation: palm out
Location: neutral space
Movement: hold hand out

walking (one person)

Handshape: 1
Orientation: palm out
Location: neutral space
Movement: bounce hand forward

go!

Handshape: 1
Orientation: palm out
Location: neutral space
Movement: bend hand out and down sharply, ending with palm down

come here, come, beckon

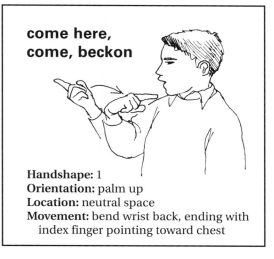

Handshape: 1
Orientation: palm up
Location: neutral space
Movement: bend wrist back, ending with index finger pointing toward chest

roam, wander

Handshape: 1
Orientation: palm out
Location: neutral space
Movement: meander hand forward

up (SM); upstairs (DM)

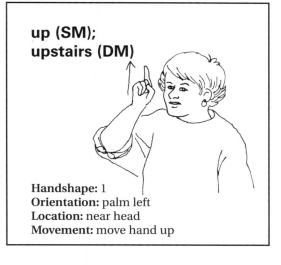

Handshape: 1
Orientation: palm left
Location: near head
Movement: move hand up

down (SM); downstairs (DM)

Handshape: 1
Orientation: palm in
Location: neutral space
Movement: move hand down

**there,
over there**

Handshape: 1
Orientation: palm out
Location: neutral space
Movement: double bounce hand
    toward referent

far, cannon

Handshape: 1
Orientation: palm left
Location: neutral space
Movement: jab index finger sharply
    forward and back

where

Handshape: 1
Orientation: palm out
Location: neutral space
Movement: shake hand side to side
Nonmanual signal: body leans forward;
    head tilts right; "questioning" frown

comma

Handshape: 1
Orientation: palm out
Location: neutral space
Movement: trace shape of a comma
    with index finger

you

Handshape: 1
Orientation: palm down
Location: neutral space
Movement: jab finger toward referent
Nonmanual signal: eyes on referent

they, them

Handshape: 1
Orientation: palm down
Location: neutral space
Movement: arc index finger from left to
    right toward referents
Nonmanual signal: eyes on person to
    whom you are speaking

she, he, her, him, it

Handshape: 1
Orientation: palm left
Location: neutral space
Movement: point index finger at referent
Nonmanual signal: eyes on person to whom you are speaking

someone, some-body, something

Handshape: 1
Orientation: palm in
Location: neutral space
Movement: move hand in small circle

only one, sole

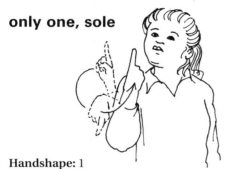

Handshape: 1
Orientation: palm out
Location: neutral space
Movement: swing hand down and around, ending with palm in

always

Handshape: 1
Orientation: palm in
Location: neutral space
Movement: make two large circles with hand

one dollar

Handshape: 1
Orientation: palm out
Location: neutral space
Movement: twist hand around, ending with palm in

scold, reprimand

Handshape: 1
Orientation: palm left
Location: neutral space
Movement: wag hand twice
Nonmanual signal: body leans forward; head tilts right; "frowning" expression

circle, cycle

Handshape: 1
Orientation: palm angled out
Location: neutral space
Movement: draw a large circle with
    index finger

insult

Handshape: 1
Orientation: palm down
Location: neutral space
Movement: twist hand right while moving
    index finger sharply up and forward

face, appearance, looks

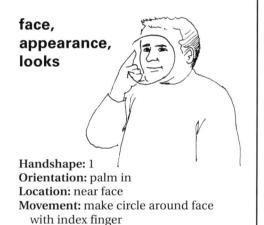

Handshape: 1
Orientation: palm in
Location: near face
Movement: make circle around face
    with index finger

crazy

Handshape: 1
Orientation: palm down
Location: near temple
Movement: circle index finger around
    temple

wonder, reckon, speculate, thoughtful

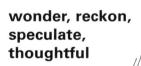

Handshape: 1
Orientation: palm in
Location: near forehead
Movement: move hand in small circles
Nonmanual signal: "pensive" expression
Note: See page 314 for a two-hand
    variation of this sign.

who, whom

Handshape: 1
Orientation: palm in
Location: near mouth
Movement: circle mouth with index finger
Nonmanual signal: body leans forward;
    head tilts right; "curious" expression

say, discourse, hearing person, public, remark, speak, statement

Handshape: 1
Orientation: palm left
Location: near mouth
Movement: circle hand out twice

think (SM); brain, mind (DM)

Handshape: 1
Orientation: palm left
Location: temple
Movement: tap temple twice with index finger

cent, penny

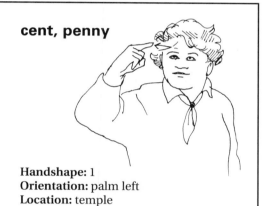

Handshape: 1
Orientation: palm left
Location: temple
Movement: bounce index finger off right temple

for

Handshape: 1
Orientation: palm left
Location: forehead
Movement: swing hand out and around

intelligent, smart

Handshape: 1
Orientation: palm left
Location: index finger on forehead
Movement: bend wrist forward
Nonmanual signal: head tilts back
Note: See page 147 for a variation of this sign.

black

Handshape: 1
Orientation: palm down
Location: forehead
Movement: brush side of index finger across forehead, and twist hand back, ending with palm in

Germany

Handshape: 1
Orientation: palm out
Location: forehead
Movement: tap back of hand against forehead twice
Note: This is the preferred sign for Germany, used by Germans.

deaf

Handshape: 1
Orientation: palm in
Location: index finger at corner of mouth
Movement: arc index finger back and tap near ear
Note: This sign can be made ear to chin. See page 129 for a variation of this sign.

hear (SM); sound (DM)

Handshape: 1
Orientation: palm in
Location: ear
Movement: tap index finger on ear twice
Nonmanual signal: head tilts left

boring, monotonous, tedious

Handshape: 1
Orientation: palm out
Location: index fingertip on nose
Movement: twist hand in
Nonmanual signal: mouth open; tongue protruding

mouse

Handshape: 1
Orientation: palm left
Location: nose
Movement: brush tip of nose twice with index finger

don't care, don't mind

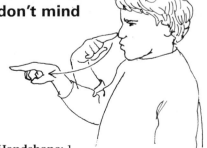

Handshape: 1
Orientation: palm in
Location: index fingertip on nose
Movement: swing hand out and around

false, fake (SM); artificial, mock (adj.) (DM)

Handshape: 1
Orientation: palm left
Location: nose
Movement: bend wrist down so index finger brushes past nose

tooth

Handshape: 1
Orientation: palm in
Location: mouth
Movement: point index finger at front teeth

red

Handshape: 1
Orientation: palm down
Location: mouth
Movement: brush index finger down chin

candy

Handshape: 1
Orientation: palm down
Location: index finger on cheek
Movement: twist hand forward and back twice

sour, bitter

Handshape: 1
Orientation: palm left
Location: index fingertip on chin
Movement: twist wrist left
Nonmanual signal: lips pursed; "sour" expression

single (person)

Handshape: 1
Orientation: palm left
Location: chin
Movement: brush index finger down left side of chin, then down right side of chin

lonely

Handshape: 1
Orientation: palm left
Location: mouth
Movement: brush side of index finger down mouth twice
Nonmanual signal: head and eyes lowered; "sad" expression

miss (regret the loss of), disappoint

Handshape: 1
Orientation: palm in
Location: chin
Movement: hit chin with index fingertip
Nonmanual signal: head tilts back; "sad" expression

tell

Handshape: 1
Orientation: palm in
Location: mouth
Movement: arc index finger out, ending with palm angled up

command, direct, order

Handshape: 1
Orientation: palm in
Location: index fingertip on lower lip
Movement: move hand right, then bend hand sharply down

didn't mean that, didn't say that

Handshape: 1
Orientation: palm out
Location: near mouth
Movement: smack back of index finger against mouth
Nonmanual signal: head shakes "no"

lie, fib (liar)

Handshape: 1
Orientation: palm down
Location: right side of chin
Movement: sharply brush index finger across chin
Nonmanual signal: head tilts back and right

am, are, be

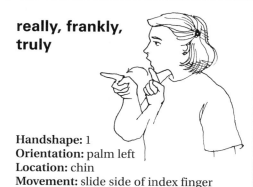

Handshape: 1
Orientation: palm left
Location: mouth
Movement: move hand straight out
Note: Do not use when signing manual
English.

really, frankly, truly

Handshape: 1
Orientation: palm left
Location: chin
Movement: slide side of index finger
up and off chin, ending with index
finger pointing forward
Nonmanual signal: "serious" expression

absolute, actual, certain, genuine, indeed, real, sure, true

Handshape: 1
Orientation: palm left
Location: chin
Movement: move hand straight out

thirst, thirsty (SM); lust (DM)

Handshape: 1
Orientation: palm in
Location: neck
Movement: slide index finger down neck
Nonmanual signal: head tilts back;
"thirsty" expression

swallow

Handshape: 1
Orientation: palm left
Location: under chin
Movement: slide edge of
index finger down neck
Nonmanual signal: head tilts back
Note: See page 326 for a two-hand
variation of this sign.

we, us

Handshape: 1
Orientation: palm in
Location: index finger on right side of chest
Movement: arc index finger across to left
side of chest

me, I

Handshape: 1
Orientation: palm in
Location: chest
Movement: touch chest with index finger

China, Chinese

Handshape: 1
Orientation: palm in
Location: index finger below left shoulder
Movement: bounce index fingertip across chest, then down to waist
Note: This is the preferred sign for China, used by Chinese people.

one hundred

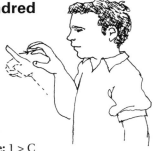

Handshape: 1 > C
Orientation: palm out
Location: neutral space
Movement: bring hand back and change to C handshape

one-half

Handshape: 1 > V
Orientation: palm in
Location: neutral space
Movement: move hand down while changing to V handshape

huh?, really?

Handshape: 1 > X
Orientation: palm out
Location: neutral space
Movement: bend index finger into X handshape twice
Nonmanual signal: "questioning" expression

government, politics

Handshape: 1 > X > 1
Orientation: palm left
Location: near head
Movement: circle index finger down, bending finger, then straighten finger and touch forehead

summer

Handshape: 1 > X
Orientation: palm down
Location: forehead
Movement: wipe index finger across forehead, ending in X handshape

suspect, superstition

Handshape: 1 > X
Orientation: palm in
Location: forehead
Movement: bend index finger, scratching forehead twice

dream

Handshape: 1 > X
Orientation: palm down
Location: forehead
Movement: bend index finger down and up several times while moving hand out to right

puzzled, perplexed

Handshape: 1 > X
Orientation: palm out
Location: back of hand on forehead
Movement: bend index finger to X handshape
Nonmanual signal: head tilts back; mouth open; brows furrowed in puzzlement

ugly, homely

Handshape: 1 > X
Orientation: palm down
Location: under nose
Movement: slide index finger under nose, ending in X handshape
Note: See page 330 for a two-hand variation of this sign.

eternal, forever, everlasting

Handshape: 1 > Y
Orientation: palm down
Location: forehead
Movement: twist wrist forward, changing to Y handshape

sun, sunshine

Handshape: 1 > 5
Orientation: palm out
Location: above head
Movement: draw a circle with index finger, then move
   hand toward head while opening to 5 handshape

broad-minded
(compound: think + general)

Handshape: 1 > B : B
Orientation: right palm left; left palm right
Location: right index fingertip on forehead; left
   hand in neutral space
Movement: bring right hand down while changing
   to B handshape, palms facing, fingers touching,
   then swing fingers away from each other
Nonmanual signal: slightly wide eyes

narrow-minded
(compound: think + narrow)

Handshape: 1 > B : B
Orientation: right palm left; left palm right
Location: right index fingertip on forehead; left
   hand in neutral space
Movement: bring right hand down while changing
   to B handshape, palms facing, hands apart, then
   bend fingers in toward each other
Nonmanual signal: brows furrowed, "serious"
   expression

witness, eyewitness
(compound: eye + prove)

Handshape: 1 > B : B
Orientation: right palm in; left palm up
Location: right hand below eye; left hand in
  neutral space
Movement: bring right hand down while changing
  to B handshape, palm up, and slap into left palm
Nonmanual signal: lips taut, "earnest" expression

deaf
(compound: hear + close)

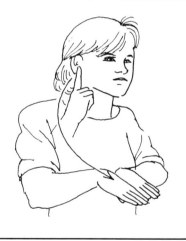

Handshape: 1 > B : B
Orientation: right palm left; left palm down
Location: right index finger below ear; left hand in
  neutral space
Movement: bring right hand down while changing
  to B handshape, and move index fingers together
Note: See page 122 for a variation of this sign.

pledge, commit, guarantee,
promise, vow, swear
(compound)

Handshape: 1 > Open B : B
Orientation: right palm left; left palm down
Location: right index finger on mouth; left hand in
  neutral space
Movement: move right hand down, changing to Open B
  handshape, then bump wrist against left hand
Nonmanual signal: pursed lips
Note: See page 130 for a variation of this sign.

public school
(compound: say + school)

Handshape: 1 > Open B : Open B
Orientation: right palm in; left hand in neutral space
Location: near mouth
Movement: circle hand out twice, then move hand down while changing to Open B handshape and clap hands

promise, commit, guarantee,
pledge, vow, swear
(compound)

Handshape: 1 > Open B : S
Orientation: right palm left; left palm in
Location: right index finger on mouth; left hand in neutral space
Movement: move right hand down, changing to Open B handshape, then slap right palm down on left hand
Nonmanual signal: pursed lips
Note: See page 129 for a variation of this sign.

anticipate, expect, hope
(compound: think + hope)

Handshape: 1 > Open B > Bent B : Open B > Bent B
Orientation: right palm left; left palm right
Location: right index finger on forehead; left hand in neutral space
Movement: move right hand out while changing to Open B handshape, palms facing, and bend both hands down and up twice

believe
(compound: think + marry)

Handshape: 1 > C : C
Orientation: right palm left; left palm up
Location: right index finger on forehead; left hand
   in neutral space
Movement: bring right hand down while changing
   to C handshape and clasp hands together

decide, determine,
resolve, verdict
(compound: think + judge)

Handshape: 1 > F : F
Orientation: right palm left; left palm right
Location: right index finger on forehead; left hand
   in neutral space
Movement: move right hand down while changing
   to F handshape, palm left, even with left hand,
   and move both hands down

loud
(compound: hear + noise)

Handshape: 1 > S : S
Orientation: right palm left; left palm down
Location: right index finger at ear; left
   hand in neutral space
Movement: move right hand down, changing to S
   handshape, then move hands side to side in unison
Nonmanual signal: "pained" expression

noise, noisy
(compound: hear + vibrate)

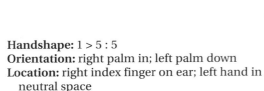

Handshape: 1 > 5 : 5
Orientation: right palm in; left palm down
Location: right index finger on ear; left hand in
   neutral space
Movement: move right hand down, even with left
   hand, and shake both hands

disagree, differ
(compound: think + opposite)

Handshape: 1 > 1 : 1
Orientation: right palm left; left palm right
Location: right index finger on forehead; left hand
   in neutral space
Movement: bring right hand down so index fingertips
   touch, then move hands away from each other

agree, concur, correspond
(compound: think + same)

Handshape: 1 > 1: 1
Orientation: right palm left; left palm down
Location: right index finger on forehead; left hand
   in neutral space
Movement: bring right hand down so index fingers
   touch
Nonmanual signal: head nods "yes"

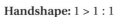
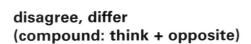

blush, embarrass, flushed
(compound: red + embarrass)

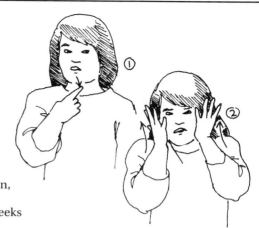

Handshape: 1 > 5 : 5
Orientation: palms in
Location: right index finger on lower lip
Movement: brush right index finger down chin,
   then change to 5 handshape, both hands
   near jaw, and move hands up in front of cheeks
Nonmanual signal: "embarrassed" expression

confident, trust
(compound: think + trust)

Handshape: 1 > 5 > S : 5 > S
Orientation: right palm in; left palm right
Location: right index finger near
   forehead; left hand in neutral space
Movement: tap right index finger on forehead, then
   move hand down, changing to 5 handshape, palm left,
   slightly above left hand; bring hands together, closing
   to S handshape, ending with right hand on top of left hand

vehicle,
moving vehicle

Handshape: 3
Orientation: palm left
Location: neutral space
Movement: move hand forward
Note: The hand moves in the direction and
   way that vehicle under discussion moves.

lousy

Handshape: 3
Orientation: palm left
Location: nose
Movement: loop hand to right, then
   bring sharply down

rooster

Handshape: 3
Orientation: palm left
Location: forehead
Movement: tap thumb twice on forehead

spit

Handshape: 3
Orientation: palm left
Location: mouth
Movement: arc hand sharply out and down

receptive

Handshape: 3 > Bent 3
Orientation: palm left
Location: near temple
Movement: bend index and middle fingers as thumb touches under eye twice

devil, demon, devilish, mischievous, Satan

Handshape: 3 > Bent 3
Orientation: palm out
Location: thumb on temple
Movement: bend and straighten index and middle fingers twice
Note: See page 333 for a two-hand variation of this sign.

insect, bug

Handshape: 3 > Bent 3
Orientation: palm left
Location: thumb on nose
Movement: bend and straighten index and middle fingers twice

jail

Handshape: 4
Orientation: palm in
Location: near face
Movement: move hand in toward face

talk

Handshape: 4
Orientation: palm left
Location: chin
Movement: double bounce index finger
lightly on chin

**invent,
create,
devise,
improvise**

Handshape: 4
Orientation: palm left
Location: index fingertip on forehead
Movement: arc hand up and out
Nonmanual signal: head tilts back

**ignore,
disregard,
neglect**

Handshape: 4
Orientation: palm left
Location: index fingertip on nose
Movement: arc hand out to side, then
bring down sharply
Nonmanual signal: head tilts left

**Scotland,
Scotch,
Scots**

Handshape: 4
Orientation: palm in
Location: upper arm
Movement: brush fingers across width
of arm, then flip over and brush back
of hand down toward elbow

**approximately,
about, around,
thereabouts,
estimate (v.)**

Handshape: 5
Orientation: palm out
Location: neutral space
Movement: move hand in a circle twice

**area,
around here**

Handshape: 5
Orientation: palm down
Location: neutral space
Movement: move hand in a circle twice

spell, alphabet, fingerspell

Handshape: 5
Orientation: palm down
Location: neutral space
Movement: move hand in small circles while randomly wiggling fingers

long ago, former, used to be

Handshape: 5
Orientation: palm left
Location: near shoulder
Movement: circle hand back so thumb brushes down shoulder twice
Nonmanual signal: body leans back; "cha" mouth utterance

insane

Handshape: 5
Orientation: palm down
Location: near head
Movement: circle hand around twice
Nonmanual signal: head tilts right; mouth open; tongue protruding

lettuce, cabbage

Handshape: 5
Orientation: palm left
Location: head
Movement: hit head twice with heel of hand

father, dad

Handshape: 5
Orientation: palm left
Location: forehead
Movement: tap thumb twice on forehead

grandfather

Handshape: 5
Orientation: palm left
Location: thumb on forehead
Movement: bounce hand out in double arc

**man,
gentleman**

Handshape: 5
Orientation: palm left
Location: forehead
Movement: tap thumb on forehead
   and then on chest
Nonmanual signal: shoulders thrust
   back; erect posture

parents

Handshape: 5
Orientation: palm left
Location: forehead
Movement: tap thumb on forehead
   and then on chin
Note: This sign can be reversed.

**mother,
mom**

Handshape: 5
Orientation: palm left
Location: chin
Movement: tap thumb twice on chin

grandmother

Handshape: 5
Orientation: palm left
Location: thumb on chin
Movement: bounce hand out in double arc

**woman,
female,
lady**

Handshape: 5
Orientation: palm left
Location: chin
Movement: tap thumb on chin and
   then chest
Nonmanual signal: shoulders thrust
   back; erect posture

**farm,
agriculture,
bum, ranch,
sloppy**

Handshape: 5
Orientation: palm left
Location: left side of chin
Movement: brush thumb across chin

dirty, filthy, soiled

Handshape: 5
Orientation: palm down
Location: under chin
Movement: randomly wiggle fingers
Nonmanual signal: mouth open;
   tongue protruding

color

Handshape: 5
Orientation: palm in
Location: chin
Movement: wiggle fingertips randomly
   while tapping chin

swell, awesome, you're a riot (slang)

Handshape: 5
Orientation: palm left
Location: chest
Movement: randomly wiggle fingers,
   keeping thumb on chest
Nonmanual signal: body leans back

indignant, appalled

Handshape: 5
Orientation: palm left
Location: thumb on chest
Movement: bend hand down sharply
Nonmanual signal: lips pursed

fancy, elegant, refined, courteous

Handshape: 5
Orientation: palm left
Location: chest
Movement: brush thumb up chest twice
Nonmanual signal: "genteel" expression

fine

Handshape: 5
Orientation: palm left
Location: chest
Movement: arc hand out and down
Nonmanual signal: shoulders thrust back

pregnant

Handshape: 5
Orientation: palm in
Location: abdomen
Movement: move hand out

leave, go away, gone

Handshape: 5 > Flattened O
Orientation: palm in
Location: neutral space
Movement: pull hand to right, closing
    to Flattened O handshape

and

Handshape: 5 > Flattened O
Orientation: palm in
Location: neutral space
Movement: move hand right, closing
    to Flattened O handshape

Africa, African

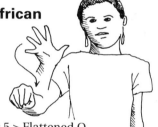

Handshape: 5 > Flattened O
Orientation: palm out
Location: neutral space
Movement: swirl fingers right and down,
    closing to Flattened O handshape
Note: This is the preferred sign, used by
    Africans to refer to themselves.

asleep, nap

Handshape: 5 > Flattened O
Orientation: palm in
Location: near face
Movement: close fingers to Flattened O
    handshape
Note: See the following sign for the
    adjective form.

drowsy, sleepy

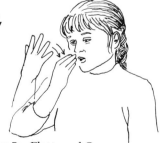

Handshape: 5 > Flattened O
Orientation: palm in
Location: near face
Movement: bring hand down slowly,
    closing fingers to thumb twice
Nonmanual signal: droopy eyes

**pretty,
beautiful,
gorgeous,
lovely**

Handshape: 5 > Flattened O
Orientation: palm left
Location: near face
Movement: slowly sweep fingers around
    face, closing to Flattened O handshape
Nonmanual signal: head tilts back

shut up

Handshape: 5 > Flattened O
Orientation: palm left
Location: near face
Movement: sharply bring hand to
    mouth, closing fingers to thumb,
    ending with fingertips on mouth
Nonmanual signal: "angry" expression

**Jewish,
Hebrew**

Handshape: 5 > Flattened O
Orientation: palm in
Location: chin
Movement: brush fingers off chin twice,
    closing to Flattened O handshape

peach

Handshape: 5 > Flattened O
Orientation: palm in
Location: cheek
Movement: brush fingers down and off
    cheek twice, closing to Flattened O
    handshape

**experience,
expert**

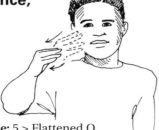

Handshape: 5 > Flattened O
Orientation: palm right
Location: cheek
Movement: brush fingers down cheek
    and pull hand right twice, closing to
    Flattened O handshape

wolf

Handshape: 5 > Flattened O
Orientation: palm in
Location: face
Movement: brush fingers off nose and
    mouth, closing to Flattened O handshape

catch (disease),
prone to catch a disease

Handshape: 5 > Flattened O
Orientation: palm down, fingers forward
Location: neutral space
Movement: move hand sharply in to chest, closing to
　Flattened O handshape
Nonmanual signal: body leans away from repelling
　reference; "disgusted" expression

white (object)

Handshape: 5 > Flattened O
Orientation: palm in
Location: chest
Movement: move hand out from chest, closing to
　Flattened O handshape

oversleep
(compound: sleep + way-past-sunrise)

Handshape: 5 > Flattened O > F : Open B (passive)
Orientation: right palm in; left palm down
Location: right hand near face; left hand in neutral
　space
Movement: close fingers to thumb in front of face,
　then change to F handshape while moving hand
　under and then above passive arm

commonplace, big deal (slang), boring, nothing to it, old hat (slang), trivial

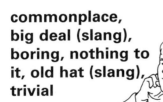

Handshape: 5 > S
Orientation: palm left
Location: left cheek
Movement: slide back of hand under chin to right cheek, closing to S handshape
Nonmanual signal: "bored" expression

channel, knob

Handshape: Bent 5
Orientation: palm out
Location: neutral space
Movement: twist arm side to side several times

crazy for (slang), crave, favorite

Handshape: Bent 5
Orientation: palm in
Location: near face
Movement: shake hand slightly side to side
Nonmanual signal: "excited" expression

dizzy

Handshape: Bent 5
Orientation: palm in
Location: near face
Movement: slowly circle face with hand
Nonmanual signal: body wobbles

grouchy, ill-tempered, irritable, moody

Handshape: Bent 5
Orientation: palm in
Location: near face
Movement: keeping hand taut, bend fingertips in and out a few times
Nonmanual signal: "angry" expression

lion

Handshape: Bent 5
Orientation: palm down
Location: above head
Movement: slide hand back along head
Nonmanual signal: shoulders thrust back, erect posture

comb

Handshape: Bent 5
Orientation: palm left
Location: head
Movement: brush fingertips down hair twice

radio

Handshape: Bent 5
Orientation: palm left
Location: ear
Movement: twist hand side to side several times
Nonmanual signal: head tilts right
Note: See page 353 for a two-hand variation of this sign.

crazy, insane

Handshape: Bent 5
Orientation: palm left
Location: near temple
Movement: twist arm back and forth several times
Nonmanual signal: mouth open; tongue protruding

eat fruit

Handshape: Bent 5
Orientation: palm in
Location: below chin
Movement: twist wrist back twice, brushing past mouth

mad, angry, cross

Handshape: Bent 5
Orientation: palm in
Location: near face
Movement: bring hand in to face in sharp, quick motion
Nonmanual signal: "angry" expression

scream, cry out, shout, yell

Handshape: Bent 5
Orientation: palm in
Location: near chin
Movement: sharply arc hand up and out
Nonmanual signal: mouth mimics a scream

hot

Handshape: Bent 5
Orientation: palm in
Location: near mouth
Movement: sharply swing hand out and around, ending palm down
Nonmanual signal: blow air out of mouth

grass, hay

Handshape: Bent 5
Orientation: palm angled up
Location: chin
Movement: brush heel of hand up and off chin twice

captain, boss, coach, general, officer

Handshape: Bent 5
Orientation: palm down
Location: shoulder
Movement: tap shoulder twice with fingertips

anger, fury, mad

Handshape: Bent 5
Orientation: palm in
Location: chest
Movement: swing hand up sharply
Nonmanual signal: "angry" expression

disgust, nauseating, obnoxious, revolting

Handshape: Bent 5
Orientation: palm in
Location: chest
Movement: move hand in small circles
Nonmanual signal: "disgusted" expression

take, get

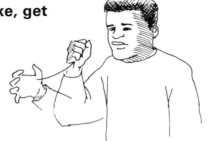

Handshape: Bent 5 > S
Orientation: palm left
Location: neutral space
Movement: bring hand in sharply, closing to S handshape

arrest, catch

Handshape: Bent 5 > S
Orientation: palm out
Location: neutral space
Movement: move hand out and down, closing to S handshape

curse, swear

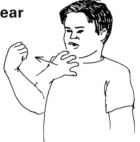

Handshape: Bent 5 > S
Orientation: palm in
Location: chin
Movement: pull hand out sharply, closing to S handshape

memorize

Handshape: Bent 5 > S
Orientation: palm left
Location: forehead
Movement: move hand out to the right, closing to S handshape
Nonmanual signal: lips taut

cherish, treasure, value

Handshape: Bent 5 > S
Orientation: palm in
Location: fingertips on chin
Movement: sharply close fingers to S handshape
Nonmanual signal: "hungry" expression

gulp, oops

Handshape: Bent 5 > S
Orientation: palm in
Location: fingertips on neck
Movement: sharply close fingers to S handshape
Nonmanual signal: "embarrassed" expression

suppress, restrain (feelings)

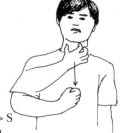

Handshape: Bent 5 > S
Orientation: palm in
Location: neck
Movement: slide fingertips down to chest, slowly closing to S handshape
Nonmanual signal: lips taut; body taut
Note: See page 362 for a two-hand variation of this sign.

**feeble-minded,
senile**

Handshape: Bent 5 > 5
Orientation: palm left
Location: forehead
Movement: straighten and bend fingers twice
Nonmanual signal: mouth open; tongue prominent

warm

Handshape: Bent 5 > 5
Orientation: palm in
Location: chin
Movement: brush fingers up and out,
  opening to 5 handshape

light (n.)

Handshape: 8 > Open 8
Orientation: palm in
Location: chin
Movement: flick middle finger up and
  off chin

pest, nuisance

Handshape: Open 8
Orientation: palm out
Location: neutral space
Movement: jab middle finger toward
  referent and back
Nonmanual signal: "annoyed" expression
Note: This sign is also used for the ASL
  idiom, SICK, YOU.

**mercy,
empathy,
pity,
sympathy**

Handshape: Open 8
Orientation: palm out
Location: neutral space
Movement: move hand forward in two
  small circles
Nonmanual signal: head lowered; "sad"
  expression

sick of it (slang)

Handshape: Open 8
Orientation: palm in
Location: middle finger on forehead
Movement: twist hand left
Nonmanual signal: "disgusted" expression

clever, bright, intelligent, smart

Handshape: Open 8
Orientation: palm in
Location: forehead
Movement: swing hand around, ending palm out
Nonmanual signal: head tilts up and to the right
Note: See page 121 for a variation of this sign.

taste, flavor

Handshape: Open 8
Orientation: palm in
Location: lower lip
Movement: tap middle finger on lower lip twice
Nonmanual signal: mouth open; tongue protruding

favorite, prefer, rather

Handshape: Open 8
Orientation: palm in
Location: chin
Movement: sharply bounce middle finger off chin
Nonmanual signal: lips taut

lucky

Handshape: Open 8
Orientation: palm in
Location: chin
Movement: swing hand around, ending palm down
Nonmanual signal: lips taut

tend, disposed to, tendency, inclined

Handshape: Open 8
Orientation: palm in
Location: middle finger on chest
Movement: move hand out, away from chest
Nonmanual signal: "pah" mouth utterance; body leans forward

**feel,
sense (SM),
emotion,
feeling,
sensation
(DM)**

Handshape: Open 8
Orientation: palm in
Location: near chest
Movement: brush middle finger up
   and off chest in two circular motions

**kind,
benevolent,
kindly,
warm-
hearted**

Handshape: Open 8
Orientation: palm in
Location: below left shoulder
Movement: move middle finger in a
   small circle, then touch chest

**touching,
heartfelt,
poignant**

Handshape: Open 8
Orientation: palm in
Location: near chest
Movement: bring hand to chest with an
   exaggerated motion and touch chest
Nonmanual signal: lips taut

heart

Handshape: Open 8
Orientation: palm in
Location: near heart
Movement: double bounce middle finger
   on chest

sensitive

Handshape: Open 8
Orientation: palm in
Location: middle finger on chest
Movement: twist hand around, ending
   palm down
Nonmanual signal: right shoulder lifts up;
   head tilts right; "cz" mouth movement

**sort, kind,
type,
species**

Handshape: Open 8
Orientation: palm in
Location: middle finger on chest,
   below left shoulder
Movement: arc hand across to right
   side of chest

delicious

Handshape: Open 8 > 8
Orientation: palm in
Location: mouth
Movement: move hand out, rubbing middle finger and thumb together
Nonmanual signal: eyes widen; smile

like

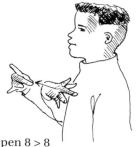

Handshape: Open 8 > 8
Orientation: palm in
Location: chest
Movement: move hand out, closing thumb and middle finger
Nonmanual signal: "happy" expression

don't like

Handshape: Open 8 > 8 > 5
Orientation: palm in
Location: chest
Movement: move hand out, closing thumb and middle finger, then twist hand around and flick middle finger off thumb

Two-Hand
Signs

with, accompany

Handshape: A : A
Orientation: palms facing
Location: neutral space
Movement: bring hands together

steady date, go steady

Handshape: A : A
Orientation: palms facing; hands touching
Location: neutral space
Movement: double bounce hands forward

association, agency

Handshape: A : A
Orientation: palms out; thumbs touching
Location: neutral space
Movement: swing hands around, ending
   with fingers touching

area

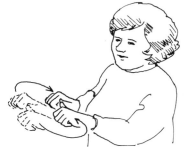

Handshape: A : A
Orientation: palms down; thumbs touching
Location: neutral space
Movement: draw semicircles with thumbs,
   ending with thumbs touching

pull

Handshape: A : A
Orientation: palms facing; left hand in
   front of right
Location: neutral space
Movement: tug hands toward body

golf

Handshape: A : A
Orientation: palms facing; right hand on left
Location: near right shoulder
Movement: swing hands down and up
Nonmanual signal: head tilts right

dig, shovel

Handshape: A : A
Orientation: right palm down; left palm up
Location: neutral space
Movement: arc hands up toward left shoulder

cabinet

Handshape: A : A
Orientation: palms facing
Location: near head
Movement: swing hands around, ending with palms in

able, can, may (SM); ability, capable, competent, possible (DM)

Handshape: A : A
Orientation: palms out
Location: neutral space
Movement: bend wrists down

attempt, audition, effort, endeavor, persist, try

Handshape: A : A
Orientation: palms down
Location: neutral space
Movement: arc hands up and forward
Nonmanual signal: "serious" expression

algebra

Handshape: A : A
Orientation: right palm left; left palm down
Location: neutral space
Movement: brush hands together twice

army, bear arms (soldier)

Handshape: A : A
Orientation: palms in; right hand above left
Location: neutral space
Movement: double bounce hands on chest
Nonmanual signal: shoulders thrust back; erect posture

coat, jacket, sweater

Handshape: A : A
Orientation: palms in
Location: thumbs on shoulders
Movement: arc hands down to chest
Nonmanual signal: shoulders hunch

bath, bathe, wash

Handshape: A : A
Orientation: palms in
Location: chest
Movement: brush hands up and down chest

bind, knot, tie

Handshape: A : A
Orientation: palms facing
Location: neutral space
Movement: move hands to mimic tying a knot

drum, play drums

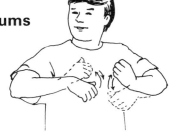

Handshape: A : A
Orientation: palms in
Location: neutral space
Movement: bend wrists alternately up and down

wash

Handshape: A : A
Orientation: right palm down; left palm up
Location: neutral space
Movement: rub hands together in circular motion

chew

Handshape: A : A
Orientation: right palm down; left palm up
Location: neutral space
Movement: grind knuckles against one another

pass by

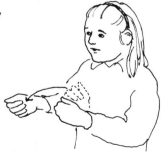

Handshape: A : A
Orientation: palms facing; right hand behind left hand
Location: neutral space
Movement: brush right hand past left hand

guitar

Handshape: A : A
Orientation: palms in
Location: right hand near waist; left hand near shoulder
Movement: twist right hand up and down

each (SM); every (DM)

Handshape: A : A
Orientation: right palm left, right hand behind left hand; left palm right
Location: neutral space
Movement: slide right hand down back of left thumb

zip (SM); zipper (DM)

Handshape: A : A
Orientation: palms in
Location: waist
Movement: slide right hand up chest

polish, rub, sandpaper, shine shoes

Handshape: A : Open B
Orientation: right palm down; left palm up
Location: neutral space
Movement: slide right hand back and forth across left palm

knock

Handshape: A : Open B
Orientation: palms facing
Location: neutral space
Movement: knock right knuckles on left palm twice

iron, press

Handshape: A : Open B
Orientation: right palm in; left palm up
Location: neutral space
Movement: slide right hand back and forth across left palm

expert, adept, experienced, sharp, skill, talent

Handshape: A : Open B
Orientation: right palm in, right hand gripping edge of left hand; left palm right
Location: neutral space
Movement: pull right hand sharply off left hand
Nonmanual signal: lips taut

dollar

Handshape: A : Open B
Orientation: right palm down, right hand gripping top of left hand; left palm in
Location: neutral space
Movement: slide right hand along left hand

lead, guide

Handshape: A : Open B
Orientation: right palm left, right hand gripping left hand fingertips; left palm right
Location: neutral space
Movement: pull left hand forward with right hand

turtle

Handshape: A : Open B
Orientation: right palm left; left palm down, left hand on top of right hand
Location: neutral space
Movement: move right thumb up and down twice

hide, conceal, take cover

Handshape: A : Open B
Orientation: right palm left; left palm down
Location: right thumb on lower lip; left hand in
   neutral space
Movement: slide right thumb down chin and below
   left palm, ending with right thumb showing
Nonmanual signal: shoulders rounded; head
   lowered

cracker, matzoh (passive)

Handshape: A : passive
Orientation: right palm in; left palm right
Location: right hand near left elbow; left
   hand in neutral space
Movement: tap right hand on left elbow
   twice

banana

Handshape: A : 1
Orientation: right palm down; left
   palm out
Location: neutral space
Movement: brush right hand down left
   index finger twice

practice, drill, exercise, rehearse

Handshape: A : 1
Orientation: right palm down; left palm in
Location: neutral space
Movement: brush right hand back and forth along
   left index finger
Nonmanual signal: body tense; head tilted left;
   lips taut

trick, betray, cheat, deceive, defraud, fraud

Handshape: A : 1
Orientation: right palm out, right hand behind left hand; left palm right
Location: neutral space
Movement: sharply knock right hand on left index finger
Nonmanual signal: lips pursed

give up, forfeit, relinquish, surrender, yield

Handshape: A > 5 : A > 5
Orientation: palms in
Location: neutral space
Movement: thrust hands up, changing to 5 handshape
Nonmanual signal: head and body thrown back; "discouraged" expression

without

Handshape: A > 5 : A > 5
Orientation: palms facing; hands touching
Location: neutral space
Movement: separate hands, changing to 5 handshape

bless

Handshape: A > 5 : A > 5
Orientation: palms facing
Location: lips
Movement: move hands down and out, changing to 5 handshape
Nonmanual signal: head lowered

shape, figure, form, image, sculpture, statue

Handshape: Open A : Open A
Orientation: palms facing
Location: neutral space
Movement: wiggle hands and move them down

challenge, opportunity

Handshape: Open A : Open A
Orientation: palms down
Location: neutral space
Movement: arc hands up, ending with palms in and fingers touching

**continue,
endure, ever,
permanent,
persevere,
persist,
remain,
stay, still**

Handshape: Open A : Open A
Orientation: palms down, thumbs
   touching
Location: neutral space
Movement: slowly push hands forward

**deposit,
down payment**

Handshape: Open A : Open A
Orientation: palms down, thumbs
   touching
Location: neutral space
Movement: separate hands, ending with
   thumbs down

**deny
(declare
untrue)**

Handshape: Open A : Open A
Orientation: palms facing
Location: chin
Movement: move thumbs out and down
Nonmanual signal: head shakes "no"

**live, address,
alive, life,
reside,
survive**

Handshape: Open A : Open A
Orientation: palms in
Location: neutral space
Movement: brush hands up chest

**sweetheart,
beau, lover**

Handshape: Open A : Open A
Orientation: palms in, knuckles touching
Location: left side of chest
Movement: bend thumbs down and up
   twice

**baptism,
Baptist,
baptize**

Handshape: Open A : Open A
Orientation: palms facing
Location: neutral space
Movement: bend wrists to the right
   and back up

associate, fellowship, interact, socialize

Handshape: Open A : Open A
Orientation: right palm out, thumb down; left palm in, thumb up
Location: neutral space
Movement: circle thumbs around each other

which, or, whether

Handshape: Open A : Open A
Orientation: palms in
Location: neutral space
Movement: move hands up and down, alternating positions
Nonmanual signal: torso leans forward; head tilts right; eyebrows knit; lips pursed

science

Handshape: Open A : Open A
Orientation: palms out, thumbs down
Location: neutral space
Movement: circle hands back and down, alternating positions

puzzle (game)

Handshape: Open A : Open A
Orientation: palms down
Location: neutral space
Movement: move thumbs down twice, alternating hands

**compete,
contest, race,
rivalry,
sports, vie**

Handshape: Open A : Open A
Orientation: palms facing, knuckles
  touching
Location: neutral space
Movement: rotate hands back and
  forth, alternating positions

**ambitious,
assertive,
aggressive**

Handshape: Open A : Open A
Orientation: palms in
Location: chest
Movement: brush hands against chest in
  circular motions, alternating positions
Nonmanual signal: lips taut; "earnest"
  expression

**act, audition, drama, perform,
play, show, theater**
(actor, actress, performer)

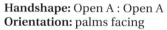

Handshape: Open A : Open A
Orientation: palms facing
Location: chest
Movement: circle alternating hands back and
  down, brushing backs of thumbs against chest

**brag,
show off**

Handshape: Open A : Open A
Orientation: palms down
Location: waist
Movement: bounce alternating thumbs
  on waist twice
Nonmanual signal: torso leans back;
  chest puffs out

most

Handshape: Open A : Open A
Orientation: palms facing, knuckles
  touching
Location: neutral space
Movement: brush right knuckles up
  and above left hand

behind, in back of

Handshape: Open A : Open A
Orientation: right palm down, closer to body; left palm right
Location: neutral space
Movement: swing right hand up and behind left thumb

ahead

Handshape: Open A : Open A
Orientation: palms facing, right hand behind left hand
Location: neutral space
Movement: move right hand past left hand

far, distant

Handshape: Open A : Open A
Orientation: palms facing, knuckles touching
Location: neutral space
Movement: arc right hand forward with an exaggerated motion
Nonmanual signal: body leans back; "cha" mouth utterance

avoid, evade, shirk

Handshape: Open A : Open A
Orientation: palms facing
Location: neutral space
Movement: rapidly wiggle right hand back

chase, follow, pursue

Handshape: Open A : Open A
Orientation: right palm left, hand behind left hand; left palm right
Location: neutral space
Movement: spiral right hand toward left hand while left hand moves forward

remember,
memory,
recall,
recollect,
remind

Handshape: Open A : Open A
Orientation: palms down
Location: right thumb on temple; left
   hand in neutral space
Movement: bring right hand down
   until thumbs touch

danger, injure,
peril, threat,
violate

Handshape: Open A : A
Orientation: right palm left; left palm in
Location: neutral space
Movement: brush right thumb against
   back of left hand twice
Nonmanual signal: "serious" expression

doorbell, bell,
ring bell

Handshape: Open A : Open B
Orientation: right palm in; left palm right
Location: neutral space
Movement: press right thumb into left
   palm twice

carve,
sculpt

Handshape: Open A : Open B
Orientation: right palm down; left palm
   right
Location: neutral space
Movement: dig right thumb into left
   palm twice

impress, emphasis,
emphasize, stress

Handshape: Open A : Open B
Orientation: right palm out, thumb on left palm;
   left palm right
Location: neutral space
Movement: twist hand forward
Nonmanual signal: lips taut; "earnest" expression

page, dictionary

Handshape: Open A : Open B
Orientation: right palm down, thumb on left palm; left palm right
Location: neutral space
Movement: brush thumb up left palm twice

letter, mail

Handshape: Open A : Open B
Orientation: right palm in; left palm right
Location: right thumb on lower lip; left hand in neutral space
Movement: bring right hand down, ending with thumb on left palm

surgery, operation

Handshape: Open A : Open B
Orientation: right palm down, thumb near left thumb; left palm right
Location: neutral space
Movement: brush right thumb down left palm

help, aid, assist, benefit, rehabilitate

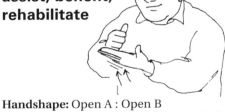

Handshape: Open A : Open B
Orientation: right palm left, hand on left hand; left palm up
Location: neutral space
Movement: lift right hand up with left hand
Nonmanual signal: "earnest" expression

blame, fault, guilt (SM); accuse (DM)

Handshape: Open A : Open B
Orientation: right palm left; left palm down
Location: neutral space
Movement: brush right hand sharply across back of left hand
Nonmanual signal: lips taut

establish, erect, form (v.), install, set up

Handshape: Open A : Open B
Orientation: palms down, right hand above left hand
Location: neutral space
Movement: swing right hand up and bring down on top of left hand

establish, erect, form (v.), implement, install, set up

Handshape: Open A : S
Orientation: palms down
Location: neutral space
Movement: swing right hand up and bring down on top of left hand

gasoline, gas

Handshape: Open A : S
Orientation: right palm down, hand above left hand; left palm right
Location: neutral space
Movement: insert thumb into left fist

defecate, bowel movement, feces

Handshape: Open A : S
Orientation: right palm left, thumb tucked in bottom of left hand; left palm right
Location: neutral space
Movement: slide right thumb out of left hand
Nonmanual signal: nose wrinkled; "disgusted" expression

close, shut

Handshape: B : B
Orientation: palms out, arms parallel
Location: neutral space
Movement: bring hands together

open (horizontal)

Handshape: B : B
Orientation: palms down; index fingers touching
Location: neutral space
Movement: arc hands up and over, ending with palms angled up

open (vertical)

Handshape: B : B
Orientation: palms out; index fingers touching
Location: neutral space
Movement: arc hands back, ending with palms facing

behavior

Handshape: B : B
Orientation: palms down
Location: neutral space
Movement: swing hands side to side in unison

corner

Handshape: B : B
Orientation: palms facing; fingertips angled toward each other
Location: neutral space
Movement: tap fingertips together twice

quiet, calm

Handshape: B : B
Orientation: right palm left; left palm right; hands crossed
Location: mouth
Movement: arc hands down and apart, ending with palms down
Nonmanual signal: lips taut

blanket

Handshape: B : B
Orientation: palms down, fingertips facing
Location: neutral space
Movement: bounce hands against chest twice

relief

Handshape: B : B
Orientation: palms down, right hand above left hand
Location: chest
Movement: slide hands down chest
Nonmanual signal: lips rounded; exaggerated exhale

satisfied, content, gratified

Handshape: B : B
Orientation: palms down; right hand above left hand
Location: neutral space
Movement: tap hands against chest
Nonmanual signal: lips pursed; "contented" expression

trouble, anxious, cares, concern, fret, worry

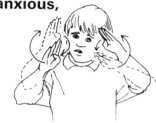

Handshape: B : B
Orientation: palms angled toward each other
Location: head
Movement: circle hands inward in alternating motions
Nonmanual signal: "worried" expression

window, open window

Handshape: B : B
Orientation: palms in; edge of right hand on left index finger
Location: neutral space
Movement: move right hand up and down

open door (SM); door (DM)

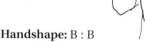

Handshape: B : B
Orientation: palms out, index fingers touching
Location: neutral space
Movement: arc right hand back, ending with palm left

specialize, field, major (study), specialty

Handshape: B : B
Orientation: right palm left, edge of right hand on left hand; left palm right
Location: neutral space
Movement: slide right hand forward along left index finger
Nonmanual signal: "earnest" expression

kick, soccer

Handshape: B : B
Orientation: right palm left, fingertips down; left palm right
Location: neutral space
Movement: swing right hand up, knocking into left hand

partial to, favorite

Handshape: B : B
Orientation: right palm in, fingertips on left index finger; left palm out
Location: neutral space
Movement: tap right fingertips against left index finger twice

autumn, fall (passive)

Handshape: B : passive
Orientation: right palm down, near left elbow; left arm across body
Location: neutral space
Movement: brush right hand down left elbow twice

slippers

Handshape: B : C
Orientation: right palm down, hand above left hand; left palm up
Location: neutral space
Movement: slide right hand into left hand twice

busy, business

Handshape: B : S
Orientation: right palm out; left palm down
Location: neutral space
Movement: brush heel of right hand back and forth against left index finger

partial to (an individual)

Handshape: B : 1
Orientation: right palm left, fingertips touching left index finger; left palm out
Location: neutral space
Movement: tap right fingertips on left index finger twice

advance, forward, go ahead, onward, proceed

Handshape: Open B : Open B
Orientation: palms in
Location: neutral space
Movement: glide hands forward
Nonmanual signal: "mm" mouth utterance

floor

Handshape: Open B : Open B
Orientation: palms down, index fingers
   touching
Location: neutral space
Movement: separate hands

children

Handshape: Open B : Open B
Orientation: palms down
Location: neutral space
Movement: bounce hands apart

swimming

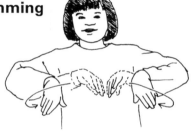

Handshape: Open B : Open B
Orientation: palms down; index fingers
   touching
Location: neutral space
Movement: circle hands out and around

not, do not, don't do that

Handshape: Open B : Open B
Orientation: palms down, hands crossed
Location: neutral space
Movement: separate hands sharply
Nonmanual signal: frown with "stern"
   expression

rise, arise, raise, stand up (to audience)

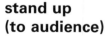

Handshape: Open B : Open B
Orientation: palms up
Location: neutral space
Movement: lift both hands up in unison

here, present

Handshape: Open B : Open B
Orientation: palms up
Location: neutral space
Movement: move hands together and
   apart in short quick motions

things

Handshape: Open B : Open B
Orientation: palms up, hands close together
Location: neutral space
Movement: bounce hands apart
Note: See page 51 for a one-hand variation.

offer, introduce (a topic), propose, recommend, suggest

Handshape: Open B : Open B
Orientation: palms up
Location: neutral space
Movement: arc hands up and forward in unison

bring, carry, deliver

Handshape: Open B : Open B
Orientation: palms up
Location: neutral space
Movement: arc hands left

volleyball

Handshape: Open B : Open B
Orientation: palms up
Location: near sides of head
Movement: push hands up twice

Sunday

Handshape: Open B : Open B
Orientation: palms out
Location: neutral space
Movement: circle hands out twice

attention, concentrate, focus, pay attention

Handshape: Open B : Open B
Orientation: palms facing
Location: near temples
Movement: move hands forward sharply

way, corridor, hallway, method, path, road, strategy, street, trail

Handshape: Open B : Open B
Orientation: palms facing, fingers forward
Location: neutral space
Movement: move hands forward

allow, condone, grant, let, may, permit, tolerate

Handshape: Open B : Open B
Orientation: palms facing, fingers down
Location: neutral space
Movement: arc hands forward and up, ending with fingers forward

person, agent, individual

Handshape: Open B : Open B
Orientation: palms facing, fingers forward
Location: in front of shoulders
Movement: move hands down

arrange, order (n.), plan, prepare

Handshape: Open B : Open B
Orientation: palms facing, fingers forward
Location: neutral space
Movement: loop hands right
Nonmanual signal: lips pursed; "thoughtful" expression

narrow

Handshape: Open B : Open B
Orientation: palms facing, fingers forward
Location: neutral space
Movement: move hands forward
Nonmanual signal: "cz" mouth utterance

wide, broad, width

Handshape: Open B : Open B
Orientation: palms facing, fingers forward
Location: neutral space
Movement: move hands apart
Nonmanual signal: "cha" mouth utterance

encourage, cheer, uplift

Handshape: Open B : Open B
Orientation: palms up; wrists bent back
Location: neutral space
Movement: push hands toward each other in two small motions
Nonmanual signal: lips pursed

convince, cornered

Handshape: Open B : Open B
Orientation: palms angled up
Location: neutral space
Movement: chop hands down sharply
Nonmanual signal: lips pursed

abhor, avoid, detest, hate, loathe

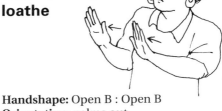

Handshape: Open B : Open B
Orientation: palms out
Location: neutral space
Movement: push hands sharply to left side
Nonmanual signal: body leans away from repelling reference; "disgusted" expression

introduce (person)

Handshape: Open B : Open B
Orientation: palms up, fingers forward
Location: neutral space
Movement: arc hands to center, ending with fingertips facing
Nonmanual signal: lips pursed

bet

Handshape: Open B : Open B
Orientation: palms up, fingers forward
Location: neutral space
Movement: flip hands over with exaggerated
   motion, ending with palms down
Nonmanual signal: body and head lean back;
   eyes widen

dark, darken, dim

Handshape: Open B : Open B
Orientation: palms in
Location: near face
Movement: cross hands in front of face
Nonmanual signal: shoulders rounded;
   head lowered

compare, distinguish

Handshape: Open B : Open B
Orientation: palms facing
Location: near face
Movement: rock hands back and forth,
   several times

house, residence

Handshape: Open B : Open B
Orientation: palms facing; fingertips
   touching
Location: neutral space
Movement: move hands apart and down

city, community, town, village

Handshape: Open B : Open B
Orientation: palms facing, fingertips
   close together
Location: neutral space
Movement: tap fingertips together
   several times while moving hands left

general

Handshape: Open B : Open B
Orientation: palms facing, fingertips forward and touching
Location: neutral space
Movement: separate hands
Nonmanual signal: lips pursed

hinge

Handshape: Open B : Open B
Orientation: palms in, fingertips touching
Location: neutral space
Movement: close and open hands

butterfly

Handshape: Open B : Open B
Orientation: palms in, hands crossed and thumbs clasped
Location: neutral space
Movement: flutter hands

boat, go by boat

Handshape: Open B : Open B
Orientation: palms up, hands touching
Location: neutral space
Movement: bounce hands forward

ask, inquire, request

Handshape: Open B : Open B
Orientation: palms facing, fingers forward
Location: neutral space
Movement: bend wrists up, then bring hands together, ending with palms touching

pray, amen

Handshape: Open B : Open B
Orientation: palms touching
Location: near face
Movement: arc hands in toward body
Nonmanual signal: head lowers as hands move down

**book,
open a book**

Handshape: Open B : Open B
Orientation: palms touching, fingers
  forward
Location: neutral space
Movement: separate hands, ending with
  little fingers touching

**applaud, clap,
commend,
congratulate,
praise**

Handshape: Open B : Open B
Orientation: right palm down, hand
  above left hand; left palm up
Location: neutral space
Movement: clap hands twice

**divide,
go-Dutch (slang),
split**

Handshape: Open B : Open B
Orientation: palms in, hands crossed
Location: neutral space
Movement: move hands apart

**sandwich (SM);
picnic (DM)**

Handshape: Open B : Open B
Orientation: palms down, right hand on
  top of left hand
Location: near mouth
Movement: move hands toward mouth twice

pants, slacks

Handshape: Open B : Open B
Orientation: palms facing, fingers down
Location: near left thigh
Movement: slide hands down in front of left thigh,
  then repeat motion on right thigh

prevent (me),
block (me)

Handshape: Open B : Open B
Orientation: right palm left, hand crossed in front of left hand; left palm right
Location: neutral space
Movement: hit edge of left hand with right index finger, then bring hands in toward body
Nonmanual signal: body and head thrown back; "discouraged" expression

block, defend,
guard,
prevent,
protect

Handshape: Open B : Open B
Orientation: right palm left, hand crossed behind left hand; left palm right
Location: neutral space
Movement: push hands forward sharply
Nonmanual signal: lips pursed

baby, infant

Handshape: Open B : Open B
Orientation: palms up, right hand inside left hand
Location: neutral space
Movement: rock arms side to side

lean, drawn

Handshape: Open B : Open B
Orientation: palms facing
Location: face
Movement: slide fingers down face
Nonmanual signal: cheeks sucked in

grateful,
appreciative,
thankful

Handshape: Open B : Open B
Orientation: palms in
Location: right fingertips on mouth; left hand in neutral space
Movement: move both hands forward
Nonmanual signal: body leans forward; "grateful" expression

beloved, care for, devotion, love, revere

Handshape: Open B : Open B
Orientation: palms in; hands crossed;
  right hand on left hand
Location: left side of chest
Movement: rest hands on heart

rest, relax, retire

Handshape: Open B : Open B
Orientation: palms in, arms crossed
Location: chest
Movement: rest hands on chest
Nonmanual signal: "contented" expression

body, physical

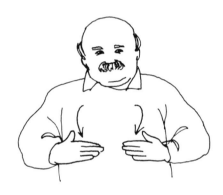

Handshape: Open B : Open B
Orientation: palms in
Location: chest
Movement: tap fingertips on chest, then on waist

happy, delight, glad, joy, merry

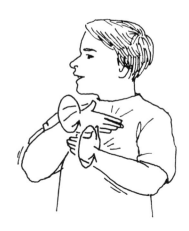

Handshape: Open B : Open B
Orientation: palms in, right hand above left hand
Location: chest
Movement: brush hands up and off chest twice
Nonmanual signal: smile

enjoy, appreciate, joy, pleasure

Handshape: Open B : Open B
Orientation: palms in, right hand above left hand
Location: chest
Movement: move hands in small opposing circles on chest
Nonmanual signal: smile

breathe, exhale

Handshape: Open B : Open B
Orientation: palms in, right hand above left hand
Location: chest
Movement: move hands out and back to chest twice
Nonmanual signal: chest expands and contracts; blow air out repeatedly

admit, acquiesce, confess, consent, give in, willing, yield

Handshape: Open B : Open B
Orientation: palms in, right hand above left hand
Location: neutral space
Movement: arc hands up and forward, ending with palms angled up
Nonmanual signal: body leans forward; head lowered; "contrite" expression

box, package, room

Handshape: Open B : Open B
Orientation: palms facing, fingers forward
Location: neutral space
Movement: move hands down, then bend wrists in, palms in, and move hands down

become

Handshape: Open B : Open B
Orientation: right palm down, hand on left palm; left palm up
Location: neutral space
Movement: flip hands over, ending with left palm on right palm

peace

Handshape: Open B : Open B
Orientation: right palm down, hand on top of left palm; left palm up
Location: neutral space
Movement: twist hands slowly, reversing palm positions, then separate hands, ending with palms down
Nonmanual signal: "serene" expression

die, dead, death, expire

Handshape: Open B : Open B
Orientation: right palm up; left palm down
Location: neutral space
Movement: flip hands over
Nonmanual signal: "sad" expression

may, maybe, might, perhaps

Handshape: Open B : Open B
Orientation: palms up
Location: neutral space
Movement: move hands alternately up and down
Nonmanual signal: shoulders shrug; eyes widen

service, serve, wait on

Handshape: Open B : Open B
Orientation: palms up
Location: neutral space
Movement: slide hands alternately back and forth twice

serve (*server, waiter, waitress*)

Handshape: Open B : Open B
Orientation: palms up
Location: near head
Movement: slide hands alternately back and forth

walk

Handshape: Open B : Open B
Orientation: palms down
Location: neutral space
Movement: bend hands alternately up and down at the wrist

stairs, steps

Handshape: Open B : Open B
Orientation: palms down, right hand higher than left hand
Location: neutral space
Movement: move left hand above right hand, then right hand above left hand, and repeat

ancestors, generations

Handshape: Open B : Open B
Orientation: palms in, one hand in front of the other
Location: near right shoulder
Movement: circle hands around each other while moving them back
Nonmanual signal: right shoulder tilts back

hands, manual

Handshape: Open B : Open B
Orientation: palms in, right hand behind left hand
Location: neutral space
Movement: brush back of right hand down left palm, then brush back of left hand down right palm

descendants, generations, posterity

Handshape: Open B : Open B
Orientation: palms in, one hand in front of the other
Location: near right shoulder
Movement: circle hands around each other while moving them forward
Nonmanual signal: body leans forward

anyhow, anyway, despite, doesn't matter, indifferent, nevertheless, regardless, whenever

Handshape: Open B : Open B
Orientation: palms in, right hand in front of left hand
Location: neutral space
Movement: slap right fingers against left fingers, then slap left fingers against right fingers

ambitious, diligent, eager, enthusiastic, industrious, Methodist, zealous

Handshape: Open B : Open B
Orientation: palms together
Location: neutral space
Movement: rub hands back and forth several times
Nonmanual signal: "earnest" expression

heaven

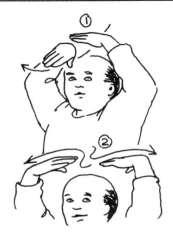

Handshape: Open B : Open B
Orientation: palms down
Location: above head
Movement: move right hand under left, then circle hands in opposite directions
Nonmanual signal: eyes gaze upward

kind, generous, gracious, merciful

Handshape: Open B : Open B
Orientation: palms in, right hand closer to body
Location: left side of chest
Movement: circle hands around each other while slowly moving them forward
Nonmanual signal: body leans forward; "grateful" expression

towel, wash

Handshape: Open B : Open B
Orientation: palms in
Location: face
Movement: move hands alternately up and down several times

complete, end

Handshape: Open B : Open B
Orientation: right palm left, hand above left hand; left palm in
Location: neutral space
Movement: slide edge of right hand across and off left index finger, then bring hand down

confront, approach, face to face

Handshape: Open B : Open B
Orientation: palms facing, right hand closer to body
Location: neutral space
Movement: arc right hand up to face left hand
Nonmanual signal: "serious" expression

below, background, basic, basis, beneath, bottom, basement, foundation, underneath

Handshape: Open B : Open B
Orientation: palms down, right hand below left hand
Location: neutral space
Movement: circle right hand counterclockwise under left hand

---

bake, oven

Handshape: Open B : Open B
Orientation: right palm up, hands perpendicular; left palm down
Location: neutral space
Movement: slide right hand under left hand

---

above, over

Handshape: Open B : Open B
Orientation: palms down, right hand below left hand
Location: neutral space
Movement: arc right hand in toward body, then above left hand

---

on

Handshape: Open B : Open B
Orientation: palms down, right hand above left hand
Location: neutral space
Movement: move right hand down on top of left hand

---

off

Handshape: Open B : Open B
Orientation: palms down, right hand crossed on top of left hand
Location: neutral space
Movement: lift right hand off left hand

than

Handshape: Open B : Open B
Orientation: palms down, hands angled toward each other, right hand above left hand
Location: neutral space
Movement: slap fingers of right hand on and past fingers of left hand

enter, entrance, go into

Handshape: Open B : Open B
Orientation: palms down, hands angled toward each other
Location: neutral space
Movement: slide right hand under left hand

warn, admonish, advise, alert, caution, forewarn

Handshape: Open B : Open B
Orientation: palms down, hands angled toward each other, right hand above left hand
Location: neutral space
Movement: smack back of left hand twice with fingers of right hand

surface, cover, superficial

Handshape: Open B : Open B
Orientation: palms down, right hand crossed on top of left hand
Location: neutral space
Movement: slide right hand back and forth along left hand

operate, execute, run

Handshape: Open B : Open B
Orientation: right palm up, hand below left hand; left palm down
Location: neutral space
Movement: quickly brush right fingers up and off left fingertips twice

time out

Handshape: Open B : Open B
Orientation: right palm left, fingertips under left hand; left palm down
Location: neutral space
Movement: hit middle of left palm twice with right fingertips

OPEN B 🕭 2-Hand SIGNS

**wood,
saw**

Handshape: Open B : Open B
Orientation: right palm left, edge of hand on back of left hand; left palm down
Location: neutral space
Movement: slide edge of right hand back and forth across back of left hand

**across,
cross over,
over**

Handshape: Open B : Open B
Orientation: right palm left, hand behind left hand; left palm in
Location: neutral space
Movement: cross right hand over left hand

**laid off,
discharge,
dismiss,
excuse**

Handshape: Open B : Open B
Orientation: right palm down, fingertips on left palm; left palm up
Location: neutral space
Movement: sharply slide right fingers down and off left hand
Nonmanual signal: lips pursed

**clean, nice,
plain, pure,
simple**

Handshape: Open B : Open B
Orientation: right palm down, palm on top of left palm; left palm up
Location: neutral space
Movement: slide right palm across left hand
Nonmanual signal: lips pursed

wash dishes

Handshape: Open B : Open B
Orientation: right palm down, hand on top of left hand; left palm up
Location: neutral space
Movement: move right hand counter-clockwise on left palm

**paper,
manuscript,
newspaper,
page**

Handshape: Open B : Open B
Orientation: right palm down, hand above left hand; left palm down
Location: neutral space
Movement: smack heel of right hand twice against heel of left hand

school

Handshape: Open B : Open B
Orientation: right palm down, hand above left hand; left palm down
Location: neutral space
Movement: clap palms together twice

college, university

Handshape: Open B : Open B
Orientation: right palm down, fingertips on left palm; left palm up
Location: neutral space
Movement: spiral right hand up

cheese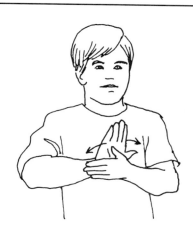

Handshape: Open B : Open B
Orientation: right palm out, heel of right hand on left palm; left palm in
Location: neutral space
Movement: twist right wrist back and forth several times

cook, fry, kitchen, pancake

Handshape: Open B : Open B
Orientation: right palm down, hand crossed on top of left palm; left palm up
Location: neutral space
Movement: flip right hand over and back on left palm

proof, evidence

Handshape: Open B : Open B
Orientation: palms up, right hand above left hand
Location: neutral space
Movement: smack back of right hand down sharply on left palm

arrive, reach

Handshape: Open B : Open B
Orientation: palms in, right hand near shoulder
Location: neutral space
Movement: arc right hand forward and down slowly, landing on left palm

new, modern

Handshape: Open B : Open B
Orientation: palms up, hands angled toward each other
Location: neutral space
Movement: slide back of right hand across left palm

almost, about, nearly

Handshape: Open B : Open B
Orientation: palms angled up, right hand in front of left hand
Location: neutral space
Movement: brush back of left fingers twice with right fingers
Nonmanual signal: "cz" mouth utterance

rights, privileges

Handshape: Open B : Open B
Orientation: right palm left, right pinky and ring fingertips on left palm; left palm up
Location: neutral space
Movement: slide edge of right hand across left palm, ending with fingertips up
Nonmanual signal: "serious" expression

all right, okay

Handshape: Open B : Open B
Orientation: right palm left, edge of hand on left palm; left palm up
Location: neutral space
Movement: brush edge of right hand across left palm twice

stop, cease, halt

Handshape: Open B : Open B
Orientation: right palm left, hand above left hand; left palm up
Location: neutral space
Movement: bring right hand down sharply on left palm
Nonmanual signal: "serious" expression

against, discriminate, oppose, prejudice, sue

Handshape: Open B : Open B
Orientation: right palm in, fingertips pointed at left palm; left palm right
Location: neutral space
Movement: hit left palm sharply with fingertips of right hand
Nonmanual signal: "serious" expression

paint

Handshape: Open B : Open B
Orientation: palms facing
Location: neutral space
Movement: brush right fingertips up and down left hand

fish

Handshape: Open B : Open B
Orientation: right palm left; left palm right, fingertips on right wrist
Location: neutral space
Movement: bend right wrist left and right

cheap, inexpensive

Handshape: Open B : Open B
Orientation: palms facing
Location: neutral space
Movement: slap right fingers down and off left palm

psychology

Handshape: Open B : Open B
Orientation: right palm left, hand above left hand; left palm out
Location: neutral space
Movement: bring right hand down between left thumb and index finger twice

average, medium, range, temperate

Handshape: Open B : Open B
Orientation: right palm left, edge of hand resting on left index finger; left palm in
Location: neutral space
Movement: slide right hand back and forth along left index finger several times
Nonmanual signal: "mm" mouth utterance

share

Handshape: Open B : Open B
Orientation: right palm left, slightly above left hand; left palm in
Location: neutral space
Movement: swing edge of right hand back and forth along left index finger twice

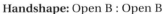

between

Handshape: Open B : Open B
Orientation: right palm left, edge in crease of left
   thumb; left palm in
Location: neutral space
Movement: slide right hand between thumb and
   knuckle of left index finger

**disrupt, hinder, impede,
intercept, interfere, interrupt,
obstruct, prevent (SM); annoy,
bother, disturb (DM)**

Handshape: Open B : Open B
Orientation: right palm left, hand above left hand;
   left palm in
Location: neutral space
Movement: bring right hand down sharply on edge
   of left hand
Nonmanual signal: "angry" expression

**after,
beyond,
next**

Handshape: Open B : Open B
Orientation: palms in, palm of right hand
   against left hand
Location: neutral space
Movement: arc right hand forward and
   down

---

after, next

Handshape: Open B : Open B
Orientation: palms in, back of right
   hand against left palm
Location: neutral space
Movement: arc right hand up and over
   left hand

before

Handshape: Open B : Open B
Orientation: palms in, back of right hand against left palm
Location: neutral space
Movement: move right hand toward body

---

all, entire, whole

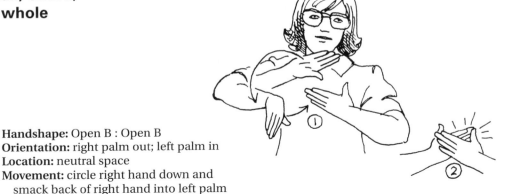

Handshape: Open B : Open B
Orientation: right palm out; left palm in
Location: neutral space
Movement: circle right hand down and smack back of right hand into left palm

---

approach, close to, near, neighbor, next door, next to

Handshape: Open B : Open B
Orientation: palms in, right hand behind left hand
Location: neutral space
Movement: hit back of right hand against left palm twice
Nonmanual signal: "cz" mouth utterance; shoulders raised

gate, fence

Handshape: Open B : Open B
Orientation: palms in, fingertips touching
Location: neutral space
Movement: swing right hand out and back twice

some, part

Handshape: Open B : Open B
Orientation: right palm left, edge of hand on left palm; left palm up
Location: neutral space
Movement: slide right hand back in an arc on left palm

videotape (v.), camcorder

Handshape: Open B : Open B
Orientation: right palm down, hand on left palm; left palm right
Location: in front of face
Movement: slightly bend right fingers down and up twice
Nonmanual signal: right shoulder raised

birth, born

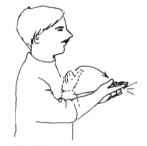

Handshape: Open B : Open B
Orientation: palms up
Location: right hand close to chest; left hand in neutral space
Movement: arc right hand forward and down, landing on left palm

worsen, decrease, downhill, regress (passive)

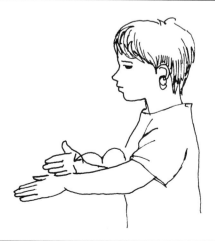

Handshape: Open B : passive
Orientation: right palm in, hand on left arm; left palm down
Location: neutral space
Movement: bounce right hand down left arm
Nonmanual signal: "sad" expression

improve, appreciate, upgrade (passive)

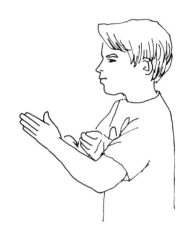

Handshape: Open B : passive
Orientation: right palm in, hand on left wrist; left palm down
Location: neutral space
Movement: bounce right hand up left arm
Nonmanual signal: smile

power, authority, energy, might (passive)

Handshape: Open B : passive
Orientation: right palm out, index finger against left upper arm; left palm up
Location: neutral space
Movement: arc right hand down, ending with hand resting in left elbow crease, palm in

midnight (passive)

Handshape: Open B : passive
Orientation: right palm left, arm relaxed at side; left palm down, fingertips in crease of right elbow
Location: neutral space
Movement: move right hand left slightly

morning (passive)

Handshape: Open B : passive
Orientation: right palm up, arm outstretched; left palm in, hand in crease of right elbow
Location: neutral space
Movement: bend right arm up slightly

noon (passive)

Handshape: Open B : passive
Orientation: right palm left, elbow slightly above left hand; left palm down
Location: neutral space
Movement: bring right arm down to rest elbow on back of left hand

afternoon (passive)

Handshape: Open B : passive
Orientation: right palm out, arm against left wrist; left palm down
Location: neutral space
Movement: tap right arm against left arm twice

all day (passive)

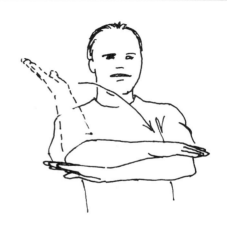

Handshape: Open B : passive
Orientation: right palm left, elbow on back of left hand; left palm down
Location: neutral space
Movement: dramatically bring right arm down to rest on left arm
Nonmanual signal: "cha" mouth utterance

all night (passive)

Handshape: Open B : passive
Orientation: right palm out; left palm down, fingers under right elbow
Location: neutral space
Movement: swing right arm clockwise, ending with palm up
Nonmanual signal: "cha" mouth utterance

all afternoon (passive)

Handshape: Open B : passive
Orientation: right palm out; left palm down, fingers under right elbow
Location: neutral space
Movement: bend right arm down

table, desk (passive)

Handshape: Open B : passive
Orientation: palms down; right arm above left arm
Location: neutral space
Movement: tap arms together twice

sing, music (passive)

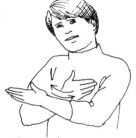

Handshape: Open B : passive
Orientation: right palm in, above left arm; left palm right
Location: neutral space
Movement: swing right hand back and forth

good, well

Handshape: Open B : Open B
Orientation: palms in
Location: right hand on mouth; left hand in neutral space
Movement: move right hand out and smack back of hand on left palm
Nonmanual signal: smile

humble

Handshape: Open B : Open B
Orientation: right palm left; left palm down
Location: right hand on lips; left hand in neutral space
Movement: pass right fingertips slowly under left hand
Nonmanual signal: head lowered

straight, faithful, integrity

Handshape: Open B : B
Orientation: right palm left, pinky on top of left index finger; left palm right
Location: neutral space
Movement: slide right hand straight out

slight (insult)

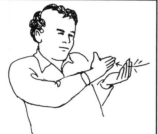

Handshape: Open B : Bent B
Orientation: right palm left, hand in front of left hand; left palm up, fingers bent
Location: neutral space
Movement: sharply slap left fingers with right fingers
Nonmanual signal: "wounded" expression

cover, lid

Handshape: Open B : S
Orientation: right palm down, hand above left hand; left palm in
Location: neutral space
Movement: move right hand down to cover left hand

blow up, blow one's top (slang), hot temper

Handshape: Open B : S
Orientation: right palm down, hand on left hand; left palm in
Location: neutral space
Movement: lift right hand up while wiggling fingers, then bring hand down sharply on left hand

full, complete

Handshape: Open B : S
Orientation: right palm down; left palm in, hand closer to body
Location: neutral space
Movement: brush right hand across top of left fist

**fire,
terminate**

Handshape: Open B : S
Orientation: right palm up, directly
above left hand; left palm in
Location: neutral space
Movement: sharply brush back of right
hand across top of left fist
Nonmanual signal: "serious" expression

flag

Handshape: Open B : 1
Orientation: right palm left; left palm
right, index finger on right wrist
Location: neutral space
Movement: bend right wrist back and
forth several times

**pressure, oppress,
stress (an individual)**

Handshape: Open B : 1
Orientation: right palm down, hand on left hand; left
palm right
Location: neutral space
Movement: press right hand sharply down on left hand
Nonmanual signal: lips pursed
Note: See page 345 for a variation of this sign.

**convince
(an individual)**

Handshape: Open B : 1
Orientation: right palm up; left palm out
Location: neutral space
Movement: move right hand to strike left
index finger
Nonmanual signal: lips pursed

through

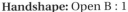

Handshape: Open B : 5
Orientation: right palm left; left palm in
Location: neutral space
Movement: slide right fingers between
left index and middle fingers

depart, leave, withdraw

Handshape: Open B > A : Open B > A
Orientation: palms down, hands angled to left
Location: neutral space
Movement: sharply pull hands in toward body, closing to A handshape

donkey, mule, stubborn

Handshape: Open B > Bent B : Open B > Bent B
Orientation: palms out
Location: thumbs on temples
Movement: bend right and left fingers down twice
Nonmanual signal: lips taut

hypocrite, two-faced

Handshape: Open B > Bent B : Open B > Bent B
Orientation: palms down, right palm on left hand
Location: neutral space
Movement: bend right and left fingers down
Nonmanual signal: "sarcastic" expression

call, summon

Handshape: Open B > A : Open B
Orientation: palms down, right hand above left hand
Location: neutral space
Movement: tap right fingers on back of left hand, then brush fingers off left hand, ending in an A handshape

pie

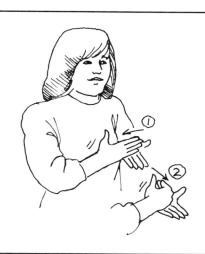

Handshape: Open B > Bent B : Open B
Orientation: right palm left; left palm up
Location: neutral space
Movement: slide edge of right hand from left index finger to heel of left palm, then bend hand and slide hand from base of left thumb to left pinky

center, intermediate, middle

Handshape: Open B > Bent B : Open B
Orientation: right palm down, hand above left hand; left palm up
Location: neutral space
Movement: circle right fingers above left palm, then bend fingers and hit center of palm

frequent, often

Handshape: Open B > Bent B : Open B
Orientation: palms up
Location: neutral space
Movement: flip right hand over twice, bending fingers, and hit center of left palm
Nonmanual signal: "cha" mouth utterance
Note: See page 207 for a variation of this sign.

pet (v.), tame, stroke (SM); pet (n.)(DM)

Handshape: Open B > Bent B : Open B
Orientation: palms down, right palm on left hand
Location: neutral space
Movement: stroke right fingers on back of left hand twice

accumulate, collect, earn, harvest, reap (SM); salary, income (DM)

Handshape: Open B > S : Open B
Orientation: right palm in; left palm up
Location: neutral space
Movement: slide right hand rapidly down left palm, closing to S handshape

not guilty
(compound: not + accuse)

Handshape: Open B > A : Open B
Orientation: palms down, hands crossed
Location: neutral space
Movement: separate hands, then change right hand
to A handshape and brush right hand across back
of left hand
Nonmanual signal: head shakes "no" during first
part of sign

injustice
(compound: not + equal)

Handshape: Open B > Bent B : Open B > Bent B
Orientation: palms down, hands crossed
Location: neutral space
Movement: separate hands, then change hands to
Bent B handshape, and bring hands together twice
Nonmanual signal: head shakes "no" during first part
of sign

limit, capacity,
reserved, restrict

Handshape: Bent B : Bent B
Orientation: palms in; right hand above left hand
Location: neutral space
Movement: twist wrists out, ending with right fingers
above left fingers
Nonmanual signal: "mm" mouth utterance

BENT B ✥ 2-Hand SIGNS

demote, debase, lower

Handshape: Bent B : Bent B
Orientation: palms facing
Location: neutral space
Movement: sharply move hands down in unison

promote, advance

Handshape: Bent B : Bent B
Orientation: palms facing
Location: neutral space
Movement: dramatically arc hands up in unison

even

Handshape: Bent B : Bent B
Orientation: palms facing, fingertips almost touching
Location: neutral space
Movement: separate hands

equal, equivalent, fair, justice

Handshape: Bent B : Bent B
Orientation: palms facing
Location: neutral space
Movement: tap fingertips together twice

heavy

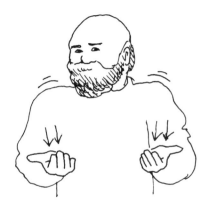

Handshape: Bent B : Bent B
Orientation: palms up
Location: neutral space
Movement: double bounce hands down
Nonmanual signal: body leans forward; head lowers; "strained" expression

how

Handshape: Bent B : Bent B
Orientation: palms down, index and middle
   fingernails touching
Location: neutral space
Movement: twist hands around, ending with
   palms up
Nonmanual signal: body leans forward; head tilts
   right; "puzzled" expression

separate, apart, part

Handshape: Bent B : Bent B
Orientation: palms in; fingernails touching
Location: neutral space
Movement: separate hands

hope, anticipate, expect

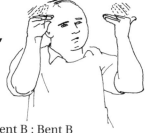

Handshape: Bent B : Bent B
Orientation: palms facing; right hand
   near head
Location: neutral space
Movement: bend fingers down and up twice
Nonmanual signal: head tilts back; eyes
   look up and left

sandwich (SM); picnic (DM)

Handshape: Bent B : Bent B
Orientation: palms in, fingertips toward mouth, right
   hand on left hand
Location: near mouth
Movement: move hands in twice toward mouth
Nonmanual signal: mouth open

responsibility, burden, fault, load, obligation

Handshape: Bent B : Bent B
Orientation: palms in, fingertips on right shoulder
Location: right shoulder
Movement: tap shoulder twice with fingertips
Nonmanual signal: "serious" expression; head tilts right
Note: This sign can be made with the right hand only.

have, possess

Handshape: Bent B : Bent B
Orientation: palms in
Location: neutral space
Movement: bring hands in to chest

tired, exhausted, weary

Handshape: Bent B : Bent B
Orientation: palms down, fingertips on chest
Location: chest
Movement: twist hands forward and down, ending with fingers almost pointing up
Nonmanual signal: shoulders rounded; head lowered

young, youth

Handshape: Bent B : Bent B
Orientation: palms in, fingertips on chest
Location: chest
Movement: brush fingers up and off chest twice
Nonmanual signal: shoulders thrust back; erect posture

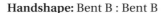

balance, scales

Handshape: Bent B : Bent B
Orientation: palms facing
Location: neutral space
Movement: move hands up and down alternately

build, construct

Handshape: Bent B : Bent B
Orientation: palms down
Location: neutral space
Movement: alternately overlap hands while moving them up

process, procedure, progress

Handshape: Bent B : Bent B
Orientation: palms in; right hand closer to body
Location: neutral space
Movement: alternately circle hands around each other while moving them forward

exceed

Handshape: Bent B : Bent B
Orientation: palms facing, fingertips touching
Location: neutral space
Movement: arc right hand up and above left hand

easy, simple

Handshape: Bent B : Bent B
Orientation: palms up, right hand below left
Location: neutral space
Movement: brush right fingers against fingers of left hand twice
Nonmanual signal: lips pursed

little
(size of object)

Handshape: Bent B : Open B
Orientation: right palm out, hand above left hand;
   left palm up
Location: neutral space
Movement: double bounce right hand slightly
Nonmanual signal: shoulders rounded; eyes look at
   hands

reduce, decrease,
diminish, discount,
less, lessen

Handshape: Bent B : Open B
Orientation: right palm out; left palm up
Location: right hand near face; left hand in
   neutral space
Movement: move right hand down
Nonmanual signal: shoulders raised; "cz"
   mouth utterance

doctor,
physician

Handshape: Bent B : Open B
Orientation: right palm down; left palm up
Location: neutral space
Movement: tap right fingers twice against
   left wrist

soap

Handshape: Bent B : Open B
Orientation: right palm down; left palm up
Location: neutral space
Movement: scrape right fingertips down
   left palm twice

scrape

Handshape: Bent B > Open B : Open B
Orientation: right palm down; left palm up
Location: neutral space
Movement: slide right fingertips down left
   hand twice

again, repeat

Handshape: Bent B : Open B
Orientation: palms up
Location: neutral space
Movement: flip right hand over, ending
   with fingertips in center of left palm

thousand

Handshape: Bent B : Open B
Orientation: right palm down, hand
   above left hand; left palm up
Location: neutral space
Movement: bring right fingertips down to
   touch left palm

million

Handshape: Bent B : Open B
Orientation: right palm down, hand
   above left hand; left palm up
Location: neutral space
Movement: bounce right fingertips from
   left palm to fingertips

frequently, often

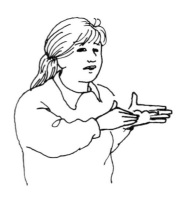

Handshape: Bent B : Open B
Orientation: right palm left, fingertips on left palm;
   left palm right
Location: neutral space
Movement: bounce right fingertips down left hand
Note: See page 200 for a variation of this sign.

BENT B ✎ 2-Hand SIGNS

excuse (n.), exempt, forgiveness, pardon (n.), parole (SM); pardon, excuse, forgive (v.) (DM)

Handshape: Bent B : Open B
Orientation: right palm down, fingertips on left palm; left palm up
Location: neutral space
Movement: slide right fingers down and off left fingertips

mortgage, installments, layaway

Handshape: Bent B : Open B
Orientation: right palm in, hand on left palm; left palm up
Location: neutral space
Movement: slide right hand down left fingertips twice

list, chapter, course, lesson, outline

Handshape: Bent B : Open B
Orientation: right palm left, hand on left fingertips; left palm in
Location: neutral space
Movement: bounce right hand down left hand

bread

Handshape: Bent B : Open B
Orientation: palms in; right hand in front of left
Location: neutral space
Movement: slice down back of left fingers with right fingers twice

England, English

Handshape: Bent B : Open B
Orientation: palms down; hands crossed
Location: neutral space
Movement: slightly pull hands in toward body twice

slow

Handshape: Bent B : Open B
Orientation: palms down; right fingertips on left fingertips
Location: neutral space
Movement: slowly slide right fingers back toward left wrist
Nonmanual signal: "mm" mouth utterance

from now on, from this point on

Handshape: Bent B : Open B
Orientation: right palm in, hand on back of left hand; left palm in
Location: neutral space
Movement: arc right hand forward

night (passive)

Handshape: Bent B : passive
Orientation: palms down, right hand above left hand
Location: neutral space
Movement: hit heel of right palm against back of left hand twice

remind (one person)

Handshape: Bent B : 1
Orientation: right palm out, hand behind left hand; left palm right
Location: neutral space
Movement: sharply tap right fingertips on left index finger twice
Nonmanual signal: "serious" expression

bury, cemetery, grave

Handshape: Bent B > Open B : Bent B > Open B
Orientation: palms down
Location: neutral space
Movement: swing hands up, straightening them, and pull them back toward body

send, dispatch, refer, send away

Handshape: Bent B > Open B : Open B
Orientation: palms down; right fingertips on left hand
Location: neutral space
Movement: flick right fingertips off left hand

reject, cast off

Handshape: Bent B > Open B : Open B
Orientation: right palm in, hand on left palm; left palm up
Location: neutral space
Movement: sweep right hand sharply off left hand, straightening hand and ending with palm down
Nonmanual signal: "hurt" expression

binoculars

Handshape: C : C
Orientation: palms facing
Location: eyes
Movement: twist hands in twice

coconut

Handshape: C : C
Orientation: right palm left, hand above left hand; left palm right
Location: near right ear
Movement: twist wrists slightly back and forth

do, action, activity, deed, demeanor

Handshape: C : C
Orientation: palms down
Location: neutral space
Movement: swing hands in unison left and right twice

class, association, company, group, organization

Handshape: C : C
Orientation: palms out, thumbs touching
Location: neutral space
Movement: swing hands around, ending with palms in

decorate, fancy

Handshape: C : C
Orientation: palms out
Location: neutral space
Movement: spiral hands up

bowl (dish)

Handshape: C : C
Orientation: palms up, hands nearly
   touching
Location: neutral space
Movement: arc hands up

calculus

Handshape: C : C
Orientation: right palm left, hand above
   left hand; left palm right
Location: neutral space
Movement: brush hands against each
   other twice

client, consumer, customer

Handshape: C : C
Orientation: palms facing, thumbs on
   chest
Location: chest
Movement: slide hands down to waist

marry

Handshape: C : C
Orientation: right palm
    angled out; left palm angled in
Location: neutral space
Movement: bring hands together

communicate

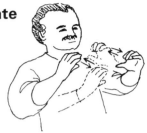

Handshape: C : C
Orientation: palms facing, right hand
    near lips
Location: face
Movement: alternately move hands back
    and forth

comfortable

Handshape: C : C
Orientation: palms facing, left fingers on
    right fingers
Location: neutral space
Movement: slowly slide left fingers down
    right fingers, then slide right fingers hand
    down left fingers
Nonmanual signal: "contented" expression

hamburger

Handshape: C : C
Orientation: right palm down, hand above left hand;
    left palm up
Location: neutral space
Movement: bring right hand down on left palm, then
    flip hands and bring left hand down on right palm

certify

Handshape: C : Open B
Orientation: right palm left, hand above left palm; left palm up
Location: neutral space
Movement: smack right hand down sharply on left palm

can, bottle, cup, glass, tumbler

Handshape: C : Open B
Orientation: right palm left, hand on left palm; left palm up
Location: neutral space
Movement: double bounce right hand on left palm

cake

Handshape: C : Open B
Orientation: right palm down, fingertips on left palm; left palm up
Location: neutral space
Movement: slide right hand down left hand
Note: See next sign and page 82 for variations of this sign.

cake

Handshape: C : Open B
Orientation: right palm down, fingertips on left palm; left palm up
Location: neutral space
Movement: move right hand up slightly
Note: See previous sign and page 82 for variations of this sign.

cream, skim (v.)

Handshape: C : Open B
Orientation: right palm left, hand on left fingertips; left palm up
Location: neutral space
Movement: slide right hand down left palm, ending palm in

picture, photograph

Handshape: C : Open B
Orientation: right palm out; left palm right
Location: neutral space
Movement: smack right hand against left palm

constitution, commandments

Handshape: C : Open B
Orientation: right palm out, thumb against left fingers; left palm right
Location: neutral space
Movement: bounce right hand down left hand

paragraph

Handshape: C : Open B
Orientation: palms facing
Location: neutral space
Movement: tap right fingertips against left palm

chapter

Handshape: C : Open B
Orientation: right palm left, hand against left palm; left palm right
Location: neutral space
Movement: bounce right hand down left hand

computer

Handshape: C : Open B
Orientation: right palm out, thumb above left wrist; left palm down
Location: neutral space
Movement: bounce right hand up left arm in small spirals

church

Handshape: C : S
Orientation: right palm out, hand above left hand; left palm down
Location: neutral space
Movement: double bounce right hand on left hand

chocolate

Handshape: C : S
Orientation: right palm out, thumb on left hand; left palm down
Location: neutral space
Movement: circle right hand on left hand

culture

Handshape: C : 1
Orientation: palms out, right thumb on left index finger
Location: neutral space
Movement: swing right hand around left index finger, ending palm in

force, coerce, compel, impel

Handshape: C : 1
Orientation: right palm out; left palm down, index finger at wrist of right hand
Location: neutral space
Movement: bend right wrist down
Nonmanual signal: right shoulder tilts forward; "serious" expression

president, superintendent

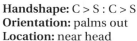

Handshape: C > S : C > S
Orientation: palms out
Location: near head
Movement: arc hands down and out, closing to S handshape
Nonmanual signal: shoulders thrust back; erect posture

hot dog, frankfurter

Handshape: C > S : C > S
Orientation: palms down, hands almost touching
Location: neutral space
Movement: move hands apart, closing to S handshape

summarize, abbreviate, brief, condense

Handshape: C > S : C > S
Orientation: palms facing, right hand higher than left hand
Location: neutral space
Movement: bring hands together, closing to S handshape and ending with right hand on left hand

sausage

Handshape: C > S > C > S : C > S > C > S
Orientation: palms down, hands almost touching
Location: neutral space
Movement: close and open hands twice while moving them apart

deflate, flat tire

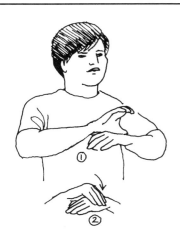

Handshape: C > Flattened O : Open B
Orientation: right palm out, thumb on left hand; left palm down
Location: neutral space
Movement: close right fingers down on left hand

copy, photocopy, Xerox, xerography

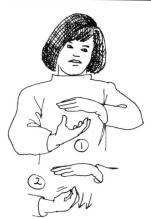

Handshape: C > Flattened O : Open B
Orientation: right palm up, hand below left palm; left palm down
Location: neutral space
Movement: move right hand down twice, closing to Flattened O handshape

subtract, deduct, eliminate, remove

Handshape: C > S : Open B
Orientation: right palm down, fingertips on left palm; left palm right
Location: neutral space
Movement: slide right fingertips down and off left palm, closing to S handshape

expire, all gone, run out

Handshape: C > S : Open B
Orientation: right palm in, hand on left palm; left palm up
Location: neutral space
Movement: slide right hand down left hand, closing to S handshape

tackle, catch, nab

Handshape: C > S : H
Orientation: right palm left; left palm in, fingertips down
Location: neutral space
Movement: grab left fingers with right hand

incompetent, dumb, moron, thick-skulled, unskilled

Handshape: C > 5 : S
Orientation: palms down, right thumb inside left hand
Location: neutral space
Movement: sharply bend right wrist back, opening to 5 handshape
Nonmanual signal: "disparaging" expression

divorce

Handshape: D : D
Orientation: palms facing
Location: neutral space
Movement: twist hands out, ending with palms out

decoder

Handshape: D : D
Orientation: palms facing, fingertips touching
Location: neutral space
Movement: arc hands apart and back together twice

date (social)

Handshape: D : D
Orientation: palms facing
Location: neutral space
Movement: tap fingertips together twice

department

Handshape: D : D
Orientation: palms facing; fingertips touch
Location: neutral space
Movement: swing hands around, ending with fingers touching

describe, define, direction

Handshape: D : D
Orientation: palms facing
Location: neutral space
Movement: move hands alternately back and forth

diamond

Handshape: D : Open B
Orientation: palms down
Location: neutral space
Movement: double bounce right hand
   down on left ring finger

dictionary

Handshape: D : Open B
Orientation: right palm down, hand
   above left palm; left palm up
Location: neutral space
Movement: brush right fingertips on
   left palm twice

doctor, physician

Handshape: D : Open B
Orientation: right palm down, hand
   above left hand;
Location: neutral space
Movement: tap right fingertips on left
   wrist twice

develop

Handshape: D : Open B
Orientation: palms facing, right fingertips
   on left palm
Location: neutral space
Movement: slide right hand up and off
   left palm

day (passive)

Handshape: D : passive
Orientation: right palm left, elbow on left
   hand; left palm down
Location: neutral space
Movement: bring right hand down to rest
   on left arm

what's happening?
what?
what are you doing?

Handshape: D > Baby O : D > Baby O
Orientation: palms up
Location: neutral space
Movement: open and close index fingers
   and thumbs, several times
Nonmanual signal: body leans forward;
   head tilts right; "puzzled" expression

effort

Handshape: E : E
Orientation: palms in
Location: neutral space
Movement: arc hands down and out,
   ending with palms out
Nonmanual signal: "earnest" expression

education, educate

Handshape: E : E
Orientation: palms facing
Location: forehead
Movement: double bounce hands forward

evaluate, evaluation, examination

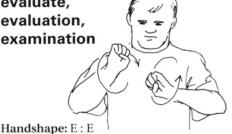

Handshape: E : E
Orientation: palms out
Location: neutral space
Movement: alternate hands in circling
   toward center
Nonmanual signal: "serious" expression

emotion

Handshape: E : E
Orientation: palms in
Location: chest
Movement: brush knuckles up chest
   while making alternating circles

encyclopedia

Handshape: E : Open B
Orientation: right palm down, hand
   above left hand; left palm up
Location: neutral space
Movement: brush right hand across left
   palm twice

engaged (to be married)

Handshape: E : Open B
Orientation: palms down; right hand
   above left hand
Location: neutral space
Movement: move right hand in a circle
   and then land on left ring finger

environment

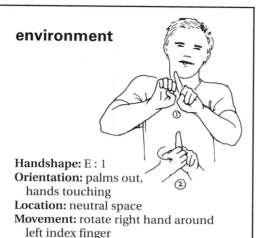

Handshape: E : 1
Orientation: palms out, hands touching
Location: neutral space
Movement: rotate right hand around left index finger

nothing, nothing special nothing to it, petty

Handshape: F : F
Orientation: palms out
Location: neutral space
Movement: shake hands side-to-side several times
Nonmanual signal: lips pursed; body and head lean back

exact, perfect, precise

Handshape: F : F
Orientation: palms facing, right hand closer to body
Location: neutral space
Movement: bend wrists toward each other in a short, quick motion
Nonmanual signal: lips tight

feedback

Handshape: F : F
Orientation: palms facing
Location: neutral space
Movement: bend wrists toward each other twice

free

Handshape: F : F
Orientation: right palm left; left palm right, wrists crossed
Location: neutral space
Movement: swing hands out and around, ending with palms out

family

Handshape: F : F
Orientation: palms out, thumbs touching
Location: neutral space
Movement: circle hands around, ending with pinkies touching

important, imperative, significant, value, vital, worth

Handshape: F : F
Orientation: palms facing; thumbs touching
Location: neutral space
Movement: arc hands up, ending with thumbs touching, palms out
Nonmanual signal: head tilted back; "serious" expression

caption, subtitle

Handshape: F : F
Orientation: palms facing, thumbs touching
Location: neutral space
Movement: move hands apart and back together twice

sentence

Handshape: F : F
Orientation: palms facing, thumbs touching
Location: neutral space
Movement: separate hands in wiggling motion

belong, affiliate, attach, connect, enlist, join, unite, participate

Handshape: F : F
Orientation: palms facing
Location: neutral space
Movement: bring hands together, interlocking thumbs and index fingers

cooperate

Handshape: F : F
Orientation: palms facing, thumbs and index fingers interlocked
Location: neutral space
Movement: circle hands right

connection, relationship

Handshape: F : F
Orientation: right palm out; left palm in, thumbs and index fingers interlocked
Location: neutral space
Movement: move hands back and forth twice

cat

Handshape: F : F
Orientation: palms facing
Location: cheeks
Movement: brush hands across and
off cheeks twice
Note: See page 71 for a one-hand variation
of this sign.

describe, define, explain

Handshape: F : F
Orientation: palms facing
Location: neutral space
Movement: move hands alternately back
and forth
Nonmanual signal: lips pursed; body and
head lean back

judge, if

Handshape: F : F
Orientation: palms facing
Location: neutral space
Movement: alternately move hands up
and down
Nonmanual signal: lips tight; "strained"
expression

exchange, replace, trade

Handshape: F : F
Orientation: palms facing, right hand
closer to body
Location: neutral space
Movement: arc hands around each
other to reverse positions

interpret, translate

Handshape: F : F
Orientation: right palm out; left palm in, thumbs
and index fingers touching
Location: neutral space
Movement: twist wrists to switch hand positions

Olympics

Handshape: F : F
Orientation: right palm out; left palm in, thumbs and index fingers interlocked
Location: neutral space
Movement: unlock hands and reverse positions

chain

Handshape: F : F
Orientation: right palm out; left palm in, thumbs and index fingers interlocked
Location: neutral space
Movement: unlock hands and reverse positions several times while moving hands right

ghost, soul, spirit

Handshape: F : F
Orientation: right palm down; left palm up, thumbs and index fingers touching
Location: neutral space
Movement: spiral right hand up

unfair

Handshape: F : F
Orientation: palms facing, right hand above left hand
Location: neutral space
Movement: bring right hand down, brushing right thumb and index finger past left thumb and index finger
Nonmanual signal: "annoyed" expression

defer, delay, postpone, procrastinate, put off

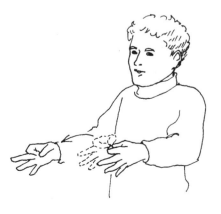

Handshape: F : F
Orientation: palms facing, thumbs and index fingers touching
Location: neutral space
Movement: arc right hand deliberately forward
Nonmanual signal: lips pursed; "annoyed" expression

field (profession)

Handshape: F : B
Orientation: right palm down, thumb and index finger on base of left index finger; left palm right
Location: neutral space
Movement: slide right hand along left index finger

very religious, religion, religious

Handshape: F : B
Orientation: right palm down, hand above left hand; left palm up
Location: neutral space
Movement: sharply brush right fingertips down and off left palm

count

Handshape: F : Open B
Orientation: palms facing; right thumb and index finger on left palm
Location: neutral space
Movement: slide right hand down left hand

flunk, fail, forbid

Handshape: F : Open B
Orientation: right palm out; left palm right
Location: neutral space
Movement: sharply smack right hand on left palm

pen, write

Handshape: F : Open B
Orientation: right palm down, thumb and index finger on left hand; left palm up
Location: neutral space
Movement: draw circles down left palm with right thumb and index finger

vote, elect, election, nominate

Handshape: F : O
Orientation: right palm down; left palm in
Location: neutral space
Movement: dip right fingertips into left hand twice

tea

Handshape: F : O
Orientation: right palm down, thumb and index finger in left hand; left palm in
Location: neutral space
Movement: circle right thumb and index finger around left thumb and index finger

watch

Handshape: F : S
Orientation: palms down, right hand above left wrist
Location: neutral space
Movement: tap right hand on left wrist twice

foreign (passive)

Handshape: F : passive
Orientation: palms down, right hand at left elbow
Location: neutral space
Movement: make small circles on left elbow with right hand

except, unique

Handshape: F : 1
Orientation: right palm down, thumb and index finger grasping left index finger; left palm in
Location: neutral space
Movement: pull left index finger up with right hand
Nonmanual signal: body and head thrust back; lips pursed

detach, break-up, disassociate, disconnect

Handshape: F > 5 : F > 5
Orientation: palms facing, thumbs and index
   fingers interlocked
Location: neutral space
Movement: release fingers and separate hands

worthless, insignificant, trivial, unimportant

Handshape: F > 5 : F > 5
Orientation: palms facing, hands almost touching
Location: neutral space
Movement: sharply flick fingertips apart and
   separate hands, ending palms down
Nonmanual signal: smirk

ring

Handshape: Open F : Open B
Orientation: palms down, right hand
   above left hand
Location: neutral space
Movement: slide right thumb and index
   finger down left ring finger

meat, beef, content (n.), steak, substance

Handshape: Open F : Open B
Orientation: right palm down; left palm in
Location: neutral space
Movement: grip left hand with right thumb
   and index finger and shake hands slightly

story, narrate, statement, tell a story

Handshape: Open F > F : Open F > F
Orientation: palms facing
Location: neutral space
Movement: bring hands together, interlocking thumbs and index fingers, then move hands apart and repeat

find, discover

Handshape: Open F > F : Open B
Orientation: right palm down, hand below left hand; left palm right
Location: neutral space
Movement: move right hand up past left hand, closing thumb and index finger

choose, choice, either, select

Handshape: Open F > F : V
Orientation: right palm out, hand closer to body; left palm in
Location: neutral space
Movement: pluck left index finger with right thumb and index finger, then repeat on left middle finger

frame

Handshape: G : G
Orientation: palms out, hands touching
Location: neutral space
Movement: separate hands, then move them down and back together

group

Handshape: G : G
Orientation: palms facing
Location: neutral space
Movement: swing hands around, ending with palms in

grammar

Handshape: G : G
Orientation: palms facing
Location: neutral space
Movement: separate hands in wiggling motion

geometry

Handshape: G : G
Orientation: right palm left, hand on left hand; left palm right
Location: neutral space
Movement: brush hands against each other twice

graduate

Handshape: G : Open B
Orientation: right palm down, hand above left hand; left palm up
Location: neutral space
Movement: flip right hand over and land in left palm

magazine, booklet, brochure, leaflet, manual, pamphlet

Handshape: G : Open B
Orientation: right palm up, fingers gripping edge of left hand; left palm right
Location: neutral space
Movement: slide right hand along left hand twice
Note: See page 260 for a variation of this sign.

word, vocabulary

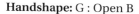

Handshape: G : 1
Orientation: palms facing
Location: neutral space
Movement: tap right fingertips on left index finger twice

wake up

Handshape: G > L : G > L
Orientation: palms facing
Location: near eyes
Movement: open fingers up into L handshape
Note: See page 256 for a variation of this sign.

gossip, rumor

Handshape: G > Baby O : G > Baby O
Orientation: palms out
Location: right hand on mouth; left hand in neutral space
Movement: circle hands clockwise, opening and closing fingers repeatedly

print, newspaper, publish

Handshape: G > Baby O : Open B
Orientation: right palm down, thumb on left palm; left palm up
Location: neutral space
Movement: close right index finger and thumb twice

rabbit

Handshape: H : H
Orientation: palms facing, hands touching
Location: neutral space
Movement: bend fingers down twice

egg

Handshape: H : H
Orientation: palms facing, fingers crossed
Location: neutral space
Movement: twist wrists down

bacon

Handshape: H : H
Orientation: palms down, fingertips touching
Location: neutral space
Movement: separate hands while wiggling index and middle fingers

highway, freeway, interstate, thoroughfare, throughway, thruway

Handshape: H : H
Orientation: palms facing, hands touching
Location: neutral space
Movement: brush hands past each other twice

named, called

Handshape: H : H
Orientation: palms facing, fingers crossed
Location: neutral space
Movement: arc hands out and down

bandit, burglar, crook, thief

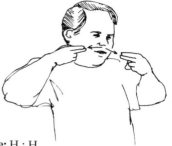

Handshape: H : H
Orientation: palms in, fingertips touching
Location: below nose
Movement: separate hands
Note: This sign is sometimes formed with an agent marker.

innocent

Handshape: H : H
Orientation: palms in
Location: mouth
Movement: move hands down, ending with palms up

heritage

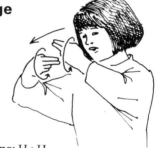

Handshape: H : H
Orientation: palms in
Location: near shoulder
Movement: circle hands around each other while moving them forward

hurry, haste, rush

Handshape: H : H
Orientation: palms facing
Location: neutral space
Movement: alternate hands in moving up and down rapidly
Nonmanual signal: body leans forward; "concerned" expression

closet, locker

Handshape: H : H
Orientation: right palm out; left palm in, fingers crossed
Location: neutral space
Movement: turn hands over, reversing positions

build, construct

Handshape: H : H
Orientation: palms down, right fingers on left fingers
Location: neutral space
Movement: alternately slap fingers on top of each other while moving hands up

weigh, pound, scale, weight

Handshape: H : H
Orientation: palms facing, fingers crossed
Location: neutral space
Movement: move right hand slightly up and down

sharp

Handshape: H : H
Orientation: palms facing, right hand above left hand
Location: neutral space
Movement: sharply brush right fingers off left fingers

knife

Handshape: H : H
Orientation: palms facing, fingers crossed
Location: neutral space
Movement: saw right fingers back and forth across left index finger

brief, short

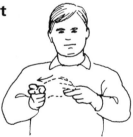

Handshape: H : H
Orientation: palms facing, fingers crossed
Location: neutral space
Movement: slide right fingers off left index
finger

name (n.)

Handshape: H : H
Orientation: palms facing, fingers crossed
Location: neutral space
Movement: double bounce right hand on
left fingers

decrease, lose weight

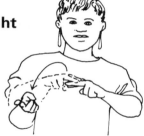

Handshape: H : H
Orientation: palms down, fingers crossed
Location: neutral space
Movement: flip right hand off left hand,
ending with palm up

increase, add (on), gain, onto, raise

Handshape: H : H
Orientation: right palm up, hand below
left hand; left palm down
Location: neutral space
Movement: flip right hand over to rest on
top of left fingers

sit, be seated (SM); chair, seat (DM)

Handshape: H : H
Orientation: palms down, right fingers
above left fingers
Location: neutral space
Movement: double bounce right fingers
down on left fingers

train, railroad

Handshape: H : H
Orientation: palms down, fingers crossed
Location: neutral space
Movement: slide right fingers down and
back left fingers several times

spoon, soup

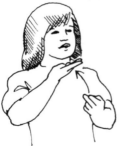

Handshape: H : H
Orientation: palms up, right fingers on left fingers
Location: neutral space
Movement: scoop right hand up toward mouth

stamp, postage

Handshape: H : H
Orientation: right palm in; left palm up
Location: right hand at mouth; left hand in neutral space
Movement: flip right hand down and land on left fingers
Note: See page 236 for a variation of this sign.

fun

Handshape: H: H
Orientation: right palm in; left palm down
Location: right hand on nose; left hand in neutral space
Movement: flip right hand down to rest on left fingers
Nonmanual signal: smile; eyes widen

spoon, ice cream, soup

Handshape: H : Open B
Orientation: palms up, right hand above left hand
Location: neutral space
Movement: brush right fingers off left palm and up toward mouth

butter

Handshape: H : Open B
Orientation: right palm down, wrist bent down; left palm up
Location: neutral space
Movement: brush right fingertips off left palm twice
Note: Right fingers can bend each time.

sign (SM); contract, signature (DM)

Handshape: H : Open B
Orientation: palms up
Location: neutral space
Movement: flip right hand over to smack fingers on left palm

screwdriver

Handshape: H : Open B
Orientation: right palm down, fingertips on left palm; left palm right
Location: neutral space
Movement: twist right fingertips back and forth twice

holy

Handshape: H : Open B
Orientation: right palm down, hand above left hand; left palm up
Location: neutral space
Movement: slide right hand down in an arc on left hand
Nonmanual signal: "solemn" expression

honest, frank, sincere, truthful

Handshape: H : Open B
Orientation: right palm left, middle finger on left palm; left palm up
Location: neutral space
Movement: slide edge of right middle finger down and off left palm

university

Handshape: H : Open B
Orientation: right palm down, fingers on left palm; left palm facing up; right hand on left
Location: neutral space
Movement: spiral right hand above left hand

nurse

Handshape: H : Open B
Orientation: right palm down, fingertips above left wrist; left palm up
Location: neutral space
Movement: tap right fingertips on left wrist twice

natural, naturally, of course

Handshape: H : Open B
Orientation: palms down, right hand above left hand
Location: neutral space
Movement: circle right hand over left hand, then drop fingertips on left hand

stamp, postage

Handshape: H : Open B
Orientation: right palm in; left palm up
Location: right fingertips on lips; left hand in neutral space
Movement: flip right hand down and smack fingers on left palm
Note: See page 234 for a variation of this sign.

get into bed

Handshape: H : C
Orientation: right palm up; left palm down
Location: neutral space
Movement: slide right fingers inside left hand

join, enlist, participate

Handshape: H : O
Orientation: right palm in; left palm right
Location: neutral space
Movement: insert right fingers into left hand

quit, drop out, resign, retire

Handshape: H : O
Orientation: palms in, right fingers inside left hand
Location: neutral space
Movement: pull right fingers out of left hand, ending with fingers up
Nonmanual signal: body leans away from repelling reference; "disgusted" expression

nation (native)

Handshape: H : S
Orientation: palms down, right hand above left hand
Location: neutral space
Movement: circle right hand above left hand, then drop fingertips on left hand

bandage, Band-Aid

Handshape: H : S
Orientation: palms down, right fingers on pinky edge of left hand
Location: neutral space
Movement: slide right fingers across left hand

use, utilize, wear

Handshape: H : S
Orientation: right palm out, heel on left hand; left palm down
Location: neutral space
Movement: circle right hand clockwise on left hand twice

used to, usually

Handshape: H : S
Orientation: right palm out, heel on left hand; left palm down
Location: neutral space
Movement: move both hands down

couch
(compound: sit + long seat)

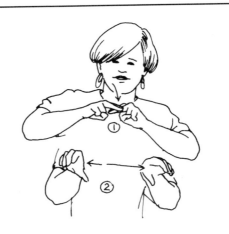

Handshape: H > C : H > C
Orientation: palms down, right fingers above left
   fingers
Location: neutral space
Movement: drop right fingers on left fingers, then
   change both hands to C handshape, hands
   touching, and separate hands

Bible
(compound: holy + book)

Handshape: H > Open B : Open B
Orientation: right palm down, hand above left hand; left
   palm up
Location: neutral space
Movement: slide right hand down in an arc on left hand,
   then bring hands together and open them

too late
(compound: train + gone)

Handshape: H > G > Baby O : H
Orientation: palms down; fingers crossed
Location: neutral space
Movement: slide right fingers along left fingers, then
   change right hand to G handshape and slide off
   left hand, closing thumb and index finger
Nonmanual signal: "pah" mouth utterance

spaghetti, line, string, thread, twine

Handshape: I : I
Orientation: palms in; pinkies touch
Location: neutral space
Movement: separate hands with a spiraling motion

independent, independence

Handshape: I : I
Orientation: right palm left; left palm right, wrists crossed
Location: neutral space
Movement: sharply separate hands, ending with palms out
Nonmanual signal: body and head thrust back; "satisfied" expression

isolated, lonely, talk to oneself

Handshape: I : I
Orientation: palms in; hands touching
Location: near face
Movement: tap hands together twice
Nonmanual signal: lips pursed; "sad" expression

individual

Handshape: I : I
Orientation: palms facing
Location: neutral space
Movement: move hands down

paranoid

Handshape: I : I
Orientation: palms in
Location: near head
Movement: spiral hands up alternately
Nonmanual signal: body leans back and sways;
   tongue protruding

egotism, conceited

Handshape: I : I
Orientation: right palm left; left palm right
Location: right hand on chest; left hand in neutral
   space
Movement: tap hands on chest with alternating
   motion
Nonmanual signal: chest puffs out; shoulders
   alternately tilt back and forth; lips pursed

**end,
final,
last**

Handshape: I : I
Orientation: palms facing
Location: neutral space
Movement: slice right pinky down through
   left pinky

**institute,
residential
school, school
for the deaf**

Handshape: I : I
Orientation: right palm left, right hand
   on left hand; left palm right
Location: neutral space
Movement: tap right hand on left hand
   twice

thin, skinny, slender

Handshape: I : I
Orientation: palms in, pinky fingers touching
Location: neutral space
Movement: move right hand down
Nonmanual signal: cheeks sucked in

international

Handshape: I : I
Orientation: right palm left, right hand on left hand; left palm right
Location: neutral space
Movement: circle right hand completely around left hand

jam, jelly

Handshape: I : Open B
Orientation: right palm down, right hand above left hand; left palm up
Location: neutral space
Movement: brush right pinky down heel of left palm twice

art, draw, design *(artist, designer, illustrator)*

Handshape: I : Open B
Orientation: palms facing, right pinky on left palm
Location: neutral space
Movement: squiggle right pinky down left palm

place, location, position

Handshape: K : K
Orientation: palms facing, middle fingers touching
Location: neutral space
Movement: arc hands back, ending with middle fingers touching

person

Handshape: K : K
Orientation: palms out
Location: neutral space
Movement: move both hands down

permission, allow, let, may, permit, tolerate

Handshape: K : K
Orientation: palms down
Location: neutral space
Movement: swing hands up

party

Handshape: K : K
Orientation: palms down
Location: neutral space
Movement: swing hands left and right

perfect, precise

Handshape: K : K
Orientation: palms facing; right hand closer to body and above left
Location: neutral space
Movement: bring middle fingers together
Nonmanual signal: lips pursed

supervise, care for, take care of (caregiver, supervisor)

Handshape: K : K
Orientation: right palm left, hand on left hand; left palm right
Location: neutral space
Movement: circle hands clockwise

borrow

Handshape: K : K
Orientation: right palm left, hand on left hand; left palm right
Location: neutral space
Movement: arc hands back toward chest

lend, loan

Handshape: K : K
Orientation: right palm left, hand on left hand; left palm right
Location: neutral space
Movement: arc hands forward

multiply, arithmetic, calculate, figure

Handshape: K : K
Orientation: right palm left, hand on left hand; left palm right
Location: neutral space
Movement: brush hands past each other twice

worse

Handshape: K : K
Orientation: palms facing
Location: neutral space
Movement: arc hands toward each other, then brush past each other
Nonmanual signal: "pained" expression

people, humanity, mankind, public

Handshape: K : K
Orientation: palms out
Location: neutral space
Movement: circle hands out, alternating hands

kind, sort, type

Handshape: K : K
Orientation: right palm left, hand on left hand; left palm right
Location: neutral space
Movement: rotate hands around each other, ending in original position

careful, be careful

Handshape: K : K
Orientation: right palm left, hand above left hand; left palm right
Location: neutral space
Movement: double bounce right hand on left hand
Nonmanual signal: body leans forward; "urgent" expression

keep, maintain

Handshape: K : K
Orientation: right palm left, hand above left hand; left palm right
Location: neutral space
Movement: bring right hand down on left hand

pure, professional

Handshape: K : B
Orientation: right palm left, middle finger on base of left thumb; left palm right
Location: neutral space
Movement: slide right middle finger off left index finger
Nonmanual signal: "cz" mouth utterance

fail, flop

Handshape: K : Open B
Orientation: palms up, right hand on left palm
Location: neutral space
Movement: slide right hand across left palm
Nonmanual signal: "sad" expression

graduate school

Handshape: K : Open B
Orientation: palms angled in, right hand above left palm
Location: neutral space
Movement: double bounce right hand on left wrist

psychiatry (psychia-trist)

Handshape: K : Open B
Orientation: right palm down, middle finger above left wrist; left palm up
Location: neutral space
Movement: tap right middle finger on left wrist twice

piece

Handshape: K : Open B
Orientation: right palm down, middle finger on left palm; left palm up
Location: neutral space
Movement: slide right middle finger across left palm

poison

Handshape: K : Open B
Orientation: right palm down, middle finger on left palm; left palm up
Location: neutral space
Movement: wiggle right hand side to side
Nonmanual signal: "sour" expression

principle

Handshape: K : Open B
Orientation: right palm down, hand on left palm; left palm right
Location: neutral space
Movement: bounce right hand down to left wrist

kitchen

Handshape: K : Open B
Orientation: right palm down, hand on left palm; left palm up
Location: neutral space
Movement: flip right hand over twice, ending with palm up

program

Handshape: K : Open B
Orientation: right palm down, middle finger on heel of left palm; left palm in
Location: neutral space
Movement: slide right middle finger up left palm and over fingertips, then slide down back of left hand

poetry (passive)

Handshape: K : passive
Orientation: right palm down, hand above left arm; left palm right
Location: neutral space
Movement: swing right hand back and forth over left arm

Passover

Handshape: K : S
Orientation: right palm out; left palm down
Location: neutral space
Movement: arc right hand over left hand, ending palm down

principal

Handshape: K : S
Orientation: palms down, right hand above left hand
Location: neutral space
Movement: circle right hand over left hand, then drop middle finger on left hand

profession

Handshape: K : 1
Orientation: right palm down, middle finger on left hand; left palm right
Location: neutral space
Movement: slide right middle finger off left index finger

license

Handshape: L : L
Orientation: palms out, thumbs touching
Location: neutral space
Movement: tap thumbs twice

language

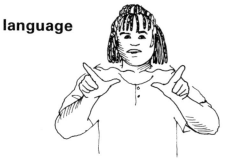

Handshape: L : L
Orientation: palms out, thumbs touching
Location: neutral space
Movement: separate hands with slight
   wiggling motion

gun,
rifle (SM);
hunt (DM)

Handshape: L : L
Orientation: palms facing; index fingers
   angled up
Location: neutral space
Movement: bend wrists down, ending
   with index fingers out

robbery,
hold-up,
shoot

Handshape: L : L
Orientation: palms facing
Location: neutral space
Movement: move hands forward

vagina

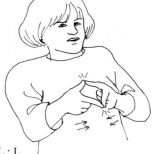

Handshape: L : L
Orientation: palms facing, thumbs and
   index fingers almost touching
Location: neutral space
Movement: tap fingertips twice

live, life,
survive

Handshape: L : L
Orientation: palms in
Location: waist
Movement: brush hands up chest

sister

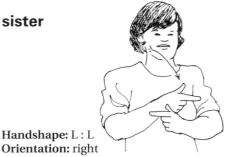

Handshape: L : L
Orientation: right palm left; left palm right
Location: right thumb on cheek; left hand in neutral space
Movement: bring right hand down to rest on left hand

brother

Handshape: L : L
Orientation: right palm left; left palm right
Location: right thumb on temple; left hand in neutral space
Movement: bring right hand down to rest on left hand

law (attorney, lawyer)

Handshape: L : Open B
Orientation: palms facing, right palm on left fingertips
Location: neutral space
Movement: bounce right hand down left palm

later, after awhile, subsequently

Handshape: L : Open B
Orientation: right palm out, thumb on left palm; left palm right
Location: neutral space
Movement: bend right hand down

ban, forbid, prohibit

Handshape: L : Open B
Orientation: right palm out; left palm right
Location: neutral space
Movement: swing right hand around and smack into left palm
Nonmanual signal: "stern" expression

aide, assistant

Handshape: L : S
Orientation: right palm hand below left hand; left palm right
Location: neutral space
Movement: tap right thumb on bottom of left hand twice

fast

Handshape: L > Bent L : L > Bent L
Orientation: palms facing
Location: neutral space
Movement: bend index fingers while
  sharply pulling hands back
Nonmanual signal: body jerks back

Japan, Japanese

Handshape: L > Baby O : L > Baby O
Orientation: palms facing, thumbs and index
  fingers touching
Location: neutral space
Movement: separate hands and close thumbs
  and index fingers

linguistics

Handshape: L > S : L > S
Orientation: palms out; thumbs touching
Location: neutral space
Movement: wiggle hands apart, changing
  to S handshape

plate, platter, dish

Handshape: Bent L : Bent L
Orientation: palms facing
Location: neutral space
Movement: move hands down slightly

lucky

Handshape: Bent L : Bent L
Orientation: palms up
Location: neutral space
Movement: slide hands in to center and
   out twice
Nonmanual signal: head leans back
Note: This is a regional sign.

**card,
placard**

Handshape: Bent L : Bent L
Orientation: palms down, hands touching
Location: neutral space
Movement: separate hands

**conceited, arrogant, big
shot (slang), egotistical,
swelled head (slang)**

Handshape: Bent L : Bent L
Orientation: palms in, index fingertips on
   forehead
Location: forehead
Movement: move hands off head with an
   exaggerated motion
Nonmanual signal: body leans back;
   "disgusted" expression

glasses, eyeglasses

Handshape: Bent L : Bent L
Orientation: palms facing
Location: eyes
Movement: tap thumbs under eyes twice
Note: See page 251 for a variation of this sign.

huge, big, enormous, great, immense

Handshape: Bent L : Bent L
Orientation: palms facing
Location: neutral space
Movement: arc hands apart in spiral motion
Nonmanual signal: "cha" mouth utterance

camera, photograph (v.), take pictures

Handshape: Bent L : Bent L
Orientation: palms facing
Location: near eyes
Movement: bend right index finger twice

article (written)

Handshape: Bent L : Open B
Orientation: palms facing
Location: neutral space
Movement: brush thumb and index
  fingertips down left palm

card, license plate

Handshape: Bent L > Baby O : Bent L >
  Baby O
Orientation: palms out, thumbs touching
Location: neutral space
Movement: separate hands, closing
  thumbs and index fingers

glasses, eyeglasses

Handshape: Bent L > Baby O : Bent L > Baby O
Orientation: palms facing
Location: thumbs and index fingertips around
  eyes
Movement: move hands off face, closing
  thumbs and index fingers
Note: See page 250 for a variation of this sign.

run

Handshape: Bent L : L > Bent L
Orientation: right palm left, index finger gripping left thumb; left palm right
Location: neutral space
Movement: bend thumbs and left index fingers while moving hands forward
Nonmanual signal: body jerks back and forth when fingers bend

mathematics

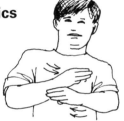

Handshape: M : M
Orientation: palms in, right hand above left hand
Location: neutral space
Movement: brush hands against each other twice

doctor, medical, physician

Handshape: M : Open B
Orientation: right palm down, hand above left wrist; left palm up
Location: neutral space
Movement: tap right fingertips on left wrist twice

-ment (suffix)

Handshape: M : Open B
Orientation: right palm out, hand on left palm; left palm right
Location: neutral space
Movement: slide right hand down left palm

none, no (quantity)

Handshape: O : O
Orientation: right palm left; left palm right, wrists crossed
Location: neutral space
Movement: separate hands
Nonmanual signal: head shakes "no"

nothing, naught

Handshape: O : O
Orientation: palms out
Location: neutral space
Movement: slide hands slightly toward
   center and out twice
Nonmanual signal: head shakes "no"

diploma, degree

Handshape: O : O
Orientation: palms down, hands touching
Location: neutral space
Movement: separate hands

organization

Handshape: O : O
Orientation: palms out, thumbs touching
Location: neutral space
Movement: swing hands around, ending
   with pinkies touching

office

Handshape: O : O
Orientation: palms
   in, right hand behind left hand
Location: neutral space
Movement: separate hands and twist
   wrists, ending with palms facing

zero, absolutely nothing

Handshape: O : Open B
Orientation: right palm in; left palm right
Location: neutral space
Movement: sharply slap right hand on left
   palm

sunrise (passive)

Handshape: O : passive
Orientation: palms down, right arm in
   front of and below left arm
Location: neutral space
Movement: bend right arm up

**sunset,
Shabbat
(passive)**

Handshape: O : passive
Orientation: right palm left arm in front
of and above left arm; left palm down
Location: neutral space
Movement: bend right arm down

opportunity

Handshape: O > K : O > K
Orientation: palms down
Location: neutral space
Movement: bend wrists up, changing to K
handshape
Nonmanual signal: eyes widen

**none,
nothing**

Handshape: O > 5 : O > 5
Orientation: palms facing, hands touching
Location: neutral space
Movement: move hands out and down,
opening to 5 handshape
Nonmanual signal: head shakes "no"

**exact,
precise,
specific**

Handshape: Baby O : Baby O
Orientation: right palm down, hand
above left hand; left palm up
Location: neutral space
Movement: circle right hand slightly, then
bring hands together
Nonmanual signal: "serious" expression

**revenge,
get even,
retaliate**

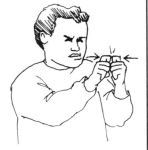

Handshape: Baby O : Baby O
Orientation: palms facing
Location: neutral space
Movement: sharply tap index fingers
together
Nonmanual signal: "angry" expression

**tear, torn,
rip**

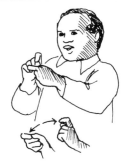

Handshape: Baby O : Baby O
Orientation: right palm out, thumb on
left thumb; left palm in
Location: neutral space
Movement: twist and bend wrists back

celebrate, anniversary, cheer, rejoice, reunion, victory, win

Handshape: Baby O : Baby O
Orientation: palms in
Location: above shoulders
Movement: twirl hands around
Nonmanual signal: smile
Note: See page 109 for a one-hand variation of this sign.

---

write

Handshape: Baby O : Open B
Orientation: right palm down, fingertips on left palm; left palm up
Location: neutral space
Movement: brush right fingertips down left palm twice

---

match

Handshape: Baby O : Open B
Orientation: right palm in, index finger on left palm; left palm right
Location: neutral space
Movement: brush right index finger up left palm

---

chicken

Handshape: Baby O : Open B
Orientation: right palm out; left palm up
Location: right hand at nose; left hand in neutral space
Movement: bring right hand down and peck on left palm

---

pencil

Handshape: Baby O : Open B
Orientation: right palm in; left palm up
Location: right hand on lips; left hand in neutral space
Movement: twist right hand around and bring down to slide across left palm

surprise, amaze, astonish, astound

Handshape: Baby O > 1 : Baby O > 1
Orientation: palms facing
Location: under eyes
Movement: move hands out while flicking index fingers up
Nonmanual signal: body and head thrust back; "surprised" expression

awake, wake up

Handshape: Baby O > 1 : Baby O > 1
Orientation: palms facing
Location: under eyes
Movement: flick index fingers up
Nonmanual signal: body and head thrust back; eyes open wide
Note: See page 229 for a variation of this sign.

spend (time)

Handshape: Baby O > 1 : Baby O > 1
Orientation: palms up
Location: neutral space
Movement: flick index fingers out while moving hands up

correspondence, letter writing

Handshape: Baby O > 1 : Baby O > 1
Orientation: palms facing
Location: neutral space
Movement: bend wrists and flick index
   fingers out twice
Nonmanual signal: lips pursed
Note: See page 262 for a variation of this sign.

teach, educate, instruct *(teacher, educator, instructor, professor)*

Handshape: Flattened O : Flattened O
Orientation: palms facing
Location: near head
Movement: double bounce hands forward

dirt, soil

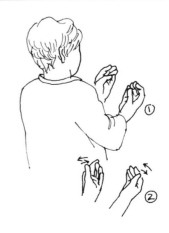

Handshape: Flattened O : Flattened O
Orientation: palms up
Location: neutral space
Movement: rub thumbs across fingertips
   repeatedly

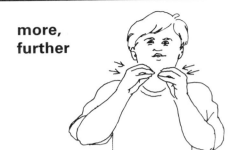

more, further

Handshape: Flattened O : Flattened O
Orientation: palms facing
Location: neutral space
Movement: tap fingertips twice

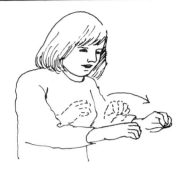

put, move

Handshape: Flattened O : Flattened O
Orientation: palms down
Location: neutral space
Movement: arc hands forward

provide, give

Handshape: Flattened O : Flattened O
Orientation: palms in
Location: neutral space
Movement: bend wrists back and move
hands forward
Note: See page 92 for a one-hand
variation of this sign.

sell, sale, vend (SM); store, market *(seller, merchant, salesclerk, vendor)* (DM)

Handshape: Flattened O : Flattened O
Orientation: palms down
Location: neutral space
Movement: flick wrists up

pack

Handshape: Flattened O : Flattened O
Orientation: palms down
Location: neutral space
Movement: alternately move hands up
and down

fix, repair

Handshape: Flattened O : Flattened O
Orientation: palms facing
Location: neutral space
Movement: brush fingertips past each
other while moving hands back and forth

number

Handshape: Flattened O : Flattened O
Orientation: right palm left; left palm in; hands touching
Location: neutral space
Movement: twist hands in opposite directions, then back to original position

budget

Handshape: Flattened O : Flattened O
Orientation: palms up, right hand closer to body
Location: neutral space
Movement: switch hand positions several times

cosmetics, make-up

Handshape: Flattened O : Flattened O
Orientation: palms in
Location: near face
Movement: move hands alternately up and down

feast, banquet, luncheon, reception

Handshape: Flattened O : Flattened O
Orientation: palms in
Location: neutral space
Movement: circle hands alternately toward mouth
Nonmanual signal: "mm" mouth utterance

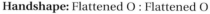

FLATTENED O ✿ **2-Hand SIGNS**

---

magazine, booklet, brochure, leaflet, manual, pamphlet

Handshape: Flattened O : Open B
Orientation: right palm up, hand gripping left hand; left palm right
Location: neutral space
Movement: slide right hand along left hand
Note: See page 229 for a variation of this sign.

---

buy, purchase *(buyer, customer, purchaser)*

Handshape: Flattened O : Open B
Orientation: palms up, right hand on left palm
Location: neutral space
Movement: arc right hand up and out

---

money, budget, economics, finance, funds

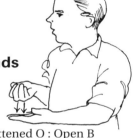

Handshape: Flattened O : Open B
Orientation: palms up, right hand on left palm
Location: neutral space
Movement: smack right hand on left palm twice

---

shop, shopping

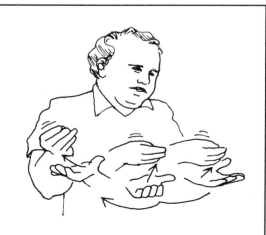

Handshape: Flattened O : Open B
Orientation: palms up, right hand on left palm
Location: neutral space
Movement: slide right hand off left hand repeatedly in different directions
Nonmanual signal: body moves left to right with movement

flexible

Handshape: Flattened O : Open B
Orientation: right palm left, hand gripping left fingers; left palm in
Location: neutral space
Movement: bend left fingertips back and forth
Nonmanual signal: lips pursed

install, investment

Handshape: Flattened O : C
Orientation: right palm out; left palm right
Location: neutral space
Movement: move right hand into left hand

in, into (SM); inside (DM)

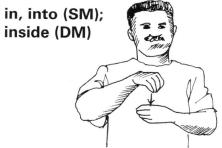

Handshape: Flattened O : O
Orientation: right palm down, hand above left hand; left palm in
Location: neutral space
Movement: move right hand into left hand

cherry, berry

Handshape: Flattened O : 5
Orientation: palms in; right fingertips gripping left pinky
Location: neutral space
Movement: twist right hand back and forth

spend, treat (v.)

Handshape: Flattened O > A : Flattened O > A
Orientation: palms up
Location: neutral space
Movement: move hands forward while sliding thumbs across and off fingertips

correspondence

Handshape: Flattened O > 5 : Flattened O > 5
Orientation: palms facing, arms at an angle
Location: neutral space
Movement: move hands toward each other and flick fingers open
Note: See page 255 for a variation of this sign.

lose, lost, misplaced

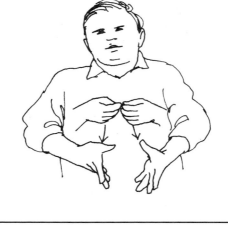

Handshape: Flattened O > 5 : Flattened O > 5
Orientation: palms in, fingers touching
Location: neutral space
Movement: move hands down, opening to 5 handshape
Nonmanual signal: head down; eyes searching; "distressed" expression

distribute, give out

Handshape: Flattened O > 5 : Flattened O > 5
Orientation: palms in; fingers touching
Location: neutral space
Movement: arc hands out while opening fingers

blossom, bloom

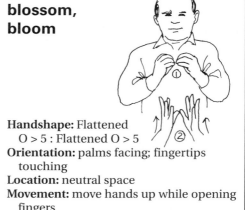

Handshape: Flattened O > 5 : Flattened O > 5
Orientation: palms facing; fingertips touching
Location: neutral space
Movement: move hands up while opening fingers

move away,
move out

Handshape: Flattened O > 5 : Flattened O > 5
Orientation: palms down
Location: neutral space
Movement: move hands across body, opening fingers
Nonmanual signal: head tilts and eyes gaze in direction
  of referent

spread,
spill

Handshape: Flattened O > 5 : Flattened O > 5
Orientation: palms down; fingertips
  touching
Location: neutral space
Movement: open hands out, spreading
  fingers

afraid,
frightened,
scared

Handshape: Flattened O > 5 : Flattened O > 5
Orientation: palms facing
Location: neutral space
Movement: move hands toward each other
  and flick fingers open
Nonmanual signal: "scared" expression

inform, information,
news, notify

Handshape: Flattened O > 5 : Flattened O > 5
Orientation: palms in
Location: right fingertips on head; left hand
  near face
Movement: arc hands down and forward,
  opening fingers

record (v.), put down, register

Handshape: Flattened O > Open B : Open B
Orientation: palms facing, right fingertips on
   left palm
Location: neutral space
Movement: open right hand and press
   against left palm

advise, affect, counsel, influence

Handshape: Flattened O > 5 : B
Orientation: palms down, right hand on left
   hand
Location: neutral space
Movement: slide right hand off left hand,
   opening hand

expensive, costly

Handshape: Flattened O > 5 : Open B
Orientation: right palm down, fingertips
   on left palm; left palm up
Location: neutral space
Movement: lift right hand and flick fingers
   open
Nonmanual signal: "cha" mouth utterance

waste, extravagant, squander

Handshape: Flattened O > 5 : Open B
Orientation: palms up, right hand on left palm
Location: neutral space
Movement: sling right hand out, opening hand
Nonmanual signal: lips pursed

rich, wealthy

Handshape: Flattened O > 5 : Open B
Orientation: right palms left, hand on left palm; left palm up
Location: neutral space
Movement: raise right hand, twisting and changing to 5 handshape
Nonmanual signal: "cha" mouth utterance

overflow

Handshape: Flattened O > 5 : Open B
Orientation: right palm out, hand on left palm; left palm in
Location: neutral space
Movement: move right hand up and over left hand, changing to 5 handshape, then wiggle fingers down

grow, develop, mature (SM); spring, plant (n.)(DM)

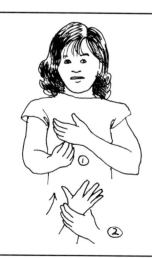

Handshape: Flattened O > 5 : C
Orientation: right palm up, hand below left hand; left palm in
Location: neutral space
Movement: move right hand up through left hand, opening fingers

feed
(compound: food + give)

Handshape: Flattened O : Flattened O
Orientation: palms in
Location: right hand at mouth; left hand in
  neutral space
Movement: move right hand down, then double
  bounce hands out

land
(compound: dirt + surface)

Handshape: Flattened O > 5 : Flattened O > 5
Orientation: palms up
Location: neutral space
Movement: rub thumbs across fingertips several
  times, then open hands, turn them over and
  circle them toward each other

relay
(operator
service)

Handshape: R : R
Orientation: right palm left, left palm
  right, wrists crossed
Location: neutral space
Movement: bend wrists down twice

ready

Handshape: R : R
Orientation: palms down
Location: neutral space
Movement: arc hands across body

doughnut

Handshape: R : R
Orientation: palms facing; fingertips touching
Location: neutral space
Movement: arc hands down, ending with palms in

response, reply, report, react

Handshape: R : R
Orientation: palms out
Location: right hand at mouth; left hand in neutral space
Movement: arc hands forward and down
Nonmanual signal: body leans forward

rest, relax

Handshape: R : R
Orientation: palms in, arms crossed
Location: chest
Movement: tap hands on chest twice
Nonmanual signal: "contented" expression

rabbi

Handshape: R : R
Orientation: palms in
Location: chest
Movement: slide fingers down chest

room

Handshape: R : R
Orientation: palms in; right hand in front of left
Location: neutral space
Movement: bend wrists back, ending with palms facing

rehabilitation

Handshape: R : Open B
Orientation: right palm down, hand on left palm; left palm up
Location: neutral space
Movement: lift left hand up

require

Handshape: R : Open B
Orientation: right palm in, fingertips on left palm; left palm right
Location: neutral space
Movement: move hands back toward body

rule, regulation

Handshape: R : Open B
Orientation: palms facing, right fingers on left fingertips
Location: neutral space
Movement: arc right hand down left palm

research

Handshape: R : Open B
Orientation: right palm in; left palm up
Location: right hand on nose; left hand in neutral space
Movement: move right hand down and brush fingers down left palm
Nonmanual signal: shoulders rounded; head lowered; "inquiring" expression

reinforce

Handshape: R : S
Orientation: palms in; right hand below left hand
Location: neutral space
Movement: hit base of left hand with right fingertips and push left hand up

power, might, strength, sturdy, tough

Handshape: S : S
Orientation: palms in
Location: neutral space
Movement: double bounce hands forward
Nonmanual signal: shoulders and head thrust back; lips pursed

ski

Handshape: S : S
Orientation: palms facing
Location: neutral space
Movement: swing arms back

cold, chilly, shiver, winter

Handshape: S : S
Orientation: palms facing
Location: neutral space
Movement: shake arms toward each other
Nonmanual signal: shoulders rounded; head lowered; "shivering" expression

can, able, may (SM); possible, capable (DM)

Handshape: S : S
Orientation: palms out
Location: neutral space
Movement: bend wrists down while moving arms down
Nonmanual signal: head nods "yes"

motorcycle, ride a motorcycle

Handshape: S : S
Orientation: palms down
Location: neutral space
Movement: twist wrists out twice

canoe

Handshape: S : S
Orientation: palms facing, arms at an angle
Location: neutral space
Movement: swing arms back to left side

carpentry (carpenter)

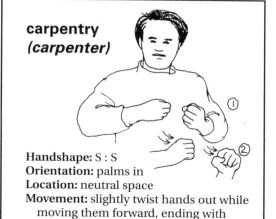

Handshape: S : S
Orientation: palms in
Location: neutral space
Movement: slightly twist hands out while moving them forward, ending with palms facing

stretch

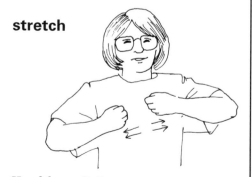

Handshape: S : S
Orientation: palms in
Location: neutral space
Movement: pull hands apart

shoes

Handshape: S : S
Orientation: palms down
Location: neutral space
Movement: tap hands together twice

hold

Handshape: S : S
Orientation: right palm left, right hand
on left hand; left palm right
Location: neutral space
Movement: shake hands slightly

baseball

Handshape: S : S
Orientation: right palm in, right hand on
left hand; left palm right
Location: neutral space
Movement: double bounce hands forward

**accustom,
bound, custom,
habit,
locked into,
tradition**

Handshape: S : S
Orientation: palms down, right hand on
left hand
Location: neutral space
Movement: move hands down

**accident,
collide,
collision**

Handshape: S : S
Orientation: palms in
Location: neutral space
Movement: smack hands into each other

**break,
fracture**

Handshape: S : S
Orientation: palms down, hands touching
Location: neutral space
Movement: swing hands up and to sides,
ending with palms facing

defend, guard, protect, shield

Handshape: S : S
Orientation: right palm left; left palm right, wrists crossed
Location: neutral space
Movement: push arms forward forcefully

free, emancipate, liberate, redeem, relief, rescue, safe, save

Handshape: S : S
Orientation: right palm left; left palm right, wrists crossed
Location: neutral space
Movement: separate hands and twist them around, ending with palms out
Nonmanual signal: body leans back; smile

embrace, dear, hug, love

Handshape: S : S
Orientation: palms in, arms crossed
Location: chest
Movement: slightly squeeze arms to chest
Nonmanual signal: smile; shoulders raised

neck (v.)

Handshape: S : S
Orientation: right palm left; left palm right, wrists crossed
Location: neutral space
Movement: bend wrists down twice
Nonmanual signal: lips pursed

car, automobile, drive

Handshape: S : S
Orientation: palms in
Location: neutral space
Movement: arc hands alternately up and down
Note: "Drive" is usually made with larger movements than "car."

bicycle, bike, ride a bicycle

Handshape: S : S
Orientation: palms down
Location: neutral space
Movement: circle hands alternately forward

Bar Mitzvah, Bat Mitzvah

Handshape: S : S
Orientation: palms in, right hand above left hand
Location: neutral space
Movement: circle hands around each other

box, fight

Handshape: S : S
Orientation: palms in, right hand closer to body
Location: neutral space
Movement: punch hands alternately toward each other

make, create, construct, manufacture, produce

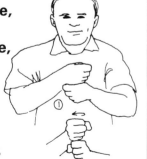

Handshape: S : S
Orientation: palms in, right hand on left hand
Location: neutral space
Movement: bend wrists back

doubt, disbelief, waver

Handshape: S : S
Orientation: palms down
Location: neutral space
Movement: move hands alternately up and down
Nonmanual signal: head tilts; "disbelieving" expression

grieve, grief, heartbreak

Handshape: S : S
Orientation: right palm down, hand on left hand; left palm up
Location: neutral space
Movement: sharply twist hands around, switching positions
Nonmanual signal: shoulders rounded; head lowered; "sad" expression

agony, suffer, suffering

Handshape: S : S
Orientation: palms in
Location: neutral space
Movement: circle hands alternately around each other, ending in original position
Nonmanual signal: shoulders rounded; head lowered; "pained" expression

stone, rock

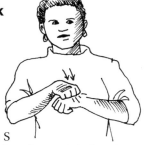

Handshape: S : S
Orientation: palms down, right hand above left hand
Location: neutral space
Movement: tap right hand on left hand twice

appointment, engagement, reservation, reserve

Handshape: S : S
Orientation: palms down, right hand above left hand
Location: neutral space
Movement: circle right hand above left hand, then drop hand down on left hand

work, employ, employment, job, labor, task, toil

Handshape: S : S
Orientation: right palm out, wrist on left wrist; left palm down
Location: neutral space
Movement: double bounce right hand on left wrist twice

year

Handshape: S : S
Orientation: right palm left, hand on left hand; left palm right
Location: neutral space
Movement: circle right hand around left hand and return to original position

hammer

Handshape: S : S
Orientation: right palm left, hand above left hand; left palm right
Location: neutral space
Movement: bend right hand down several times
Nonmanual signal: "cha" mouth utterance

fix, repair

Handshape: S : S
Orientation: palms in
Location: neutral space
Movement: brush right hand against left hand twice
Nonmanual signal: "earnest" expression

coffee

Handshape: S : S
Orientation: palms in; right hand on left hand
Location: neutral space
Movement: circle right hand counter-clockwise on left hand

umbrella

Handshape: S : S
Orientation: palms in; right hand on left hand
Location: neutral space
Movement: double bounce right hand up

support, advocate, endorse, maintain, reinforce, sponsor, sustain, uphold

Handshape: S : S
Orientation: palms in, right hand below left hand
Location: neutral space
Movement: push left hand up with right hand

exaggerate

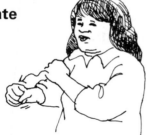

Handshape: S : S
Orientation: palms down, right hand in front of left hand
Location: neutral space
Movement: bounce right hand forward in small arcs

advertise, propaganda, publicize

Handshape: S : S
Orientation: palms down, right hand in front of left hand
Location: neutral space
Movement: move right hand forward twice
Nonmanual signal: pursed lips

defeat, conquer

Handshape: S : S
Orientation: right palm out, wrist against edge of left hand; left palm down
Location: neutral space
Movement: sharply bend right hand over left hand
Nonmanual signal: "serious" expression

certify, license, seal

Handshape: S : Open B
Orientation: right palm in, hand above left palm; left palm up
Location: neutral space
Movement: stamp left palm with edge of right fist

credit card, charge

Handshape: S : Open B
Orientation: right palm in, hand on left fingertips; left palm up
Location: neutral space
Movement: rapidly slide right hand back and forth across left palm

bell, chimes, ring bells

Handshape: S : Open B
Orientation: right palm down; left palm right
Location: neutral space
Movement: bounce right hand against left palm

state (geography), statute (law)

Handshape: S : Open B
Orientation: right palm out, hand on left fingertips; left palm right
Location: neutral space
Movement: bounce right hand once down to heel of left hand

sample, symbol

Handshape: S : Open B
Orientation: right palm out, hand against left palm; left palm right
Location: neutral space
Movement: move hands forward in two quick motions

stage (passive)

Handshape: S : passive
Orientation: right palm down, hand on left wrist; left palm down
Location: neutral space
Movement: slide right hand down to left fingertips

situation

Handshape: S : 1
Orientation: palms out
Location: neutral space
Movement: arc right hand around left index finger

abuse, hit (more than once), attack, strike (more than once)

Handshape: S : 1
Orientation: right palm in, hand closer to body; left palm right
Location: neutral space
Movement: brush right knuckles harshly back and forth against left index finger
Nonmanual signal: "angry" expression

obey

Handshape: S > 5 : S > 5
Orientation: palms in
Location: right hand on forehead; left hand in front of left cheek
Movement: move hands down and forward while opening hands

terrible, awful, dreadful, horrible

Handshape: S > 5 : S > 5
Orientation: palms out
Location: both sides of the temple
Movement: move hands straight out while opening hands
Nonmanual signal: "disgusted" expression

cause

Handshape: S > 5 : S > 5
Orientation: palms up, right hand in front of left hand
Location: neutral space
Movement: move hands forward while opening hands

bawl out

Handshape: S > 5 : S > 5
Orientation: right palm left, right hand on top of left hand; left palm right
Location: neutral space
Movement: flick fingers out sharply
Nonmanual signal: body jerks forward; "angry" expression

many, lots, multiple, numerous

Handshape: S > 5 : S > 5
Orientation: palms in
Location: neutral space
Movement: sharply thrust hands forward while flicking fingers open
Nonmanual signal: "cha" mouth utterance

how many, how much

Handshape: S > 5 : S > 5
Orientation: palms up
Location: neutral space
Movement: move hands up, flicking fingers open
Nonmanual signal: body leans forward; head tilts right; eyebrows knit

magic

Handshape: S > 5 : S > 5
Orientation: palms down
Location: neutral space
Movement: move hands forward slightly, then down, flicking fingers open

express (feelings)

Handshape: S > 5 : S > 5
Orientation: palms in
Location: chest
Movement: arc hands forward while opening hands
Nonmanual signal: lips pursed

expand, enlarge

Handshape: S > Bent 5 : S > Bent 5
Orientation: palms in; right hand on top of left hand
Location: neutral space
Movement: move hands apart while opening hands to Bent 5 handshape

fireworks

Handshape: S > 5 : S > 5
Orientation: palms out
Location: neutral space
Movement: alternately open and close hands rapidly in different locations in the air

climb, ladder

Handshape: S > Bent 5 : Bent 5 > S
Orientation: palms out
Location: neutral space
Movement: close and open hands while moving hands up in alternating motions

next year (SM); annual, yearly (DM)

Handshape: S > 1 : S
Orientation: right palm left, hand on top of left hand; left palm right
Location: neutral space
Movement: flick right index finger out as right hand moves forward

abortion

Handshape: S > 5 : Open B
Orientation: right palm up, hand against left palm; left palm angled right
Location: neutral space
Movement: move right hand sharply out and down, flicking fingers open

refuge, shelter
(compound: safe + roof)

Handshape: S > B : S > B
Orientation: palms in, wrists crossed
Location: neutral space
Movement: separate hands and twist them around, then change to B handshape, palms down, fingertips touching, and angle hands down

hill
(compound: rock + slope)

Handshape: S > Open B : S > Open B
Orientation: palms down, right hand above left hand
Location: neutral space
Movement: drop right hand onto left hand, then change to Open B handshape and outline the contours of a hillside

try

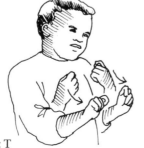

Handshape: T : T
Orientation: palms in
Location: neutral space
Movement: arc hands down and twist forward, ending with palms out
Nonmanual signal: "earnest" expression

translate, transliterate

Handshape: T : T
Orientation: right palm down, hand resting on left hand; left palm up
Location: neutral space
Movement: reverse hand positions

team

Handshape: T : T
Orientation: palms facing
Location: neutral space
Movement: swing hands around, ending
with pinkies nearly touching

time
(abstract)

Handshape: T : Open B
Orientation: right palm out, hand
against left palm; left palm right
Location: neutral space
Movement: move right hand clockwise
around left palm

Total Communication

Handshape: T : C
Orientation: palms facing
Location: neutral space
Movement: alternately move hands back
and forth

temple,
synagogue

Handshape: T : S
Orientation: right palm out; left palm down
Location: neutral space
Movement: bounce heel of right hand on
back of left hand

champagne

Handshape: T > Open A : S
Orientation: palms in, right hand on
top of left hand
Location: neutral space
Movement: move right hand quickly
upward while flicking thumb out

fast, quick,
rapid

Handshape: T > Open A : T > Open A
Orientation: palms facing
Location: neutral space
Movement: quickly flick thumbs out
while moving hands forward

transliterate, translate

Handshape: T > L : T > L
Orientation: right palm out, hand on heel of left hand; left palm in
Location: neutral space
Movement: reverse positions of hands, flicking open thumbs and index fingers

look forward to, anticipate

Handshape: V : V
Orientation: palms down, hands angled left
Location: neutral space
Movement: double bounce hands forward
Nonmanual signal: eyes widen

funeral

Handshape: V : V
Orientation: palms out, right hand behind left hand
Location: neutral space
Movement: bounce hands forward
Nonmanual signal: "sad" expression

contempt, patronize, scorn

Handshape: V : V
Orientation: palms down, hands angled left
Location: neutral space
Movement: move fingers down and up sharply
Nonmanual signal: "smirking" expression

vain, flatter, vanity

Handshape: V : V
Orientation: palms in
Location: above shoulders
Movement: bend fingers down and up twice
Nonmanual signal: shoulders thrust back; erect posture

tent, camping

Handshape: V : V
Orientation: palms facing, fingertips angled toward each other
Location: neutral space
Movement: move hands down at an angle
Note: See page 305 for a variation of this sign.

intercourse, copulate, fornicate

Handshape: V : V
Orientation: right palm down, hand above left hand; left palm up
Location: neutral space
Movement: double bounce right hand on left hand

very, extremely

Handshape: V : V
Orientation: palms facing, fingertips angled toward each other and touching
Location: neutral space
Movement: separate hands sharply
Nonmanual signal: "intense" expression

visit

Handshape: V : V
Orientation: palms up
Location: neutral space
Movement: circle hands out alternately

either, or

Handshape: V : V
Orientation: palms facing, fingertips angled toward each other
Location: neutral space
Movement: tap left index finger with right index finger, then tap left middle finger with right middle finger, repeat
Nonmanual signal: body tilts slightly side to side

save, preserve, reserve, store

Handshape: V : V
Orientation: palms in, right hand in front of left hand
Location: neutral space
Movement: hit left fingers twice with right fingers
Note: See page 288 for a variation of this sign.

indecision, uncertainty

Handshape: V : B
Orientation: right palm down, index and middle finger straddling left hand; left palm right
Location: neutral space
Movement: rock right hand side to side
Nonmanual signal: "indecisive" expression

ride (horse, bike)

Handshape: V : B
Orientation: right palm down, index and middle fingers straddling left hand; left palm right
Location: neutral space
Movement: bounce hands forward several times (horse); move hands forward (bike)

predict, forecast, foretell, omen, prophecy *(fortune-teller, prophet)*

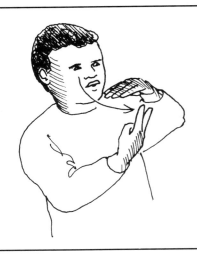

Handshape: V : Open B
Orientation: right palm in; left palm down
Location: right hand below eyes; left hand in neutral space
Movement: move right hand under and beyond left hand

drown

Handshape: V : Open B
Orientation: right palm out, fingertips wedged between left index and middle fingers; left palm down
Location: neutral space
Movement: wiggle right hand down

lose (competition)

Handshape: V : Open B
Orientation: right palm down, hand above left hand; left palm up
Location: neutral space
Movement: smack right hand down sharply on left palm
Nonmanual signal: "sad" expression

dance, party

Handshape: V : Open B
Orientation: right palm down, fingertips above left hand; left palm up
Location: neutral space
Movement: swing right hand left and right
Nonmanual signal: smile

stand

Handshape: V : Open B
Orientation: right palm down, fingertips above left palm; left palm up
Location: neutral space
Movement: move right hand down so fingertips touch left palm

fork

Handshape: V : Open B
Orientation: right palm down, finger tips above left palm; left palm up
Location: neutral space
Movement: stab left palm with right fingertips twice

recline, lie down

Handshape: V : Open B
Orientation: palms up, back of right hand on left palm
Location: neutral space
Movement: slide back of right hand across left palm
Nonmanual signal: "tired" expression

arise, get up, stand up

Handshape: V : Open B
Orientation: right palm left; left palm up
Location: neutral space
Movement: flip right fingers over to stand on left palm

fall down, fall

Handshape: V : Open B
Orientation: right palm down, hand above left hand; left palm up
Location: neutral space
Movement: flip right hand over and smack onto left palm
Nonmanual signal: body leans back

read

Handshape: V : Open B
Orientation: palms facing, fingertips up
Location: neutral space
Movement: brush right fingertips down left palm

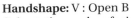

mean, imply, intend, motive, purpose, signify

Handshape: V : Open B
Orientation: right palm down, fingertips on left palm; left palm right
Location: neutral space
Movement: rotate right fingertips on left palm

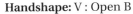

toast

Handshape: V : Open B
Orientation: palms facing; right fingertips toward left palm
Location: neutral space
Movement: stab palm and back of left hand with right fingertips by rotating both hands

twice, double, duplicate

Handshape: V : Open B
Orientation: right palm in, middle finger on left palm; left palm right, fingertips up
Location: neutral space
Movement: brush right middle finger up left palm

salt

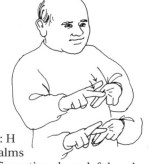

Handshape: V : H
Orientation: palms down, right fingertips above left hand
Location: neutral space
Movement: tap left fingers twice with alternating right index and middle fingers

dive

Handshape: V : H
Orientation: right palm down, fingertips on back of left fingers; left palm down
Location: neutral space
Movement: flip right hand off left hand, ending below left hand with fingertips up

watch

Handshape: V : S
Orientation: palms down; right hand on left hand
Location: neutral space
Movement: move hands forward in two quick motions

save, store, reserve, preserve

Handshape: V : S
Orientation: palms in,
  right hand in front of left hand
Location: neutral space
Movement: tap right fingertips on back of
  left hand twice
Note: See page 284 for a variation of this
  sign.

bridge (passive)

Handshape: V : passive
Orientation: right palm left, fingertips on
  left wrist; left palm down
Location: neutral space
Movement: arc right fingertips along left
  arm, ending at left elbow

sheep (passive)

Handshape: V : passive
Orientation: right palm up, fingers on left
  arm; left palm down
Location: neutral space
Movement: shear back of left arm with
  right fingertips

plumbing, wrench (plumber, mechanic)

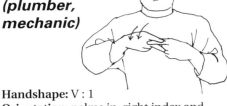

Handshape: V : 1
Orientation: palms in, right index and
  middle fingers straddling left index finger
Location: neutral space
Movement: twist right index and middle
  fingers around left index finger

apply, shelve it (slang), table it (slang)

Handshape: V : 1
Orientation: palms facing
Location: neutral space
Movement: move right hand down onto
  left index finger

vocabulary

Handshape: V : 1
Orientation: palms out,
  right fingertips above left index finger
Location: neutral space
Movement: tap right fingertips on left
  index finger twice as hands move left
  slightly

plug, electric outlet

Handshape: V : 1
Orientation: right palm down, behind left
hand; left palm out
Location: neutral space
Movement: plug right index and
middle fingers into left index finger

both

Handshape: V > H : C > S
Orientation: palms in, right hand inside left hand
Location: neutral space
Movement: move right hand down left palm, closing
left hand as right fingers come together

videotape (n.)

Handshape: V > T : Open B
Orientation: right palm out, index finger against left
palm; left palm right
Location: neutral space
Movement: circle right hand clockwise, ending in
T handshape

jump

Handshape: V > Bent V : Open B
Orientation: right palm down, fingertips on left palm; left palm up
Location: neutral space
Movement: bounce right fingertips on left palm, bending the fingers on the way up

rob, steal (passive)

Handshape: V > Bent V : passive
Orientation: palms down
Location: neutral space
Movement: sharply slide right hand from left elbow to left wrist while bending fingers

quote, caption, subject, theme, title, topic

Handshape: Bent V : Bent V
Orientation: palms out
Location: neutral space
Movement: twist wrists, ending with palms facing

dead (animal), kick the bucket (slang)

Handshape: Bent V : Bent V
Orientation: palms facing, fingers out
Location: neutral space
Movement: sharply twist wrists up
Nonmanual signal: lips pursed

analyze, analysis, research

Handshape: Bent V : Bent V
Orientation: palms down, knuckles facing
Location: neutral space
Movement: slightly straighten and bend fingers twice
Nonmanual signal: shoulders rounded; head lowered; "inquiring" expression

laid up

Handshape: Bent V : Bent V
Orientation: palms facing, fingers out
Location: left side of body
Movement: arc hands up sharply toward right shoulder
Nonmanual signal: pursed lips, body and head lean back

poison

Handshape: Bent V : Bent V
Orientation: palms in, wrists crossed
Location: neutral space
Movement: tap wrists against each other twice
Nonmanual signal: "sour" expression

tournament

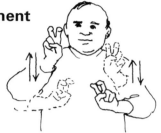

Handshape: Bent V : Bent V
Orientation: palms out, right hand higher than left hand
Location: neutral space
Movement: shift hands up and down several times

difficult, hardship

Handshape: Bent V : Bent V
Orientation: palms in, knuckles facing, right hand above left hand
Location: neutral space
Movement: brush knuckles against each other in alternating pattern
Nonmanual signal: lips tight; "strained" expression

problem

Handshape: Bent V : Bent V
Orientation: right palm down; left palm in, knuckles touching
Location: neutral space
Movement: twist hands to switch palm positions
Nonmanual signal: lips tight; "strained" expression

roller skate

Handshape: Bent V : Bent V
Orientation: palms up
Location: neutral space
Movement: slide hands alternately back
  and forth several times

tough

Handshape: Bent V : Bent V
Orientation: palms in, right hand above left
  hand
Location: neutral space
Movement: bring right hand down, brushing
  knuckles of left hand sharply
Nonmanual signal: "serious" expression

dumbfounded, open-mouthed, speechless

Handshape: Bent V : Bent V
Orientation: right palm in; left palm out, back of left
  hand against mouth
Location: in front of mouth
Movement: arc right hand down, ending with
  palm up
Nonmanual signal: mouth open; "shocked"
  expression

squirrel

Handshape: Bent V : Bent V
Orientation: right palm left; left palm right
Location: right hand above mouth; left hand in
neutral space
Movement: move right hand down to left hand,
then tap fingertips together several times
Nonmanual signal: shoulders rounded; head
lowered; cheeks puffed

hilarious, laughter, rolling in the aisles (slang)

Handshape: Bent V : Open B
Orientation: palms up, right hand on left palm
Location: neutral space
Movement: slide right hand across left palm
while straightening and bending right index
and middle fingers
Nonmanual signal: mouth open; head tilted
back

kneel

Handshape: Bent V : Open B
Orientation: right palm in, knuckles
above left palm; left palm up
Location: neutral space
Movement: move right hand down onto
left palm

get in

Handshape: Bent V : C
Orientation: right palm up; left palm right
Location: neutral space
Movement: flip right hand down to perch
on left thumb

get out

Handshape: Bent V : C
Orientation: right palm down, fingers on left thumb; left palm right
Location: neutral space
Movement: flip right hand off left thumb

hard

Handshape: Bent V : S
Orientation: right palm in, hand above left hand; left palm down
Location: neutral space
Movement: bring right hand down onto back of left hand
Nonmanual signal: lips tight

Ireland, Irish

Handshape: Bent V : S
Orientation: palms down, right fingertips above left hand
Location: neutral space
Movement: circle right hand above left hand, then land on left hand

potato

Handshape: Bent V : S
Orientation: palms down, right fingertips above left hand
Location: neutral space
Movement: tap right fingertips on back of left hand twice

nab,
caught in the act,
contact, corner (v.)

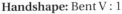

Handshape: Bent V : 1
Orientation: right palm down, hand in back of left hand; left palm right
Location: neutral space
Movement: move right hand forward to trap left index finger between right knuckles
Nonmanual signal: lips pursed

change the topic, change the subject

Handshape: Bent V > V : Bent V
Orientation: palms down, index fingers touching
Location: neutral space
Movement: arc right hand to the right, straightening bent fingers

war

Handshape: W : W
Orientation: palms down, fingertips pointing toward each other
Location: neutral space
Movement: move hands side to side in unison

winter

Handshape: W : W
Orientation: palms facing
Location: neutral space
Movement: tap pinkies and thumbs together twice

weather

Handshape: W : W
Orientation: palms facing, thumbs and pinkies touching
Location: neutral space
Movement: twist hands in opposite directions twice

world

Handshape: W : W
Orientation: right palm left, hand on top of left hand; left palm right
Location: neutral space
Movement: circle hands around each other

worship

Handshape: W : W
Orientation: right palm left; left palm down
Location: right index finger on right side of head; left hand in neutral space
Movement: right hand twists down, ending with hand on top of left hand
Nonmanual signal: "earnest" expression

dangerous, hazardous

Handshape: X : X
Orientation: palms up
Location: neutral space
Movement: flip hands over sharply
Nonmanual signal: eyes widen; "frightened" expression

give, award, contribute, present, reward (SM); gift, award, contribution, present, reward (DM)

Handshape: X : X
Orientation: palms facing, index fingers up
Location: neutral space
Movement: bend wrists forward and down

ski

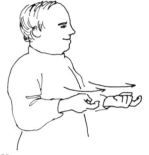

Handshape: X : X
Orientation: palms up
Location: neutral space
Movement: glide hands forward and
back slightly

**urge,
coax,
persuade,
prod**

Handshape: X : X
Orientation: palms up, right hand closer
to body
Location: neutral space
Movement: tug hands in toward body twice
Nonmanual signal: "earnest" expression

**electric,
electronics,
physics**

Handshape: X : X
Orientation: palms in, knuckles touching
Location: neutral space
Movement: hit knuckles together twice

**Spain, Spanish
(Spaniard)**

Handshape: X : X
Orientation: palms in
Location: shoulders
Movement: move hands forward, ending
with index fingers clasped

**suspend,
hold up**

Handshape: X : X
Orientation: palms down, index fingers
clasped
Location: neutral space
Movement: sharply bring wrists up

best friend

Handshape: X : X
Orientation: right palm
down; left palm up, index fingers clasped
Location: neutral space
Movement: arc hands sharply forward
and down
Nonmanual signal: lips taut; "earnest"
expression

expression, grimace

Handshape: X : X
Orientation: palms out
Location: right hand near temple; left hand near cheek
Movement: move hands alternately up and down
Nonmanual signal: lips pursed

ice skate

Handshape: X : X
Orientation: palms up
Location: neutral space
Movement: slide hands side to side twice
Nonmanual signal: body sways

change, adapt, adjust, modify

Handshape: X : X
Orientation: right palm out; left palm in; hands crossed at wrists
Location: neutral space
Movement: twist hands around, reversing palm positions

exchange, switch, trade

Handshape: X : X
Orientation: right palm left; left palm right, closer to body
Location: neutral space
Movement: rotate hands so right hand is closer to body

direct, control, discipline, govern, manage, regulate, reign, rule

Handshape: X : X
Orientation: palms facing, right hand closer to body
Location: neutral space
Movement: move hands back and forth in alternating motion
Nonmanual signal: shoulders thrust back; erect posture

friend

Handshape: X : X
Orientation: right palm down; left palm up; index fingers clasped
Location: neutral space
Movement: rotate hands to switch palm positions

pull, hitch, hook, tow

Handshape: X : X
Orientation: right palm down; left palm in; index fingers clasped
Location: neutral space
Movement: use right hand to pull left hand to the right

cards, play cards

Handshape: X : X
Orientation: palms in, right hand above left hand
Location: neutral space
Movement: brush right hand off left hand several times while moving hands right

ruin, spoil, torment

Handshape: X : X
Orientation: right palm left, above and in back of left hand; left palm right
Location: neutral space
Movement: brush right hand across left hand, arcing wrist forward and up
Nonmanual signal: "cha" mouth utterance

tease

Handshape: X : X
Orientation: right palm left, above and in back of left hand; left palm right
Location: neutral space
Movement: brush right hand across left hand twice
Nonmanual signal: head tilts right; "taunting" expression

demand, command, insist, require

Handshape: X : Open B
Orientation: right palm in, index fingertip on left palm; left palm right
Location: neutral space
Movement: sharply pull hands in toward body
Nonmanual signal: "insistent" expression

key, lock

Handshape: X : Open B
Orientation: right palm down, index finger knuckle on left palm; left palm right
Location: neutral space
Movement: twist right hand on left palm

charge, cost, expense, fee, fine, price, tax, toll

Handshape: X : Open B
Orientation: right palm in; left palm right
Location: neutral space
Movement: brush right index finger down left palm

time (passive)

Handshape: X : S
Orientation: palms down, right index finger above left wrist
Location: neutral space
Movement: tap right fingertip on left wrist twice

tempt, temptation (passive)

Handshape: X : passive
Orientation: palms in, right index finger-tip on left arm below elbow
Location: neutral space
Movement: tap right index finger on left elbow twice

from

Handshape: X : 1
Orientation: right palm left, index finger against left index finger; left palm out
Location: neutral space
Movement: pull right hand back, away from left index finger

pick on, henpeck, nag

Handshape: X : 1
Orientation: palms out
Location: neutral space
Movement: peck right index finger on left index finger twice
Nonmanual signal: lips pursed

hang, closet, hanger

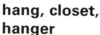

Handshape: X : 1
Orientation: palms down, right index finger crooked over left index finger
Location: neutral space
Movement: bounce right hand on left index fingertip several times

telegram, call (by TTY)

Handshape: X : 1
Orientation: right palm down, index fingertip at base of left index finger; left palm right
Location: neutral space
Movement: slide right fingertip off left index finger

sandals, thongs

Handshape: X : 5
Orientation: palms down, right index finger between left index and middle fingers
Location: neutral space
Movement: move right index finger forward and back twice

play (v.)

Handshape: Y : Y
Orientation: palms out
Location: neutral space
Movement: twist wrists in and out twice
Nonmanual signal: body bounces

now, presently, today

Handshape: Y : Y
Orientation: palms up
Location: neutral space
Movement: move hands down sharply
Nonmanual signal: "cz" mouth utterance

contrary, antagonistic, bullheaded, cantankerous

Handshape: Y : Y
Orientation: palms facing
Location: neutral space
Movement: bring heels of hands together twice
Nonmanual signal: "angry" expression

measure, ruler, size

Handshape: Y : Y
Orientation: palms down
Location: neutral space
Movement: tap thumbs together twice

still, yet

Handshape: Y : Y
Orientation: palms down
Location: neutral space
Movement: move hands forward, bending wrists up

uniform, in common, same, standard, universal

Handshape: Y : Y
Orientation: palms down, thumbs touching
Location: neutral space
Movement: move hands in a large circle

cow, bull

Handshape: Y : Y
Orientation: palms down
Location: thumbs at temples
Movement: bend wrists down and up
Note: See page 113 for a one-hand variation of this sign.

humorous, comical

Handshape: Y : Y
Orientation: right palm left; left palm right
Location: right hand in front of nose; left hand in neutral space
Movement: twist wrists up and down twice
Nonmanual signal: smile

drafting, engineering (engineer)

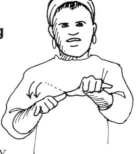

Handshape: Y : Y
Orientation: palms down, thumbs touching
Location: neutral space
Movement: twist right hand down twice

that

Handshape: Y : Open B
Orientation: right palm down; left palm up
Location: neutral space
Movement: bring right hand down onto
left palm

New York

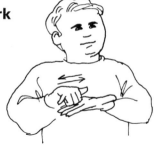

Handshape: Y : Open B
Orientation: right palm down; left palm up
Location: neutral space
Movement: slide right hand back and forth
along left palm

impossible

Handshape: Y : Open B
Orientation: right palm down; left palm up
Location: neutral space
Movement: bring right hand down sharply
onto left palm, then bounce hand up
Nonmanual signal: head shakes "no"

**fat (demeaning),
obese**

Handshape: Y : Open B
Orientation: right palm down; left palm up
Location: neutral space
Movement: rock right knuckles side to side
on left palm
Nonmanual signal: "cha" mouth utterance

**country
(foreign)
(passive)**

Handshape: Y : passive
Orientation: palms in
Location: neutral space
Movement: make a clockwise circle
with right hand in front of left elbow

big word

Handshape: Y : 1
Orientation: right palm down; left palm in
Location: neutral space
Movement: move right hand down so
knuckles hit left index finger

swear, curse

Handshape: Y : 1
Orientation: right palm down; left palm right
Location: neutral space
Movement: wiggle right hand down and off left index finger
Nonmanual signal: "cha" mouth utterance

today
(compound: now + day)

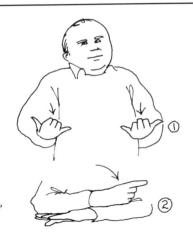

Handshape: Y > 1 : Y > B
Orientation: palms up
Location: neutral space
Movement: move hands down, then change right hand to 1 handshape, palm left, and left hand to B handshape, palm down, right elbow on left fingers, bend right arm down onto left arm

I love you
(casual)

Handshape: L-I : L-I
Orientation: palms out
Location: neutral space
Movement: shake hands slightly side to side
Nonmanual signal: smile

mock,
make fun of,
ridicule

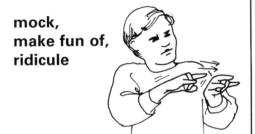

Handshape: 1-I : 1-I
Orientation: palms down, right hand closer to body, hands angled to left
Location: neutral space
Movement: double bounce hands forward
Nonmanual signal: "smirking" expression

tent, camping

Handshape: 1-I : 1-I
Orientation: palms facing, fingertips touching
Location: neutral space
Movement: move hands down at an angle
Note: See page 283 for a variation of this sign.

sarcasm, cynical, ironic

Handshape: 1-I : 1-I
Orientation: palms down
Location: right index finger on tip of nose; left hand in neutral space
Movement: move right hand down to meet left hand, then brush hands past each other
Nonmanual signal: "smirking" expression

liquor, whiskey

Handshape: 1-I : 1-I
Orientation: right palm left; left palm right
Location: neutral space
Movement: double bounce right hand down on left hand
Note: See page 306 for a variation of this sign.

trick, deceive, defraud, fraud

Handshape: 1-I : 1-I
Orientation: palms down, fingertips forward, right hand above left hand
Location: neutral space
Movement: slide right hand off left hand
Nonmanual signal: lips pursed

liquor, whiskey

Handshape: 1-I : S
Orientation: right palm in; left palm down
Location: neutral space
Movement: double bounce right hand down on left hand
Note: See page 305 for a variation of this sign.

cigarette

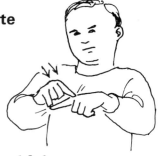

Handshape: 1-I : 1
Orientation: palms down
Location: neutral space
Movement: tap right index finger and pinky on left index finger twice

sin

Handshape: 1 : 1
Orientation: palms facing, index fingers angled toward each other
Location: index fingertips at corners of mouth
Movement: arc hands out, then rotate hands, ending with palms in

hurt, ache, injure, harm, pain

Handshape: 1 : 1
Orientation: right palm out; left palm in
Location: neutral space
Movement: twist hands in opposite directions
Nonmanual signal: shoulders rounded; "pained" expression

opposite, contrast, oppose, reverse
(enemy, foe, opponent)

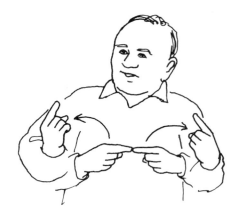

Handshape: 1 : 1
Orientation: palms in, fingertips touching
Location: neutral space
Movement: arc hands up then out to opposite sides

struggle

Handshape: 1 : 1
Orientation: palms in
Location: neutral space
Movement: move hands side to side in unison
Nonmanual signal: lips tight; "pained" expression

quake, scared

Handshape: 1 : 1
Orientation: palms down
Location: neutral space
Movement: move hands together and apart in short, quick shakes
Nonmanual signal: "frightened" expression

go to, attend

Handshape: 1 : 1
Orientation: palms out, right hand slightly behind left hand
Location: neutral space
Movement: bend wrists down while moving hands forward

come

Handshape: 1 : 1
Orientation: palms up, right hand slightly closer to body
Location: neutral space
Movement: bring hands in toward the body while bending wrists in

parallel, coincide, concurrent

Handshape: 1 : 1
Orientation: palms down, index fingers touching
Location: neutral space
Movement: move hands forward

during, meantime, meanwhile, while

Handshape: 1 : 1
Orientation: palms in, index fingers angled in
Location: neutral space
Movement: arc index fingers down and out while moving hands forward

happen, event, incident, occur

Handshape: 1 : 1
Orientation: palms up
Location: neutral space
Movement: flip hands over

accomplish, achieve, prosper, succeed, triumph

Handshape: 1 : 1
Orientation: palms in
Location: index fingers at sides of forehead
Movement: move hands forward in two spiraling
motions, ending with palms out
Nonmanual signal: shoulders and head thrust back

finally, pah!

Handshape: 1 : 1
Orientation: palms in
Location: sides of head
Movement: twist wrists out in an exagger-
ated motion, ending with palms out
Nonmanual signal: body and head thrust
back; "pah" mouth utterance

computer

Handshape: 1 : 1
Orientation: palms down
Location: neutral space
Movement: circle hands out in opposite
directions

wheelchair

Handshape: 1 : 1
Orientation: palms in
Location: outside of thighs
Movement: circle index fingers forward twice

pass by

Handshape: 1 : 1
Orientation: palms facing, right hand
    closer to body
Location: near shoulders
Movement: move hands toward and past
    each other

meet, encounter, face-to-face, one-to-one

Handshape: 1 : 1
Orientation: right palm out, right hand
    closer to body; left palm in
Location: neutral space
Movement: move hands toward each
    other until they meet

but, contrariwise, however

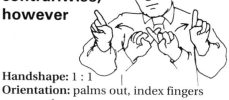

Handshape: 1 : 1
Orientation: palms out, index fingers
    crossed
Location: neutral space
Movement: arc hands out in opposite
    directions
Nonmanual signal: body and head thrust
    back; eyes widen

intersect, conflict, cross

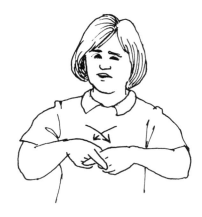

Handshape: 1 : 1
Orientation: palms in, index fingers angled
    toward each other
Location: neutral space
Movement: bring hands together so that index
    fingers cross

conflict, clash, cross-purposes

Handshape: 1 : 1
Orientation: palms down, index fingers angled up
Location: neutral space
Movement: bring hands together sharply until index fingers cross and knuckles clash
Nonmanual signal: brows furrowed; "serious" expression

same, alike, identical, similar (SM); according to, also, too (DM)

Handshape: 1 : 1
Orientation: palms down, hands parallel
Location: neutral space
Movement: bring hands together so index fingers touch

as, according to, also

Handshape: 1 : 1
Orientation: palms down, hands parallel
Location: right side of neutral space
Movement: bring hands together and tap index fingers together, then move hands to the left and tap index fingers again

since, all along, ever since, so far

Handshape: 1 : 1
Orientation: palms in, index fingers angled toward right shoulder
Location: in front of right shoulder
Movement: slowly arc hands out, ending with palms up

corn on the cob

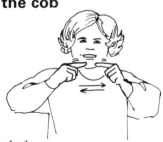

Handshape: 1 : 1
Orientation: palms down
Location: in front of mouth
Movement: move hands left and right in unison

China, Chinese, Oriental

Handshape: 1 : 1
Orientation: palms in
Location: corners of eyes
Movement: rotate fingertips back and forth
Note: See page 126 for the preferred sign.

smile

Handshape: 1 : 1
Orientation: palms facing, index fingers
   angled up
Location: corners of mouth
Movement: slide index fingers up cheeks
Nonmanual signal: smile

laugh, laughter

Handshape: 1 : 1
Orientation: palms in, index fingers
   angled toward each other
Location: corners of mouth
Movement: brush index fingers off cheeks
   twice
Nonmanual signal: mimic laughter

answer, comment, order, reply, respond

Handshape: 1 : 1
Orientation: palms out
Location: back of right index finger on
   lips; left hand in neutral space
Movement: bend wrists forward, ending
   with palms down
Nonmanual signal: body jerks forward
   slightly

announce, declare, proclaim

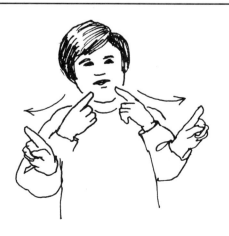

Handshape: 1 : 1
Orientation: palms in, index fingers angled
   toward each other
Location: corners of mouth
Movement: swing hands out to opposite sides,
   ending with palms out
Nonmanual signal: body leans forward;
   head tilts back

famous, fame, popular, renown

Handshape: 1 : 1
Orientation: palms in, index fingers angled toward each other
Location: corners of mouth
Movement: move hands out and spiral forward
Nonmanual signal: shoulders and head thrust back

heart (romantic)

Handshape: 1 : 1
Orientation: palms in, index fingertips touching
Location: left side of chest
Movement: outline the shape of a heart with the index fingers

knit

Handshape: 1 : 1
Orientation: right palm left; left palm out, index fingertips crossed
Location: neutral space
Movement: twist wrists forward

quarrel, argue

Handshape: 1 : 1
Orientation: palms in, right index finger up, left index finger down
Location: neutral space
Movement: shake index fingers alternately up and down
Nonmanual signal: "angry" expression

variety, assorted, different, diverse, etcetera

Handshape: 1 : 1
Orientation: palms down, right hand higher than left hand
Location: neutral space
Movement: move hands out to the sides while alternately bending wrists up and down
Nonmanual signal: body jerks slightly

crippled, lame

Handshape: 1 : 1
Orientation: palms down
Location: neutral space
Movement: move hands alternately up and down
Nonmanual signal: left shoulder dips twice

tornado

Handshape: 1 : 1
Orientation: palms in
Location: right side of body
Movement: rapidly spiral index fingers around one another while moving hands left
Nonmanual signal: lips blow out air

travel, journey, roam, trip, wander

Handshape: 1 : 1
Orientation: palms in
Location: neutral space
Movement: spiral index fingers around each other while moving hands forward
Nonmanual signal: lips pursed

stars, astrology

Handshape: 1 : 1
Orientation: palms out, right index finger against base of left thumb
Location: neutral space
Movement: alternately brush one index finger up and off the other
Nonmanual signal: gaze upward

sign language, signs

Handshape: 1 : 1
Orientation: palms in
Location: neutral space
Movement: move hands in alternating circles toward the body

stockings, socks

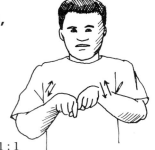

Handshape: 1 : 1
Orientation: palms down, index fingers touching
Location: neutral space
Movement: slide index fingers alternately back and forth against each other

relatives

Handshape: 1 : 1
Orientation: right palm out, right hand slightly higher than left hand; left palm in
Location: neutral space
Movement: bring index fingers together until tips touch, then rotate hands to switch positions

consider, contemplate, ponder, reckon, speculate, wonder

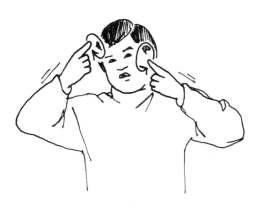

Handshape: 1 : 1
Orientation: palms in, index fingers angled up
Location: near temples
Movement: move hands in small, alternating, circles
Nonmanual signal: shoulders raise; head tilts right; "pensive" expression
Note: See page 120 for a one-hand variation of this sign.

cry, bawl, tears, weep

Handshape: 1 : 1
Orientation: palms in
Location: index fingers below eyes
Movement: brush alternating index fingers down cheeks
Nonmanual signal: "sad" expression

talk, converse with, dialogue

Handshape: 1 : 1
Orientation: right palm left; left palm right
Location: right index fingertip on lips; left hand in neutral space
Movement: move hands in opposition forward and back from mouth
Nonmanual signal: lips pursed

allergy

Handshape: 1 : 1
Orientation: palms facing, right hand slightly higher than left
Location: in front of nose
Movement: pull right hand away from nose sharply
Nonmanual signal: body pulls away from the offending source

when

Handshape: 1 : 1
Orientation: right palm down; left palm right
Location: neutral space
Movement: rotate right finger clockwise around left index finger, ending with index fingers touching
Nonmanual signal: body leans forward; head tilts right; eyebrows knit

objective, aim, ambition, goal, purpose

Handshape: 1 : 1
Orientation: right palm left; left palm out
Location: right hand at right temple; left hand in front of face
Movement: move right hand to left index finger
Nonmanual signal: head tilts right; eyes on left index finger

until

Handshape: 1 : 1
Orientation: right palm out; left palm in
Location: right hand near right shoulder; left hand in neutral space
Movement: arc right hand up then down until fingertips touch

point (n.)

Handshape: 1 : 1
Orientation: right palm left; left palm out
Location: neutral space
Movement: tap right index finger on left index finger twice

to, toward

Handshape: 1 : 1
Orientation: right palm out, right hand closer to body; left palm in
Location: neutral space
Movement: move right hand forward to meet left index finger

specific

Handshape: 1 : 1
Orientation: right palm in, right hand closer to body; left palm right
Location: neutral space
Movement: sharply hit left index fingertip with right index fingertip
Nonmanual signal: lips tight; "strained" expression; right shoulder raised

digress, distracted, off the subject

Handshape: 1 : 1
Orientation: right palm in; left palm right
Location: neutral space
Movement: move right hand toward left index finger, then bounce right index finger off left index finger, detouring to the left
Nonmanual signal: lips pursed; "annoyed" expression

**stray,
deviate,
divert**

Handshape: 1 : 1
Orientation: palms down, index fingers
   touching
Location: neutral space
Movement: slide right index finger off to
   the left

**turn back,
go back,
return,
turn around**

Handshape: 1 : 1
Orientation: right palm down, hand above
   left hand; left palm right
Location: neutral space
Movement: circle right index finger
   counterclockwise around left hand

**positive, add,
addition,
optimistic,
plus**

Handshape: 1 : 1
Orientation: right palm down; left palm
   right
Location: neutral space
Movement: bounce right index finger on
   middle of left index finger

**month (SM),
monthly (DM)**

Handshape: 1 : 1
Orientation: right palm in; left palm right
Location: neutral space
Movement: brush right index finger down
   edge of left index finger

**temperature,
fever,
thermometer**

Handshape: 1 : 1
Orientation: right palm down; left palm
   right
Location: neutral space
Movement: slide right index finger up and
   down edge of left index finger

**depend on,
rely**

Handshape: 1 : 1
Orientation: palms down, index fingers
   crossed
Location: neutral space
Movement: bounce index fingers down
   twice

cannot, can't, unable

Handshape: 1 : 1
Orientation: palms down, index fingers perpendicular, right hand above left hand
Location: neutral space
Movement: bring right index finger down, hitting left index finger
Nonmanual signal: head shakes "no"

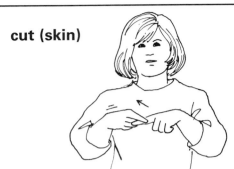

cut (skin)

Handshape: 1 : 1
Orientation: right palm in; left palm down
Location: neutral space
Movement: slide right index finger across left index finger

correct, accurate, decent, exact, proper, right

Handshape: 1 : 1
Orientation: right palm left, right hand above left hand; left palm right
Location: neutral space
Movement: bring right hand down, landing on left hand

consistent, faithful, regular

Handshape: 1 : 1
Orientation: right palm left, right hand on left hand; left palm right
Location: neutral space
Movement: bring hands down in an exaggerated motion
Nonmanual signal: lips pursed

first

Handshape: 1 : Open A
Orientation: right palm left, index finger forward; left palm right
Location: neutral space
Movement: swing right index finger around to hit left thumb

begin, commence, initiate, originate, start

Handshape: 1 : Open B
Orientation: right palm down, index finger between left index and middle fingers; left palm right
Location: neutral space
Movement: twist right index finger forward

escape, flee, get away, runaway

Handshape: 1 : Open B
Orientation: right palm out, index finger between left index and middle fingers; left palm down
Location: neutral space
Movement: sharply slide right index finger out of left hand
Nonmanual signal: "poo" mouth utterance

appear, pop up, show up

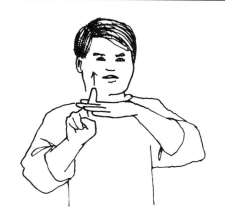

Handshape: 1 : Open B
Orientation: right palm out, right hand below left hand; left palm down
Location: neutral space
Movement: lift right index finger up between left index and middle fingers
Nonmanual signal: body and head thrust back; "surprised" expression

disappear

Handshape: 1 : Open B
Orientation: right palm out, index finger between left index and middle fingers; left palm down
Location: neutral space
Movement: slide right index finger down and away from left hand
Nonmanual signal: "surprised" expression

kill, murder

Handshape: 1 : Open B
Orientation: palms down, right hand closer to body
Location: neutral space
Movement: pass right hand under left hand, sharply brushing against left palm while moving forward
Nonmanual signal: "angry" expression

notice, observe, recognize

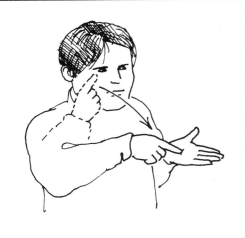

Handshape: 1 : Open B
Orientation: right palm in; left palm up
Location: right index finger on right eye; left hand in neutral space
Movement: move right hand down, ending with right index finger on left palm
Nonmanual signal: lips pursed; body and head lean back

show, demonstrate, display, exhibit (v.), illustrate, indicate, represent, signify (SM); demonstration, exhibit (n.), example (DM)

Handshape: 1 : Open B
Orientation: right palm in, index finger on left palm; left palm out
Location: neutral space
Movement: push both hands forward

this

Handshape: 1 : Open B
Orientation: right palm down, right hand above left hand; left palm up
Location: neutral space
Movement: move right index finger down to stab center of left palm

owe, afford, debt, due

Handshape: 1 : Open B
Orientation: right palm down, right hand above left hand; left palm up
Location: neutral space
Movement: move right index finger down and sharply poke left palm twice
Nonmanual signal: lips pursed

pay

Handshape: 1 : Open B
Orientation: right palm down; left palm up
Location: neutral space
Movement: brush right index finger down and off left palm

check (SM); inspect, examine, investigate, research (DM)

Handshape: 1 : Open B
Orientation: right palm down; left palm up
Location: in front of shoulders
Movement: slide right index finger off left fingertips
Nonmanual signal: shoulders rounded; head lowered; "inquiring" expression

coin, change

Handshape: 1 : Open B
Orientation: right palm down; left palm up
Location: neutral space
Movement: draw a small circle on left palm with right index finger

week (SM); weekly (DM)

Handshape: 1 : Open B
Orientation: right palm down; left palm up
Location: neutral space
Movement: place right hand on heel of left palm, then slide right hand down to left fingertips

1 •   2-Hand SIGNS

discuss

Handshape: 1 : Open B
Orientation: right palm in, index finger above left palm; left palm up
Location: neutral space
Movement: bring right index finger down and tap left palm twice

debate

Handshape: 1 : Open B
Orientation: right palm in, index finger above left palm; left palm up
Location: neutral space
Movement: bring right index finger down and tap left palm, then reverse handshapes and repeat or run down hand

last week, one week ago

Handshape: 1 : Open B
Orientation: right palm down, hand on heel of left palm; left palm up
Location: neutral space
Movement: slide right hand off left fingertips, then arc hand back toward right shoulder
Nonmanual signal: head and right shoulder tilt toward each other; "cz" mouth utterance

next week

Handshape: 1 : Open B
Orientation: right palm down, hand on heel of left palm; left palm up
Location: neutral space
Movement: slide right hand off left fingertips, then arc hand forward

cancel, correct, criticize, find fault

Handshape: 1 : Open B
Orientation: right palm down, index finger above left palm; left palm up
Location: neutral space
Movement: draw a large X on left palm with right index finger

what

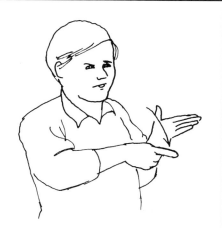

Handshape: 1 : Open B
Orientation: right palm in; left palm right
Location: neutral space
Movement: slide right index finger down
   left palm
Nonmanual signal: body leans forward;
   head tilts right; eyebrows knit

once (SM); sometimes (DM)

Handshape: 1 : Open B
Orientation: right palm in, index finger
   on left palm; left palm right
Location: neutral space
Movement: brush right index finger up
   and off left palm

occasionally,
once in a while

Handshape: 1 : Open B
Orientation: right palm in, index finger
   on left palm; left palm right
Location: neutral space
Movement: brush right index finger up
   and off left palm twice in a slow,
   elliptical motion

tall, height

Handshape: 1 : Open B
Orientation: right palm out, right hand below
   left hand; left palm right
Location: neutral space
Movement: slide right index finger up and off
   left palm
Nonmanual signal: eyes gaze upward

hour

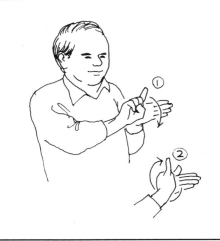

Handshape: 1 : Open B
Orientation: right palm out, edge of hand
   against left palm; left palm right
Location: neutral space
Movement: rotate right index finger around left
   palm, ending with palm in

half hour

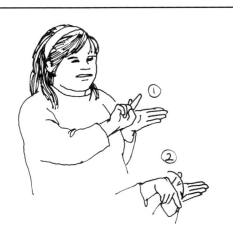

Handshape: 1 : Open B
Orientation: right palm out, edge of hand against
   left palm; left palm right
Location: neutral space
Movement: bend right wrist down, ending with
   index finger down

minute, moment

Handshape: 1 : Open B
Orientation: right palm out, edge of hand against left palm; left palm right
Location: neutral space
Movement: bend right index finger forward slightly
Nonmanual signal: right shoulder lifts up; head tilts right, "cz" mouth utterance

alarm

Handshape: 1 : Open B
Orientation: right palm angled out; left palm right
Location: neutral space
Movement: sharply smack right hand against left palm several times
Nonmanual signal: "alarmed" expression

deep, depth, detail

Handshape: 1 : Open B
Orientation: right palm down, edge of index finger on left palm; left palm right
Location: neutral space
Movement: slide right index finger across left palm and down

minus, negative

Handshape: 1 : Open B
Orientation: right palm down, hand in front of left palm; left palm out
Location: neutral space
Movement: sharply smack right index finger against left palm

day (passive)

Handshape: 1 : passive
Orientation: right palm in, index finger up, elbow on left fingertips; left palm down, arm across body
Location: neutral space
Movement: bring right arm down onto left arm

length, long (passive)

Handshape: 1 : passive
Orientation: palms down, right index finger on back of left wrist, left arm extended forward
Location: neutral space
Movement: slide right index finger along left forearm toward elbow

pail, bucket (passive)

Handshape: 1 : passive
Orientation: right palm left, index finger touching underside of left wrist; left palm in
Location: neutral space
Movement: arc right index finger along left arm, ending at left elbow

Episcopal (passive)

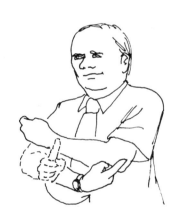

Handshape: 1 : passive
Orientation: right palm left, index finger on left wrist; left palm down, arm across body
Location: neutral space
Movement: arc right index finger out and around to left elbow

swallow

Handshape: 1 : C
Orientation: right palm left; left palm in
Location: right index finger under chin; left hand in front of neck
Movement: slide right index fingertip down neck
Note: See page 125 for a variation of this sign.

then, either, or

Handshape: 1 : L
Orientation: right palm in, index finger on left thumb; left palm right
Location: neutral space
Movement: bounce right index finger from left thumb to left index finger

about, concerning

Handshape: 1 : Flattened O
Orientation: right palm in; left palm right
Location: neutral space
Movement: circle right index finger around left fingertips

tomato

Handshape: 1 : S
Orientation: right palm in, index finger up; left palm down
Location: right index finger in front of lips; left hand in neutral space
Movement: brush right index finger down lips, then turn palm out and brush down edge of left hand

penalty, punish (passive)

Handshape: 1 : passive
Orientation: right palm down, index finger in front of left elbow; left palm down, arm across body
Location: neutral space
Movement: sharply brush right index finger down left elbow
Nonmanual signal: lips tight

might, power (passive)

Handshape: 1 : passive
Orientation: right palm down; left palm in
Location: right index fingertip on left shoulder; left hand in neutral space
Movement: arc right index finger down to crook of left arm
Nonmanual signal: lips pursed

second, secondly

Handshape: 1 : V
Orientation: right palm out, index finger above left middle finger; left palm angled right
Location: neutral space
Movement: tap right index finger on left middle finger

preparatory (year)

Handshape: 1 : 5
Orientation: right palm left, index finger near left pinky; left palm in
Location: neutral space
Movement: tap left pinky twice with right index finger

freshman

Handshape: 1 : 5
Orientation: right palm left, index finger near left ring finger; left palm right
Location: neutral space
Movement: tap right index finger on left ring finger twice

sophomore

Handshape: 1 : 5
Orientation: right palm left, index finger near left middle finger; left palm angled up
Location: neutral space
Movement: tap right index finger on left middle finger twice

junior

Handshape: 1 : 5
Orientation: right palm left; left palm right
Location: neutral space
Movement: tap right index finger on left index finger twice

among, amid

Handshape: 1 : 5
Orientation: right palm down, index finger above left index finger; left palm right
Location: neutral space
Movement: weave right index finger between left fingers, ending at left pinky

review

Handshape: 1 : 5
Orientation: right palm in, index finger on left pinky; left palm right
Location: neutral space
Movement: arc right index finger backward across left fingertips, ending at left thumb

insult

Handshape: 1 : 5
Orientation: right palm left; left palm right
Location: right hand in front of right shoulder; left hand in front of left shoulder
Movement: propel right index finger through left index and middle fingers
Nonmanual signal: tongue protrudes

skip class, absent, cut class

Handshape: 1 : Open 8
Orientation: right palm down, index finger above left middle finger; left palm down
Location: neutral space
Movement: brush right index finger sharply past left middle finger
Nonmanual signal: lips pursed
Note: See page 364 for a variation of this sign.

complex, complicated

Handshape: 1 > X : 1 > X
Orientation: palms facing, right hand behind
   left hand
Location: neutral space
Movement: move hands toward opposite shoulders
   while bending index fingers several times
Nonmanual signal: "serious" expression

ugly, homely

Handshape: 1 > X : 1 >X
Orientation: right palm left; left palm right, wrists
   crossed
Location: under nose
Movement: move hands apart while bending
   index fingers to X handshape
Nonmanual signal: "revolted" grimace
Note: See page 127 for a one-hand variation of
   this sign.

test, exam, quiz

Handshape: 1 > X : 1 > X
Orientation: palms out
Location: neutral space
Movement: move hands down, changing
   both index fingers to X handshape

pry, meddle, nosy

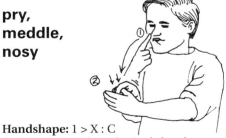

Handshape: 1 > X : C
Orientation: right palm in; left palm
   angled in
Location: right index fingertip on nose;
   left hand in neutral space
Movement: bring right index finger down
   to left palm, changing to X handshape

walk

Handshape: 3 : 3
Orientation: palms down
Location: neutral space
Movement: swing hands alternately
forward and back

awkward, clumsy

Handshape: 3 : 3
Orientation: palms
down, right hand lower than left hand
Location: neutral space
Movement: move hands alternately up
and down
Nonmanual signal: body shifts awkwardly;
bite tongue

garage

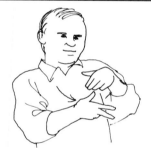

Handshape: 3 : Open B
Orientation: right palm left, hand close to
body; left palm down, fingers angled right
Location: neutral space
Movement: move right hand under left
hand

park (vehicle)

Handshape: 3 : Open B
Orientation: right palm left, hand above
left hand; left palm up
Location: neutral space
Movement: bring right hand down,
landing on left palm

ship

Handshape: 3 : Open B
Orientation: right palm left, hand on left
palm; left palm up
Location: neutral space
Movement: gently bounce hands forward

cheat

Handshape: 3 : Open B
Orientation: right palm in; left palm
down, hands parallel
Location: neutral space
Movement: move right hand left, catching
left fingers between right index and
middle fingers twice

accident (car), collide, collision

Handshape: 3 > Open A : 3 > Open A
Orientation: palms in, fingertips pointing toward each other
Location: neutral space
Movement: move hands toward each other, closing hands, until they collide
Nonmanual signal: lips tight

greedy, selfish, stingy

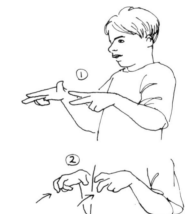

Handshape: 3 > Bent 3 : 3 > Bent 3
Orientation: palms down, hands parallel
Location: neutral space
Movement: pull hands back in a sharp, quick motion while bending index and middle fingers
Nonmanual signal: "angry" expression

mischievous, devilish

Handshape: 3 > Bent 3 : 3 > Bent 3
Orientation: palms out
Location: near temples
Movement: circle hands toward head, brushing thumbs down temples and bending index and middle fingers
Nonmanual signal: "mischievous" expression

devil, demon, Satan

Handshape: 3 > Bent 3 : 3 > Bent 3
Orientation: palms out
Location: thumbs on temples
Movement: bend index and middle fingers down twice
Nonmanual signal: "mischievous" expression
Note: See page 134 for a one-hand variation of this sign.

ticket

Handshape: Bent 3 : Open B
Orientation: right palm in; left palm up, hands parallel
Location: neutral space
Movement: move right hand left, sandwiching edge of left hand between right index and middle fingers

champion

Handshape: Bent 3 : 1
Orientation: right palm down, hand above left index finger; left palm right
Location: neutral space
Movement: bounce right palm off left index finger
Nonmanual signal: shoulders thrust back; erect posture

war, battle

Handshape: 4 : 4
Orientation: palms down, fingertips facing
Location: neutral space
Movement: move hands left and right in unison

curtains, drapes

Handshape: 4 : 4
Orientation: palms out
Location: neutral space
Movement: move hands down and slightly apart

Chanukah, Hanukkah

Handshape: 4 : 4
Orientation: palms out, index fingers touching
Location: neutral space
Movement: arc hands down and out to sides

assembly line, mass production

Handshape: 4 : 4
Orientation: right palm down, hand above left hand; left palm up
Location: neutral space
Movement: slide hands to the left in short quick motions
Nonmanual signal: "mm" mouth utterance

net, sieve

Handshape: 4 : 4
Orientation: palms in, back of right fingers against left fingers
Location: neutral space
Movement: hands slowly arc down and out to opposite sides

line, form a line, line up

Handshape: 4 : 4
Orientation: right palm left, pinky almost touching left index finger; left palm right
Location: neutral space
Movement: move right hand back toward right shoulder

jail, cage, prison

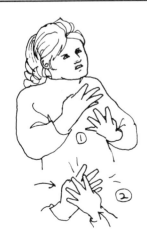

Handshape: 4 : 4
Orientation: palms in, fingers angled toward each other, right hand closer to body
Location: neutral space
Movement: smack back of right hand into left palm

well! so!

Handshape: 5 : 5
Orientation: palms in
Location: neutral space
Movement: arc hands down, ending with
   palms up
Nonmanual signal: body jerks forward; head
   tilts back; eyes widen

what?

Handshape: 5 : 5
Orientation: palms up
Location: neutral space
Movement: shake hands back and forth
   toward center
Nonmanual signal: body leans forward;
   head tilts right; eyebrows knit

catch
(catcher)

Handshape: 5 : 5
Orientation: palms up,
   right hand in front of left hand
Location: neutral space
Movement: bring hands together while
   moving in toward body
Nonmanual signal: lips tight; "strained"
   expression

chat

Handshape: 5 : 5
Orientation: right palm angled left; left
   palm angled right
Location: neutral space
Movement: shake hands down at an angle
   twice
Nonmanual signal: lips pursed; body and
   head lean back

**abandon,
desert (v.),
forsake,
leave,
leftover**

Handshape: 5 : 5
Orientation: palms facing, fingers up
Location: neutral space
Movement: bend wrists down, ending
with fingers pointing forward

**wind, breeze,
storm**

Handshape: 5 : 5
Orientation: palms facing
Location: neutral space
Movement: sway hands side to side
Nonmanual signal: mouth blows out air

**party (v.),
good time**

Handshape: 5 : 5
Orientation: palms facing, right hand
higher than left hand
Location: neutral space
Movement: shake hands exaggeratedly
out to opposite sides twice
Nonmanual signal: body sways; smile

**piano,
play piano**

Handshape: 5 : 5
Orientation: palms down
Location: neutral space
Movement: wiggle fingers as hands
move side to side in unison

**excellent, fantastic, grand,
marvelous, splendid,
wonderful**

Handshape: 5 : 5
Orientation: palms out
Location: above shoulders
Movement: double bounce hands forward
Nonmanual signal: smile

**friendly,
amiable,
cheerful,
pleasant**

Handshape: 5 : 5
Orientation: palms in
Location: in front of cheeks
Movement: wiggle fingers as hands move
back toward ears
Nonmanual signal: smile

**cool, air,
fresh**

Handshape: 5 : 5
Orientation: palms in
Location: in front of shoulders
Movement: bend wrists slightly to fan
face twice
Nonmanual signal: mouth blows out air;
body and head lean back

**sad,
dejected,
frown**

Handshape: 5 : 5
Orientation: palms in,
right hand higher than left hand
Location: in front of face
Movement: bring hands down in a sharp,
slight motion
Nonmanual signal: "sad" expression;
head lowered

**embarrass,
blush, flush**

Handshape: 5 : 5
Orientation: palms facing, fingers up
Location: in front of cheeks
Movement: move hands up cheeks slowly
Nonmanual signal: head and eyes lowered;
"embarrassed" expression

**traffic,
bumper-to-
bumper,
gridlock**

Handshape: 5 : 5
Orientation: palms down, fingertips
forward, right hand closer to body
Location: neutral space
Movement: double bounce hands forward
with exaggerated motion
Nonmanual signal: "weary" expression

**parade,
march,
procession**

Handshape: 5 : 5
Orientation: palms in, fingers pointing
down, right hand in back of left hand
Location: neutral space
Movement: move hands forward in a
marching motion

snow

Handshape: 5 : 5
Orientation: palms down
Location: above shoulders
Movement: wiggle fingers as hands slowly
  move down

**fire, arson,
burn**

Handshape: 5 : 5
Orientation: palms toward body, fingers up
Location: neutral space
Movement: wiggle fingers as hands move up
Nonmanual signal: shoulders raised

wait

Handshape: 5 : 5
Orientation: palms angled up, right
  hand closer to body
Location: neutral space
Movement: wiggle fingers

**nervous,
anxious**

Handshape: 5 : 5
Orientation: palms down
Location: neutral space
Movement: shake hands while moving
  them down
Nonmanual signal: "nervous" expression

**fear, afraid, dread,
frightened, scared, terror**

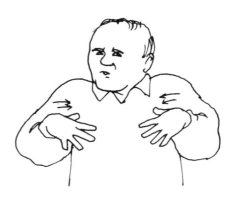

Handshape: 5 : 5
Orientation: palms in, fingertips facing
Location: in front of chest
Movement: move hands toward each other twice
Nonmanual signal: shoulders rounded;
  "frightened" expression

finish, already, done, end, over, then

Handshape: 5 : 5
Orientation: palms in
Location: neutral space
Movement: flip wrists out to sides, ending with palms out

flirt

Handshape: 5 : 5
Orientation: palms angled out
Location: in front of face
Movement: flutter fingers
Nonmanual signal: head tilts; "coy" expression

merge, mainstream

Handshape: 5 : 5
Orientation: palms angled in
Location: neutral space
Movement: move hands toward each other, then forward, ending with right hand on top of left hand and fingers forward

America

Handshape: 5 : 5
Orientation: palms angled in, fingers meshed
Location: neutral space
Movement: circle hands clockwise

wrestling

Handshape: 5 : 5
Orientation: palms facing, fingers meshed
Location: neutral space
Movement: bend wrists down slightly twice

football

Handshape: 5 : 5
Orientation: palms in
Location: neutral space
Movement: move hands toward each
other, interlocking fingers twice

**pregnant,
conceive**

Handshape: 5 : 5
Orientation: palms facing, fingers forward
Location: in front of abdomen
Movement: bring hands together, ending
with fingers interlocking

**Germany,
German**

Handshape: 5 : 5
Orientation: palms in, right hand at base
of left thumb
Location: neutral space
Movement: wiggle fingers
Note: See page 122 for the preferred sign.

moose

Handshape: 5 : 5
Orientation: palms out
Location: thumbs on temples
Movement: move hands out and up

**deer,
antlers,
elk**

Handshape: 5 : 5
Orientation: palms out
Location: thumbs near temples
Movement: tap thumbs on temples twice

**father
(honorific)**

Handshape: 5 : 5
Orientation: right palm left; left palm right
Location: right thumb at temple; left hand
in neutral space
Movement: arc hands up to the right

mother
(honorific)

Handshape: 5 : 5
Orientation: right palm left; left palm right
Location: right thumb on chin; left hand in
neutral space
Movement: arc hands up to the right

vomit, detest,
loathe

Handshape: 5 : 5
Orientation: right palm left; left palm right
Location: right thumb on lip; left hand below right hand
Movement: sharply thrust hands out and down to
the right
Nonmanual signal: tongue sticks out; head tilts away
from offender

dress (v.), wear (SM);
clothes, dress (n.),
garment, gown (DM)

Handshape: 5 : 5
Orientation: palms in
Location: thumbs on chest
Movement: brush thumbs down chest

retired, idle

Handshape: 5 : 5
Orientation: palms facing, fingertips up
Location: in front of shoulders
Movement: rest thumbs on shoulders while
   wiggling fingers
Nonmanual signal: body leans back; lips
   pursed

retired, idle (SM); holiday, leisure, retirement, vacation (DM)

Handshape: 5 : 5
Orientation: palms facing, fingers up
Location: in front of shoulders
Movement: bring hands back so thumbs hit chest
Nonmanual signal: smile

Russia, Russian

Handshape: 5 : 5
Orientation: palms down
Location: thumbs at sides of waist
Movement: tap thumbs on waist twice

flatter, manipulate

Handshape: 5 : 5
Orientation: palms out, thumbs touching
Location: neutral space
Movement: bend wrists alternately down
   and up
Nonmanual signal: head tilts; "devious"
   expression

traffic

Handshape: 5 : 5
Orientation: palms facing, fingertips up
Location: neutral space
Movement: brush fingers against each other as hands move alternately forward and back

crowded

Handshape: 5 : 5
Orientation: palms facing and touching, fingers up
Location: in front of face
Movement: press hands together and rub palms back and forth
Nonmanual signal: shoulders raised; "disgusted" expression

gray, grey

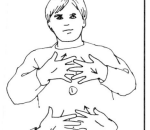

Handshape: 5 : 5
Orientation: palms in, right hand closer to body
Location: neutral space
Movement: pass fingers through each other as hands alternately move forward and back

senior

Handshape: 5 : 5
Orientation: right palm down, hand above left thumb; left palm right
Location: neutral space
Movement: bounce right palm on left thumb twice

blood

Handshape: 5 : 5
Orientation: palms in, right hand above left hand
Location: right index finger on lips; left hand in neutral space
Movement: wiggle right fingers while moving right hand down back of left fingers

film, motion picture, movie

Handshape: 5 : 5
Orientation: right palm out, heel on heel of left hand; left palm in
Location: neutral space
Movement: slide right hand back and forth on left palm several times

blurry, obscure, unclear, vague

Handshape: 5 : 5
Orientation: right palm out, palm on left palm; left palm in
Location: in front of face
Movement: rub right palm back and forth on left palm
Nonmanual signal: shoulders raised; tongue protruding

schedule

Handshape: 5 : 5
Orientation: right palm out, hand above left palm; left palm in
Location: neutral space
Movement: brush right fingertips down left palm, then flip right hand over and brush across left fingers

study

Handshape: 5 : Open B
Orientation: right palm down, hand above left hand; left palm up
Location: neutral space
Movement: wiggle right fingers
Nonmanual signal: lips taut; "earnest" expression

glory, glorious

Handshape: 5 : Open B
Orientation: right palm down, fingertips on left palm; left palm up
Location: neutral space
Movement: wiggle right fingers as hand moves up
Nonmanual signal: smile

country (passive)

Handshape: 5 : passive
Orientation: palms in, right hand in front of left elbow, left arm across body
Location: neutral space
Movement: rub right palm counterclockwise on left elbow

tree (SM); forest (passive) (DM)

Handshape: 5 : passive
Orientation: right palm left, elbow on back of left hand; left palm down
Location: neutral space
Movement: shake right hand back and forth

enough, adequate, abundant, ample, plenty, sufficient

Handshape: 5 : S
Orientation: right palm down, hand on top of left hand; left palm right
Location: neutral space
Movement: slide right palm forward and off left hand
Nonmanual signal: lips pursed; cheeks puffed

pressure, oppress, stress

Handshape: 5 : S
Orientation: right palm down, on top of left hand; left palm right
Location: neutral space
Movement: press right hand down on left hand twice
Nonmanual signal: body leans forward; head lowers; "stressed" expression
Note: See page 198 for the verb form.

mainstream (negative meaning)

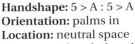

Handshape: 5 : 1
Orientation: palms down, fingertips facing
Location: neutral space
Movement: bring hands together, then forward, ending with right hand covering left index finger

helicopter

Handshape: 5 : 3
Orientation: right palm down, hand on left thumb; left palm right
Location: neutral space
Movement: shake right hand slightly as hands move forward

popular, flock to

Handshape: 5 : 1
Orientation: right palm out; left palm right, index finger up
Location: neutral space
Movement: hit right palm against left index finger twice

candle

Handshape: 5 : 1
Orientation: right palm out; left palm right, index finger on heel of right hand
Location: neutral space
Movement: flicker right fingers

dissolve, decay, fade, melt, rot

Handshape: 5 > A : 5 > A
Orientation: palms in
Location: neutral space
Movement: brush thumbs across fingertips as hands separate, ending with hands closed
Nonmanual signal: lips pursed

pants, jeans, slacks, trousers

Handshape: 5 > Bent B : 5 > Bent B
Orientation: palms in, fingertips down
Location: in front of thighs
Movement: bend fingers as hands brush
   up thighs twice

belong, annex, attach, enlist, enroll, join, unite

Handshape: 5 > F : 5 > F
Orientation: right palm out, hand closer to body;
   left palm in
Location: neutral space
Movement: bring hands together, linking thumbs
   and index fingers

damp, humid, moist, wet

Handshape: 5 > Flattened O : 5 > Flattened O
Orientation: palms in
Location: neutral space
Movement: move hands down, closing
   thumb to fingers, twice
Nonmanual signal: "disgusted" expression

total, add up, altogether, sum

Handshape: 5 > Flattened O : 5 > Flattened O
Orientation: right palm angled down,
   above left hand; left palm angled up
Location: neutral space
Movement: bring hands together in an
   exaggerated motion, closing thumbs to
   fingers as fingertips touch

football (ball)

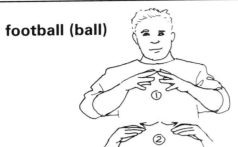

Handshape: 5 > Flattened O : 5 > Flattened O
Orientation: palms facing, fingertips touching
Location: neutral space
Movement: separate hands and close thumbs to fingers

meeting, conference, gathering

Handshape: 5 > Flattened O : 5 > Flattened O
Orientation: palms angled out
Location: neutral space
Movement: bring hands together twice, closing thumbs to fingers as fingertips touch

wedding

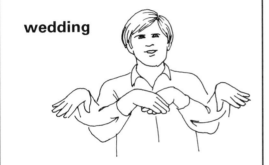

Handshape: 5 > Flattened O : 5 > Flattened O
Orientation: palms down
Location: neutral space
Movement: twist hands up and clasp hands

story, tell a story

Handshape: 5 > Flattened O : 5 > Flattened O
Orientation: palms facing
Location: neutral space
Movement: circle hands twice in toward center, closing thumbs to fingers as fingertips brush past each other

accept

Handshape: 5 > Flattened O : 5 > Flattened O
Orientation: palms down
Location: neutral space
Movement: move hands in to chest, closing thumbs to fingers
Nonmanual signal: lips pursed; "contented" expression

fascinate

Handshape: 5 > S : 5 > S
Orientation: right palm left; left palm right
Location: right index finger on nose; left hand in
neutral space
Movement: move hands down and close hands,
ending with right hand on top of left hand
Nonmanual signal: body leans forward; eyes widen;
tongue protruding

adopt, assume, host, take up

Handshape: 5 > S : 5 > S
Orientation: palms down
Location: neutral space
Movement: bend wrists up and close hands

acquire, get, obtain, procure, receive

Handshape: 5 > S : 5 > S
Orientation: right palm left, hand above
left hand; left palm right
Location: neutral space
Movement: pull hands in, closing hands
and ending with right hand on top of
left hand

arrest, capture, grab, seize

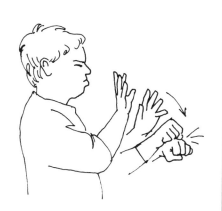

Handshape: 5 > S : 5 > S
Orientation: palms out, right hand above left hand
Location: neutral space
Movement: slowly move hands down as hands
close, ending with right hand on top of left hand
Nonmanual signal: "stern" expression

healthy, brave, bravery, courage, well

Handshape: 5 > S : 5 > S
Orientation: palms in
Location: shoulders
Movement: bring hands forward slowly, closing hands
Nonmanual signal: shoulders thrust back; posture erect; lips pursed

freeze, frost, frozen, ice

Handshape: 5 > Bent 5 : 5 > Bent 5
Orientation: palms down, fingers forward
Location: neutral space
Movement: pull hands back sharply while bending fingers
Nonmanual signal: body stiffens

pretend, deceive, fool

Handshape: 5 > A : 1
Orientation: palms out
Location: right index finger on tip of nose; left hand in neutral space
Movement: move right hand down, changing to A handshape before knuckles hit left index finger
Nonmanual signal: lips pursed

learn (student, pupil)

Handshape: 5 > Flattened O : Open B
Orientation: right palm down, fingertips on left palm; left palm up
Location: neutral space
Movement: pull right hand up to head while closing thumb to fingers
Nonmanual signal: lips taut; "earnest" expression

disappear, absent, gone, vanish

Handshape: 5 > Flattened O : C
Orientation: palms in, right wrist inside left palm
Location: neutral space
Movement: slide right hand down and below left palm, closing thumb to fingers
Nonmanual signal: "surprised" expression

include, everything, incorporate, involve, whole

Handshape: 5 > Flattened O : C
Orientation: right palm angled out, fingertips up, hand above left hand; left palm in
Location: neutral space
Movement: circle right hand clockwise, closing thumb to fingers as fingers tuck into left hand
Nonmanual signal: body jerks forward slightly

additionally, amendment, furthermore, in addition to

Handshape: 5 > Flattened O : Flattened O
Orientation: right palm down, hand below left hand; left palm right
Location: neutral space
Movement: swing right hand up, closing thumb to fingers as fingertips meet

poor

Handshape: 5 > Flattened O : passive
Orientation: right palm up, hand below left elbow; left palm in
Location: right hand at left elbow; left hand in neutral space
Movement: brush right fingers down and off left elbow twice, closing thumb to fingers
Nonmanual signal: shoulders rounded; head lowered; "pained" expression

ball, sphere

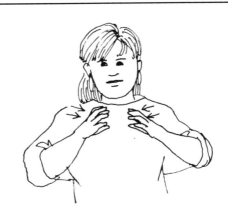

Handshape: Bent 5 : Bent 5
Orientation: palms facing
Location: neutral space
Movement: move hands together until fingertips bounce off each other

much, a lot

Handshape: Bent 5 : Bent 5
Orientation: palms facing, fingertips touching
Location: neutral space
Movement: separate hands in an exaggerated motion
Nonmanual signal: body and head jerk slightly

rain

Handshape: Bent 5 : Bent 5
Orientation: palms down
Location: above shoulders
Movement: double bounce hands down

audience

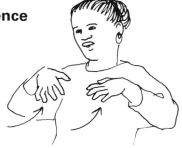

Handshape: Bent 5 : Bent 5
Orientation: palms down
Location: neutral space
Movement: move hands back and up
toward body

radio, audiology *(audiologist)*

Handshape: Bent 5 : Bent 5
Orientation: right palm left; left palm right
Location: ears
Movement: twist wrists forward and back
twice
Note: See page 143 for a one-hand
variation of this sign.

don't want

Handshape: Bent 5 : Bent 5
Orientation: palms up
Location: neutral space
Movement: sharply flip hands over,
ending with palms down
Nonmanual signal: head shakes "no"

roommate

Handshape: Bent 5 : Bent 5
Orientation: palms in, fingers facing
Location: neutral space
Movement: bring hands together and
interlock fingers twice

want, desire

Handshape: Bent 5 : Bent 5
Orientation: palms up
Location: neutral space
Movement: move arms back and forth
slightly
Nonmanual signal: "desirous" expression

spider

Handshape: Bent 5 : Bent 5
Orientation: palms down, right hand on left hand
Location: neutral space
Movement: wiggle fingers while moving hands slowly forward
Nonmanual signal: shoulders rounded; head lowered

shock, at a loss, dumbfounded

Handshape: Bent 5 : Bent 5
Orientation: palms out
Location: right hand on right temple; left hand at left shoulder
Movement: move hands out and down slowly, ending with palms down
Nonmanual signal: mouth open; "shocked" expression

sweat, perspire

Handshape: Bent 5 : Bent 5
Orientation: palms out, fingers up
Location: knuckles on forehead
Movement: bend wrists down and off forehead, ending with palms down
Nonmanual signal: "uncomfortable" expression

fat, obese

Handshape: Bent 5 : Bent 5
Orientation: right palm left; left palm right
Location: cheeks
Movement: move hands out to side with exaggerated motion
Nonmanual signal: cheeks puffed; "cha" mouth utterance

salad

Handshape: Bent 5 : Bent 5
Orientation: palms up, fingers angled toward each other
Location: neutral space
Movement: move hands up and toward each other twice

breakdown, cave in, collapse

Handshape: Bent 5 : Bent 5
Orientation: palms down, fingertips interlocked
Location: neutral space
Movement: collapse wrists down, ending with fingers down
Nonmanual signal: head lowered; "sad" expression

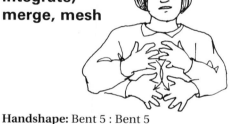

combine, blend, integrate, merge, mesh

Handshape: Bent 5 : Bent 5
Orientation: palms in, fingers angled up
Location: neutral space
Movement: bend wrists toward each other and down, ending with fingers meshed

fit, match

Handshape: Bent 5 : Bent 5
Orientation: palms in, left hand closer to body, fingers toward each other
Location: neutral space
Movement: bring hands together and interlock fingers

factory, engine, machine, motor

Handshape: Bent 5 : Bent 5
Orientation: palms in, fingertips interlocked
Location: neutral space
Movement: bend wrists down and up twice
Nonmanual signal: pursed lips

bear, grizzly

Handshape: Bent 5 : Bent 5
Orientation: palms in, arms crossed
Location: body
Movement: brush fingertips down chest twice

monkey

Handshape: Bent 5 : Bent 5
Orientation: palms in
Location: armpits
Movement: brush fingertips lightly up and off body twice

animal

Handshape: Bent 5 : Bent 5
Orientation: palms in
Location: fingertips on chest
Movement: bend fingers several times

laugh (hysterically)

Handshape: Bent 5 : Bent 5
Orientation: right palm down, hand above left palm; left palm up
Location: neutral space
Movement: move hands alternately forward and back several times
Nonmanual signal: laugh; body jerks

type, typewriter

Handshape: Bent 5 : Bent 5
Orientation: palms down
Location: neutral space
Movement: wiggle fingers while moving hands alternately up and down

storm, clouds

Handshape: Bent 5 : Bent 5
Orientation: right palm down, hand above left palm; left palm up
Location: in front of head
Movement: spiral hands to the right

mix, complicated, confused, mingle, puzzled, scramble

Handshape: Bent 5 : Bent 5
Orientation: right palm down, hand above left palm;
  left palm up
Location: neutral space
Movement: circle hands around each other
Nonmanual signal: "confused" expression

washing machine, wash (clothes)

Handshape: Bent 5 : Bent 5
Orientation: right palm down, hand
  above left palm; left palm up
Location: neutral space
Movement: twist hands in opposite
  directions

crude, rough, rude

Handshape: Bent 5 : Open B
Orientation: right palm down, fingertips on
  left palm; left palm up
Location: neutral space
Movement: slide right hand sharply down and
  off left fingertips
Nonmanual signal: "pained" expression

boil, cook

Handshape: Bent 5 : Open B
Orientation: right palm up, hand below left hand;
    left palm down
Location: neutral space
Movement: wiggle right fingers while
    moving hand in small circles
Nonmanual signal: "mm" mouth utterance

cookie

Handshape: Bent 5 : Open B
Orientation: right palm down, fingertips on left palm;
    left palm up
Location: neutral space
Movement: bounce right hand up, twist to the right, and
    land on left palm, then repeat twisting hand to the left

weak, feeble, frail

Handshape: Bent 5 : Open B
Orientation: right palm down, fingertips on left palm;
    left palm up
Location: neutral space
Movement: slowly bend right fingers until knuckles
    touch left palm twice
Nonmanual signal: shoulders rounded; head
    lowered; "pained" expression

grapes

Handshape: Bent 5 : Open B
Orientation: palms down, right fingertips on left wrist
Location: neutral space
Movement: bounce right fingertips down left hand to fingertips

beg, entreat, plea

Handshape: Bent 5 : C
Orientation: palms up, back of right hand in left palm
Location: neutral space
Movement: bend right fingers as hand slides down left palm twice
Nonmanual signal: shoulders rounded; head lowered; "pained" expression

darn, drat

Handshape: Bent 5 : O
Orientation: right palm down, thumb down; left palm right
Location: neutral space
Movement: move right hand down sharply, inserting thumb inside left hand
Nonmanual signal: body jerks; "angry" expression

popular

Handshape: Bent 5 : 1
Orientation: right palm out, hand closer to body; left palm right
Location: neutral space
Movement: smack right hand against left index finger twice

soft

Handshape: Bent 5 > Flattened O : Bent 5 > Flattened O
Orientation: palms up
Location: neutral space
Movement: gently close hands while
   moving them down slightly twice
Nonmanual signal: lips pursed

self-control,
suppress feelings

Handshape: Bent 5 > S : Bent 5 > S
Orientation: palms up, right hand above left hand
Location: chest
Movement: move hands down in deliberate motion,
   closing hands
Nonmanual signal: shoulders rounded; head lowered;
   "pained" expression
Note: See page 145 for a one-hand variation of this sign.

drawer,
open drawer

Handshape: Bent 5 > S : Bent 5 > S
Orientation: palms up
Location: neutral space
Movement: pull hands back while closing
   hands

**trust,
confidence**

Handshape: Bent 5 > S : Bent 5 > S
Orientation: palms up, right hand slightly above
    left hand
Location: neutral space
Movement: move hands slightly down and out
    while closing hands
Nonmanual signal: lips tight

cruel, mean

Handshape: Bent 5 > S : Bent 5 > S
Orientation: right palm left; left palm right
Location: right index finger on tip of nose; left hand
    in neutral space
Movement: bring right hand down and left hand up,
    closing hands, then brush hands past each other
Nonmanual signal: "angry" expression

**destroy, damage,
demolish,
devastate**

Handshape: Bent 5 > S : Bent 5 > S
Orientation: right palm down, right hand above left
    palm; left palm up
Location: neutral space
Movement: separate hands then bring back to
    center while closing hands, then sharply brush
    hands past each other
Nonmanual signal: body jerks; "angry" expression

greedy, miser, selfish, stingy

Handshape: Bent 5 > A : Open B
Orientation: right palm down, fingertips on left palm; left palm up
Location: neutral space
Movement: close right hand sharply
Nonmanual signal: shoulders raised; "disgusted" expression

pear

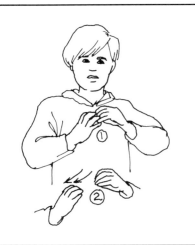

Handshape: Bent 5 > Flattened O : Flattened O
Orientation: right palm left, fingers covering left fingers; left palm right
Location: neutral space
Movement: slide right fingers down and off left fingers twice

remove, abolish, discard, subtract, take away

Handshape: Bent 5 > S > 5 : Open B
Orientation: right palm down, hand above left palm; left hand up
Location: neutral space
Movement: brush back of right fingers down left palm and close hand, then throw hand down, opening fingers

win

Handshape: Bent 5 > S : S
Orientation: right palm left, above and to the right of left hand; left palm right
Location: neutral space
Movement: swoop right hand to the left, closing hand and brushing across left hand
Nonmanual signal: smile

awful, disgusting, dreadful, horrible, terrible

Handshape: 8 > 5 : 8 > 5
Orientation: right palm left; left palm right
Location: temples
Movement: flick middle fingers out as hands move forward
Nonmanual signal: shoulders and head thrust back; "upset" expression

hate, despise, detest

Handshape: 8 > 5 : 8 > 5
Orientation: palms facing
Location: neutral space
Movement: sharply flick middle fingers out
Nonmanual signal: shoulders and head tilt away; "hateful" expression

Australia, Australian

Handshape: 8 > Open 8 : 8 > Open 8
Orientation: palms down, fingers forward
Location: neutral space
Movement: bounce hands forward and flick open middle fingers

**melon,
pumpkin,
watermelon**

Handshape: 8 > Open 8 : S
Orientation: palms down, hands crossed,
  right thumb slightly above left hand
Location: neutral space
Movement: flick right middle finger open
  and thump back of left hand

computer

Handshape: Open 8 : Open 8
Orientation: palms out
Location: neutral space
Movement: circle hands toward each other

**contact
(a person)**

Handshape: Open 8 : Open 8
Orientation: palms facing
Location: neutral space
Movement: bring middle fingers together
  and tap twice

light (weight)

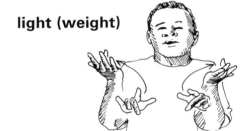

Handshape: Open 8 : Open 8
Orientation: palms down
Location: neutral space
Movement: slowly swing hands around,
  ending with palms up
Nonmanual signal: body and shoulders lift

**what's up,
affair, event,
what's new**

Handshape: Open 8 : Open 8
Orientation: palms in
Location: middle fingers on chest
Movement: flick wrists up and out off chest
Nonmanual signal: head tilts back; eyes
  widen; "mm" mouth utterance

**disappointed,
depressed,
discouraged**

Handshape: Open 8 : Open 8
Orientation: palms in
Location: middle fingers on chest
Movement: slide middle fingers down chest
Nonmanual signal: head lowered; "sad"
  expression

sick, ill

Handshape: Open 8 : Open 8
Orientation: palms in
Location: right hand in front of head; left hand in front of stomach
Movement: bring hands in sharply toward body
Nonmanual signal: "sickly" expression

disease, illness

Handshape: Open 8 : Open 8
Orientation: palms in
Location: right hand in front of head; left hand in front of chest
Movement: move hands in small circles
Nonmanual signal: lips pursed; "sad" expression

tend, inclined

Handshape: Open 8 : Open 8
Orientation: palms in, right hand above left hand
Location: middle fingers on left side of chest
Movement: move hands forward with an exaggerated motion
Nonmanual signal: body leans forward; "pah" mouth utterance

cut class, absent, miss class

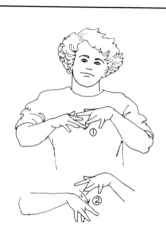

Handshape: Open 8 : Open 8
Orientation: palms down, right middle finger above left middle finger
Location: neutral space
Movement: brush right middle finger past left middle finger
Note: See page 329 for a variation of this sign.

excited

Handshape: Open 8 : Open 8
Orientation: palms in
Location: in front of chest
Movement: brush middle fingers
   alternately up and off chest
Nonmanual signal: eyes widen; "excited"
   expression

shiny, bright, glisten

Handshape: Open 8 : Open B
Orientation: palms down, hands crossed,
   right middle finger on left hand
Location: neutral space
Movement: shake right hand as it moves up
Nonmanual signal: eyes widen

touch, been there

Handshape: Open 8 : Open B
Orientation: palms down, right middle
   finger above left hand
Location: neutral space
Movement: bounce right middle finger off
   back of left hand

take advantage, rip off

Handshape: Open 8 : Open B
Orientation: right palm down, middle
   finger above left palm; left palm angled up
Location: neutral space
Movement: sharply brush right middle
   finger off left palm, ending with middle
   finger bent
Nonmanual signal: "angry" expression

medicine

Handshape: Open 8 : Open B
Orientation: right palm down, middle
   finger on left palm; left palm up
Location: neutral space
Movement: bend right hand side to side

center, middle, intermediate

Handshape: Open 8 : Open B
Orientation: right palm down, hand
   above left hand; left palm up
Location: neutral space
Movement: circle right hand above left
   hand, then drop right middle finger
   down in the center of left palm

technology
(technician)

Handshape: Open 8 : Open B
Orientation: right palm in, hand below left hand; left palm right
Location: neutral space
Movement: tap right middle finger on edge of left hand twice

early

Handshape: Open 8 : S
Orientation: palms down, hands crossed, right middle finger above left hand
Location: neutral space
Movement: slide right middle finger across back of left hand
Nonmanual signal: right shoulder raised

earth

Handshape: Open 8 : S
Orientation: palms down, hands crossed, right middle finger and thumb grip left hand
Location: neutral space
Movement: rock right hand side to side

bare, bald, blank, empty, naked, nude, vacant, void

Handshape: Open 8 : S
Orientation: palms down, knuckles forward, right middle finger above left hand
Location: neutral space
Movement: slide right middle finger down back of left hand
Nonmanual signal: raise right shoulder

interesting

Handshape: Open 8 > 8 : Open 8 > 8
Orientation: palms in, right hand above left hand
Location: middle fingers and thumbs on chest
Movement: move hands forward with an
    exaggerated motion, closing thumbs and middle
    fingers
Nonmanual signal: body leans forward; eyes
    widen; mouth open

heart attack

Handshape: Open 8 > S : Open B
Orientation: palms in
Location: right middle finger on left side of chest;
    left hand in neutral space
Movement: move right hand out, closing hand, and
    smack hand into left palm
Nonmanual signal: body rigid when fist hits

grease, fat, gravy, greasy, oil

Handshape: Open 8 > 8 : Open B
Orientation: right palm up, thumb and middle
    finger gripping edge of left hand; left palm right
Location: neutral space
Movement: brush right thumb and middle
    finger down and off edge of left hand twice
Nonmanual signal: "disgusted" expression

soda pop

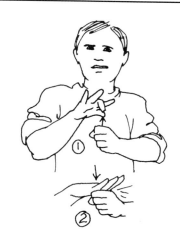

Handshape: Open 8 > 5 : S
Orientation: right palm down, middle finger inside left index finger; left palm right
Location: neutral space
Movement: lift right hand up, opening hand, then smack down on top of left hand

Jesus

Handshape: Open 8 > 5 : 5 > Open 8
Orientation: palms facing
Location: neutral space
Movement: tap right middle finger on left palm, then tap left middle finger on right palm

Bible (Christian)
(compound: Jesus + book)

Handshape: Open 8 > 5 > Open B : Open 8 > 5 > Open B
Orientation: palms facing
Location: neutral space
Movement: tap right middle finger on left palm, then tap left middle finger on right palm; change to Open B handshape, palms facing and touching, and open hands out

Index of English Glosses

Each gloss is followed by the initial handshape(s) of its corresponding sign and then by the page number where it appears. When the same gloss appears two or more times, the glosses are listed in the morphologic order of their handshapes; when the handshapes are the same, one-hand signs are listed before two-hand signs. Glosses that need an agent marker are indicated in italics.

A

H

I

X

xerography: C : Open B, 217
Xerox: C : Open B, 217

Y

year: S : S, 274
yearly: S : S, 279
yell: Bent 5, 143
yellow: Y, 113
yes: S, 97
yesterday: Open A, 44
yesterday: Y, 115
yet: Y : Y, 302
yield: A : A, 158
yield: Open B, 57
yield: Open B : Open B, 178
you: 1, 118
young: Bent B : Bent B, 204
your: B, 50
you're a riot (slang): 5, 138
yours (singular): B, 50
yours (plural): Open B, 51
yourself: Open A, 43
yourselves: Open A, 43
youth: Bent B : Bent B, 204

Z

zap: H, 75
zealous: Open B : Open B, 182
zero: O, 89
zero: O : Open B, 253
zip: A, 42
zip: A : A, 155
zip: O, 89
zipper: A, 42
zipper: A : A, 155

Acknowledgments

Producing a reference book of this nature would not have been possible without a tremendous amount of cooperation and assistance from Deaf acquaintances, Deaf service workers, interpreters, and patient teachers of American Sign Language.

One of the first teachers to become interested in this reference was Amy Falardo of West Palm Beach, Florida, whose classes I attended at Palm Beach Community College. She encouraged me and worked with me during her free periods. She gave me advice on the classification of handshapes as well as many suggestions for the arrangement of illustrations. I also owe a great deal to Beth Bystrycki, a Deaf woman from Wellington, Florida, who is very active in the Deaf Service Center of Palm Beach and the local Deaf club. She spent a great deal of her time tutoring me and was kind enough to include me in several Deaf club activities.

I would like to thank Patty Mullin, a teacher at the State University of New York in New Paltz, for her support of my idea and for generously including me in her classes.

My mother-in-law, Esther Shulman of Royal Palm Beach, deserves special thanks for the enormous amount of time she spent cutting and pasting illustrations and checking entries in the index as well as for her continued belief in me and my project.

My wife Susan was a constant source of inspiration. She never complained about the expenses or the mess or the time I devoted to the dictionary, but instead was the one person who would get me back on track whenever I became discouraged.

I would like to thank Emily Perl Kingsley, Richard Evans of Academic Study Associates, Don Metlay, and Morrie Brown for their encouragement, support, and frequent worthwhile suggestions.

The contribution of Marianne Gluszak Brown, cannot be overstated. Not only did she aid in the categorizing and placement of the more than 1600 sign illustrations, but she also supervised the selections of glosses, monitored the correctness of the illustrations, prepared original descriptions for every sign, and wrote the introductory sections on American Sign Language.

A guardian angel must have guided me to Valerie Nelson-Metlay. We could not possibly have found an artist who brought more skill to such an enormous task. Each person represented in the illustrations is unique. Each shows the wide variety of individuals one might find in the Deaf community, and each has his or her own personality with a puckish quality that makes it a joy to turn the pages. For her contribution, as well as for Marianne's, I will be forever grateful.

Finally, to Ivey Pittle Wallace, our editor at Gallaudet University Press, my sincere thanks. She recognized the value of the arrangement of our dictionary when it was first brought to her attention and supported me enthusiastically throughout the ensuing years. Without her devotion, this work would never have come to fruition.

R. T.

I want to thank my mother, Barbara Drumm, for introducing me to Richard Tennant, whom she had tutored in American Sign Language (ASL). As a student of ASL, Richard had been frustrated by the sign dictionaries then in use. I had heard similar frustrations from my students and wondered when someone would publish a dictionary that did not depend on the users already knowing an English gloss in order to find its corresponding sign. Richard showed me a rough draft of a dictionary he was working on. Here it was— a dictionary organized by ASL handshapes, not by English glosses. I should not have been surprised to find that it took a student with a student's perspective to come up with an ASL version of a two-way dictionary.

Throughout our collaboration, Richard has impressed me with his energy, tenacity, and dedication in staying true to a student perspective. I believe it helped to keep this book fresh and original.

I am grateful to Susan Tennant for her support throughout the project. Her charm and diplomacy helped us all to keep on an even keel through the occasionally rough waters of collaboration.

Additionally, I am indebted to Val Nelson-Metlay for patiently working and reworking her illustrations when my guidance as a first-time author was not always clear. When I was uncertain about the merit of my comments and suggestions, I had only to see her sweet smile, sense of humor, and the final product to realize how intuitively she was able to transcend my inexperience. As a renowned illustrator she brought the most experience to this project, and, I might add, the most grace. As luck would have it, her husband, Don Metlay, is a linguist and was keenly interested in the integrity of the book. I have not taken all of his suggestions, but they helped keep me and the book honest.

As a member of the American Sign Language Teachers Association and the Registry of Interpreters for the Deaf, I am ever aware of the contributions of my students and colleagues to my professional growth. I am particularly indebted to those who were willing to review sections of the manuscript and give me feedback. They have helped to ensure the quality and integrity of this work.

I will always be grateful to Gallaudet University Press for taking a chance on two unknown authors. I cannot thank them enough for giving us this opportunity.

I especially thank my husband, Morrie, for helping me through this project. He encouraged me to do this book when I was uncertain that I had the requisite skills to accomplish it. Among the many tasks he kindly assumed was the creation of software applications that enabled me to write the sign descriptions and to edit the work in progress. His only reward was to see the book come to fruition and to know that his wife will remember his generosity of time and spirit.

To my mother, Barbara Drumm, my father, Joe Gluszak, and my step-mother, Mabel Gluszak, I owe a debt of gratitude for raising me with a love and appreciation for sign language and the Deaf world.

And to my grandmother, Lee Green, whose unwavering support of all my endeavors has been a lifelong inspiration to me.

M.G.B.